Legal Theory Today
A Sociology of Jurisprudence

Legal Theory Today

Founding Editor

John Gardner, Professor of Jurisprudence, University College, Oxford

A Sociology of
Jurisprudence

Richard Nobles and David Schiff

·HART·
PUBLISHING

OXFORD AND PORTLAND OREGON
2006

Published in North America (US and Canada) by
Hart Publishing
c/o International Specialized Book Services
920 NE 58th Avenue, Suite 300
Portland, Oregon
97213–3644
USA
Tel: +1 503 287 3093 or toll-free: (1) 800 944 6190
Fax: +1 503 280 8832
E-mail: orders@isbs.com
Web Site: www.isbs.com

Chapter 4 is a revised version of a chapter by Richard Nobles and David Schiff
from "Law and Sociology" edited by Freeman, M. (forthcoming 2006).
By permission of Oxford University Press.

Hart Publishing, Salter's Boatyard, Folly Bridge,
Abingdon Road, Oxford OX1 4LB
Telephone: +44 (0)1865 245533 or Fax: +44 (0)1865 794882
e-mail: mail@hartpub.co.uk
WEBSITE: http//:www.hartpub.co.uk

British Library Cataloguing in Publication Data
Data Available
ISBN 13: 978–1–84113–598–4 (paperback)
ISBN 10: 1–84113–598–4 (paperback)

Typeset by Hope Services (Abingdon) Ltd.
Printed and bound in Great Britain by
TJ International, Padstow, Cornwall

Contents

Preface

In this book we examine the implications of a sociological theory, systems theory, most particularly as set out in the writings of Niklas Luhmann, for jurisprudence. This theory provides a sociological explanation for the interminable[1] debates amongst and between different schools of jurisprudence on topics such as the origin and/or source of law, the nature of law's determinacy or indeterminacy, and the role of justice. Our project is to continue the work begun by Luhmann in his book, *Das Recht der Gesellschaft.*[2]

Jurisprudential theories typically take as their object the unity or identity of law.[3] What is it that unites law, and distinguishes it from other aspects of social life? Even the most critical of theories accept that law is something different from other things that it is not, although answers as to this difference vary between the respective theories.[4] What we attempt to do is demonstrate the explanatory power and sociological enterprise of systems theory by applying it to a range of modern jurisprudential writings on the nature or basis of the unity or identity[5] of law.

---

[1] Alexy, 2002, suggests that the possible points of disagreement between natural law theorists and legal positivists can be represented in 64 separate theses. However, his estimation reflects his rather generalised analysis, and only relates to those two principal types of theorist. At a more particular level, when including other theorists, the possibilities indeed become interminable.

[2] Luhmann, 1993, trans 2004.

[3] Even when, as with the critical legal theorists (see Collins, 2002) the focus results in a sustained attempt to show law's disunity. Luhmann describes these presentations of 'the unity of the system in the system' as 'self-description'. (Luhmann, 2004, 424)

[4] Thus even if 'law is politics', such a classification still presupposes that this composite can be distinguished from other things that are not politics.

[5] In this book, hereafter, we will refer to 'unity' as an entity that represents unity as identity (rather than refer to 'unity or identity' each time we use the

Preface

Readers who have a background in jurisprudence in general, or particular writing in jurisprudence, might like to read one or more of the substantive chapters (chapters 3–6), in which the theory involved is subjected to some part of a systems theory critique, before reading chapters 1 and 2. The substantive matter of chapters 3-6 might, for some readers, be more approachable or an easier route to enable them to engage with the particular theoretical perspective being offered in this book, which is by no means straightforward, or simply accessible. That said however, one of our aims in this book is to offer an accessible set of writings about this theoretical perspective to enable the reader to engage with it, and to enable us to suggest the valuable insights that it has to offer to jurisprudential writing and its further development.

We are grateful to Professor Michael Freeman and Oxford University Press for permission to include, in an amended form, as chapter 4 of this book, our chapter 'A Sociology of Jurisprudence' published in M.D.A. Freeman (ed.) *Law and Sociology* (Oxford, Oxford University Press, 2006); and to our colleague James Penner for his discussion of that chapter with us. We wish to thank our colleagues, Hugh Collins, Nicola Lacey, Kate Malleson, and Jill Peay for reading and commenting on other chapters. Thanks also to Gunther Teubner for his support and encouragement from the beginning of the general project of which this book is the latest stage.

Richard Nobles and David Schiff, LSE, August 2005.

word 'unity'). This is the way that Luhmann seems to use the word 'Einheit', which tends to be translated as 'unity' (or sometimes entity, object, unit, or oneness). The idea of unity as identity can be distinguished from the idea of unity as completeness, perfection, or sum total.

1
Locating Jurisprudence Sociologically

The practice of law can be, and is, studied and described sociologically. Thus the sociology of law scrutinises the main institutions, structures and personnel of law (courts, tribunals, prisons, legislative and regulatory bodies, executive and administrative agencies, lawyers, judges, the police, probation officers, bailiffs, etc) and subjects them and their practices to a range of descriptions and explanations. What these institutions and structures and who these personnel are, what their practices involve and what they do, are available to be described, explained and understood, both in themselves, and in the context of broader descriptions and explanations of society, its social control mechanisms, its cohesion, its evolution, etc. And the same applies to law's rules, principles, procedures, methods of reasoning and conceptual structures. The particular rules operating in any particular society or groups of society, their underlying conceptual structure and formalisation can be studied sociologically—a paradigm example being Weber's analysis of the types of law and legal thought and their interaction—if not causal relationship—with modern capitalist society.[1]

[1] Weber's extensive sociological analysis of law has been described as taking two forms: causal and exegetical. The former looks to 'explaining how and to what extent different forces—in particular, economic forces—have contributed to the historical growth of the modes of thought and substantive doctrines characteristic of the law today.' The latter aims 'to make manifest the common thread of meaning that links certain centrally important features of the modern legal order—including all those substantive and procedural aspects of modern law that he [Weber] characterizes as "formally rational", the distinctive type of contractual association which predominates in modern legal systems (the

1

By contrast, if jurisprudence is the body of writing that has on occasion been portrayed as either the theory of law, or the philosophy of law or the science of law,[2] then there is little that requires or offers itself to a sociological explanation or understanding. Such a body of writing suggests itself as representing its object (law) in theoretical, philosophical, scientific, or other descriptive terms, with each version recommending itself as somehow or other a better representation than others. When attempts are made to attribute a common enterprise to such writing, what is characteristically attempted is a map of jurisprudence's development, or some part of its development, either historically or philosophically. Modern books of, rather than about, jurisprudence usually take this form.[3] Further, it is not uncommon for books of and on jurisprudence to assume that the subject matter to be discussed is of such obvious focus that no further elaboration or definition of what jurisprudence means is necessary.[4] We assume that a principal reason for this is that the link between jurisprudence and legal practice[5] is one that, to

"purposive contract"), and the conception of authority that underlies the modern state and its bureaucratic apparatus ("legal-rational authority").' (Kronman, 1983, 34–36). Weber's sociology of law can be found in Weber, 1954. Although there appears to have been a reluctance by many jurisprudential writers throughout the 20th century to engage with such sociological analysis, it has now become clear that Hart's classic jurisprudential text, *The Concept of Law* (1961) was 'influenced' in its formulation by Weber's writings (see Lacey, 2004, 230–1; and on 'influence', see Duxbury, 2001, 5–7).

[2] For a model example that expresses this variety of meanings and approaches, see Pound, 1959, vol 1, ch 1.

[3] Invariably jurisprudence books incorporate meta-theoretical questions about their object (law), namely methodological and epistemological questions about the possibility of, and ways of approaching, that object. Books about jurisprudence tend to focus primarily on such meta-theoretical questions; see the background thesis in Dickson, 2001.

[4] The designation 'legal theory', however, may connote many additional exercises that function beyond what is suggested here as the usual parameters of jurisprudence. See, for example, 'The Scope of Legal Theory' in Cotterrell, 1995, 275–78.

[5] Indeed some uses of the word jurisprudence imply that it is a synonym for law, or for legal practice in general, or (as with the French word *'jurisprudence'*) the body of decisions of courts in particular.

many, sets clear markers for what is being discussed.[6] However, beginning in this chapter, and within our discussion of systems theory in chapter 2, we will tease out, and thereby offer, a particular understanding of jurisprudence, which we will then apply throughout this book.

The dichotomy suggested in the above two paragraphs poses at one and the same time a complementary and a sharp division between jurisprudence and the sociology of law. Both, but in different ways, take as their object the practice of law. Each attempts to describe and account for what it identifies as legal practice by reference to different theoretical traditions and methodologies, and by addressing different questions. This dichotomy assumes that jurisprudence is not part of law's practice, but somehow represents it, or is at least grounded in it. From this perspective, while jurisprudence may offer descriptions of the object (law) that are superior, inferior or perhaps complementary to those generated by sociological research,[7] jurisprudence is not itself part of the object which needs to be described. However, this assumption is problematic.

The practice of law[8] often requires generalisations. Whether these take the form of expressing what is common to the reasoning adopted by those who claim to practice law, or the common attributes of the body of rules that characterise an area of law (*mens rea* in criminal law, consideration in contract law, etc), these generalisations are part of the practice of law. In other words, as a working practice, law could not operate in today's world, without many of its actors generalising: expressing their practice in forms that capture what is common, rather than what

---

[6] Such a link to legal practice can even be articulated in a negative form. Thus Cotterrell, 2003, 2 suggests: 'Jurisprudence is probably best defined negatively as encompassing all kinds of general intellectual inquiries about law that are not confined solely to doctrinal exegesis or technical prescription. The qualification "general" is important. If jurisprudence is unified at all it is by a concern with theoretical generalisation, in contrast to the emphasis on the particular and the immediate that characterise most professional legal practice.'

[7] Cotterrell, in many of his writings, including all of those mentioned in footnotes to this chapter, has argued consistently for the plausibility and importance of a complementary relationship between jurisprudence and sociology of law.

is specific and particular. Without such generalisation categories such as criminal law, contract law, etc, would not be possible as working assumptions for the location of particular rules, and the institutional set-up that claims to operate these rules (eg criminal as opposed to civil courts) would collapse. So, whether to understand the structure of the courts, or the political and legal differences between executive, legislative and judicial powers, or the differences between public, private, criminal and civil law, or just about any other working assumptions of legal practice, generalisation is a prerequisite.

Jurisprudence, even though it appears to start one step removed from legal practice cannot, however, be totally removed from it.[9] It is often at a telling point of a writer's theorisation that one meets the crucial link to legal practice. Some writers express this more obviously than others. Dworkin, for example, makes the explicit claim that by exploring judicial practice in hard cases one is able to see how judges are in effect theoreticians of the law, and express disagreements of a theoretical kind about the law.

> Any practical legal argument, no matter how detailed and limited, assumes the kind of abstract foundation jurisprudence offers, and when rival foundations compete, a legal argument assumes one and rejects others. So any judge's opinion is itself a piece of legal philosophy, even when the philosophy is hidden and the visible argument is dominated by citation and lists of facts. Jurisprudence is the general part of adjudication, silent prologue to any decision at law.[10]

[8] The practice of law is, as with the meaning of jurisprudence, assumed to be clearly understood, being based on common experience, even though there is recognition that at a higher level of philosophical or sociological questioning many difficult issues arise with this designation. Arguments about 'legal pluralism' have become the conventional means through which such issues have been addressed, and through which legal practice as centred on state agencies (legislative, executive or judicial) is questioned. 'Legal pluralism' is however a complex and controversial concept: see, Tamanaha, 2000, and 2001, ch 7.

[9] There is, of course, a link between jurisprudence and legal practice via the route of legal education in which future practising lawyers study the generalisations and theories of jurisprudence, as well as those of sociological understanding, in the course of their academic training.

[10] Dworkin, 1986, 90.

This does not, of course, mean that jurisprudence guides the everyday practice of law, like statutes or precedents. Quoting Powell, Luhmann makes this point humorously: '[I]t is hard to imagine many JPs thumbing through the *Summa Theologiae*[11] after a hard day at the sessions.' But, as he goes on to say: '[Legal] practice presupposes that the fundamental questions of the meaning of the system can be answered and it bases its decision-making on that . . .'.[12] Indeed, as modern jurisprudence developed in universities, it was assumed that the needs of legal practice could be enhanced by such theorisation. It is only in very recent times, when the development of general theories of law has created such a large literature, that this obvious link seems to have been broken.[13] Take the example of the first edition of Dias and Hughes' text *Jurisprudence*.[14] This volume contained an equal number of chapters on general theories of law, and analyses of the main legal conceptions: property, contract, responsibility, etc, and characteristics of legal reasoning: precedent, statutory interpretation, etc. The latter two sets of chapters is now less of the standard content of jurisprudence texts, although in the tradition of analytic legal positivism were very much the preponderant form of jurisprudential writings over the previous century.

So, the apparent dichotomy, the complementarity and, at the same time, division between jurisprudence and the sociology of law is problematic. Since law is both an idea (or ideal) and a universal practice, it is not surprising that at all levels practice and theory are intertwined. But, it is about the nature of this intertwining and how it can be understood sociologically that there tends to be a marked silence, even though some sociologies of law give a number of leading clues. These sociologies of law

---

[11] The archetypal treatise on law written by the medieval theologian, St Thomas Aquinas, 1959 edn.

[12] Luhmann, 2004, 425.

[13] Although it survives, as can be illustrated by looking at the content of books of essays on jurisprudence, see for example the *Oxford Essays in Jurisprudence* series from 1961, the first being edited by Guest.

[14] Dias and Hughes, 1957.

recognise that lawyers' understandings of what they do form a crucial part of law's existence, so that a sociology of law that fails to have regard to these understandings is somewhat impoverished in its explanatory potential. Lawyers' understandings involve some degree of generalisation, and sociologies of law that take these generalisations and understandings seriously are then concerned not only with what law does, and what legal institutions and lawyers do, but also what they say or claim to do. Here we have a potential subject for sociological exploration: the link between law, its practice, and those self-understandings that are a part of that practice.[15] Further, we have a potential link with jurisprudence. To the extent that jurisprudence takes seriously what law, legal institutions and lawyers claim they are doing, and how they operate, it contains information in its theorisations that are a part of legal practice, which can be studied sociologically.

Although it is possible to demonstrate how jurisprudence evidently can include the self-understandings of those who are involved in the practice of law, and thereby incorporates evidence of what might be available to sociological enquiry, just as all other aspects of legal practice, the terms of such enquiry need careful investigation. For, potentially, the integration of jurisprudence into legal practice is not only about the complementariness of particular theories with how well they reflect what law, legal institutions and lawyers claim that they do, but also about something less dependent on how good or bad the theory in question is at such reflection. Considered as good or bad reflection, each theory offers its own subjective account. This particular problem, of how the understanding of those involved in the practice of law is reflected in legal theories, is mirrored in the analysis and criticism of many modern jurisprudential theories, and sociological analyses. Hart's *The Concept of Law* has been subjected to extensive criticism,[16] and re-articulation,[17]

---

[15] Weber's sociological analysis of law (see n 1 above) significantly includes the 'subjective' understandings of the ideas and beliefs of legal actors as part of his causal explanation and exegetical analysis.

[16] See, for example, Fitzpatrick, 1992, ch 6, especially 197–206.

[17] See, for example, MacCormick, 1981, 32–40.

in response to this problem. He recognised that an adequate elucidation of what law is must incorporate the internal understandings of rules by both those subject to them, and those who apply them. And, within sociological analysis (including that of law), while the empirical investigation of behaviour offers apparently more potentially objective description, the investigation of individual or group understandings, whether specialist or popular, is thought to produce many additional insights, whilst at the same time raising considerable difficulties for evidence production and interpretation.[18]

How then should one account for different theories offered within jurisprudence, when each theory might present a better or worse description of the self-understanding of law, legal institutions and lawyers, but where that self-understanding is difficult to assess in itself, and can so easily appear to be nothing more than self-deception, or a form of legitimising practice?[19] Each theory, in this light, becomes no more than a subjective account of what 'really' reflects what law, legal institutions and lawyers do, or say that they do, and one likely to be historically conditioned by the prevailing legal structures operating at the time. As such each theory will tend to talk past each other, rather than engage in dialogue (as the debates within jurisprudence conventionally assume that they do). The problems identified here, that need to be overcome, are how not to view each example of jurisprudence as either subjective, or merely justificatory of existing practices. Within jurisprudence, the practice of debate suggests that it should be possible for evidence to be adduced to determine what theory better captures legal practice (is a better description), or a more accurate justification in the sense that more of the practice of law relies on it at all levels of its practices. These suggestions continue to rely on the apparent separation between jurisprudence and the

---

[18] In relation to Weber's dependence on the method of '*Verstehen*', the plausibility of relying on 'understanding' as part of his sociological analysis of law, see Andreski, 1981.

[19] Reflecting on modern jurisprudence and legal theory in these terms is the focus of many writings, for example Cotterrell, 2003; Kerruish, 1991.

subject matter of much sociology of law, namely legal practice, a separation that does not establish any more than the representation of the one in the other, rather than some integration between the two. However, is there an alternative?

Let us consider the possibility that jurisprudence is integrated as a part of legal practice, a possibility that is more likely when considering the longevity of legal history, and the potential influence of jurists on judges and other legal practitioners.[20] Let us also consider how the character of modern law is so dense and complex that the only possibility for achieving consistent decision-making is not only that legal practice operates with its own generalisations to support its aim of 'treating like cases alike' (as claimed by its practitioners and appears to be so claimed implicitly by so much of its practice), but that it can only do so within its own self-understandings of those generalisations. Like a language, law has developed a given vocabulary, grammar and syntax that, although it is still developing, can only develop from what it currently is.[21] If this were the case then jurisprudence, rather than being only tangentially related to, or a representation of, legal practice, would be an encapsulation of it, its self-description, based on its own self-observations. This could lead to the understanding of jurisprudence as an autonomous body of theory self-produced through legal practice. Such theory would not be a better or worse representation of legal practice, or the better or worse justification of such practice, but the encapsulation of its practices and justifications. Such a view of jurisprudence would make jurisprudence available for sociological investigation, not in terms of whether it represented legal practice, but how it constituted itself as object, how it distinguished itself from what it is not. To observe jurisprudence in this light does not imply that jurisprudence, as self-description, will be able at one and the same time to observe

[20] See generally Duxbury, 2001.

[21] By using this analogy we do not intend, in any way, to imply anything more than that this analogy, in this context, is a useful analogy. We certainly do not make any supposition that it is appropriate to understand law as, in fact, a language or specialist language.

itself outside or beyond the terms of law's practices, but rather how such self-description 'must identify with its conditions.'[22] This view of jurisprudence makes it available for a sociological investigation that is complementary to what is undertaken within much sociology of law.[23] The latter enterprise studies all aspects of legal practice, and it offers explanations or understandings for the evidence it adduces as to what that practice really is both at a particular and at a more general level. At its greatest level of generalisation such explanations or understandings will integrate legal practice into social practice and law into society, or at least our understanding of it. Invariably this will lead to a further elaboration of the nature, character, and evolution of society, and law's role in it.[24] However, much of this sociological analysis assumes that society or the social system can be talked about in general terms (that society is not so differentiated and uncoordinated as to make such talk relatively meaningless). It assumes a sufficiently united and holistic society, one in which the legal system is integrated with the economic system, political system, media, science, education, health, etc, under the umbrella of the social system and society at large. Such an assumption may prove plausible, but it may also prove to be untenable in the modern world. The latter view is taken by modern systems theory as developed by Niklas Luhmann,[25] which theory informs this book. It is a theory that suggests that a genuine sociology of law must first know its object, law, which

[22] Luhmann, 2004, 431.

[23] As with the meaning of jurisprudence, the meaning of sociology of law is often assumed, rather than clarified explicitly. Again, part of the reason is that the subject matter to be discussed is of such obvious focus, that no further elaboration or definition appears to be necessary. Thus what it describes, rather than what it is, usually forms the basis for its elaboration. For example, Cotterrell, 1984, 2, states: '. . . law is too important a social phenomenon to be analysed in a way that isolates it from other aspects of society and makes impossible an understanding of its social character, the complexity of its relations with other social phenomena, its "reality" as a part of life and not merely as a technique of professional practice.'

[24] The usual designation for such accounts is that of 'law and social theory'.

[25] See, in particular, his *The Differentiation of Society* (1982).

object is not a given of society—a phenomenon derived from the stage of societal or economic or political development—but something that has developed in itself, that has produced itself from its own elements, and reacts to society in its own way, without the possibility of direct integration in or direct causation of the one by the other.[26] Indeed, just as it (law) makes observations about the nature and modern character of law, so it does about the character of modern society (that is, its conception of modern society) as such. This sociology of law is part of a wider sociology that treats not only law, but politics, economics, science and the media as similarly autonomous systems that produce themselves from their own elements, including their own version of what is external to them (their environment). This theory denies that there is in modern society a meta-language in general social communication that can capture what law is, or what it does. Rather law, including jurisprudence, relies on its own structures and concept formation—namely its own distinctions—which allow it to construct itself apart from its environment (society in general, the economic system, political system, or whatever).[27]

Without the assumption of a united and holistic society, but rather one of a highly differentiated society,[28] the material of jurisprudence can be analysed as part of a sociological investigation of the theorisation of law's identity and unity in itself, as a part of the attempt by those involved in the practice of law to generalise those practices in order to establish its rules, structures, principles, or whatever, and then observe how such generalisations can be organised consistently and coherently—in

[26] This statement does not, of course, mean that law can operate outside of society, that there isn't an invariable relationship between the two, in the same way that there is such a relationship between law and the material conditions of life, the atmosphere, the physical world, the biological human organism, etc (see ch 2 below).

[27] It is beyond the needs of this analysis to address the question of what 'society' is, from this theoretical perspective, however we address this question briefly in ch 2.

[28] As we will show in ch 2, the form of differentiation represented in this theory is that of functional differentiation, rather than stratification or hierarchy.

other words how law's unity can be expressed. As a part of legal practice, jurisprudence can be represented as that part of the practice of law that intentionally attempts its own self-description: 'In self-description, the system becomes its own theme; it claims an identity of its own.'[29] At a certain stage of societal development, if modern society has become highly differentiated in its functions, then jurisprudence can be understood sociologically as law's own self-description, rather than a 'better' description in relation to some other. Luhmann himself presents such a challenge for a sociology of jurisprudence. Having recorded the alternative ways of sociology (looking at law from the outside) and jurisprudence (observing law from within), he proposes how sociology could offer an adequate account of law. To do so it needs 'To acknowledge the fact that there are self-observations and self-descriptions of the object [that are] the condition for a scientifically appropriate, realistic, and I venture to say, empirically adequate description.'[30]

In writing this sociology of jurisprudence we take up this challenge. We treat jurisprudence as part of the practice of law, as self-description of what distinguishes law, by setting its boundaries, and what unites law. We offer an attempt to apply these criteria of self-description to a number of modern jurisprudential theories to see how they deal with them, and to see what, if anything such a sociology might add to what currently is expressed as jurisprudential knowledge. Our task then is not, as with so much jurisprudential writing, to argue for what theory is a better description of law, or a better representation of legal practice, or a better representation of what lawyers claim represents or justifies their practices, but rather how each theory operates as a self-description of its object, law. Our task is not to engage in the internal dialogue within jurisprudence, which so

[29] Luhmann, 2000a, 248; and see 248–9 for a brief definition of self-description. The German word, to express this idea of self-thematisation, is *'reflexion'*. This word includes both the idea of passive reflection, but also, as a reflex, an active response. Jurisprudence texts thus produced can be described as 'autological'.

[30] Luhmann, 2004, 60.

often fails actually to debate, because the participants talk past each other by adopting their different starting positions as to the meaning of law. Rather our task might allow us to see what a 'new jurisprudence' informed by such a sociological critique might look like, and what its principal questions might be.

It follows that we treat jurisprudential theories from a constructivist perspective.[31] Namely, how they constitute themselves from their own elements—their self-observations and self-descriptions; how they capture what they can and cannot deny from being part of the system that they are observing. We do not evaluate those theories for their ability to construct the world inside or outside of law. Whether they have a more realistic view of law, or of politics, or the economy, or society, is neither their rationale, nor the means by which they need to be assessed. The need for law's self-descriptions to include external description follows inevitably from the nature of distinction. Law can only be described by reference to what it is not: its other. The external description contained within jurisprudence has much in common with a variety of social theories. But if one accepts that all systems (and not just law) generate self-descriptions (which inevitably include distinctions—descriptions of what they are not) then there is little point (sociologically) in evaluating, for example, whether a jurisprudential theory's account of politics is superior to a political theory's description of politics, or which gives the superior description of law. The extent to which other social theories are better or worse at constituting their object than jurisprudential ones depends on whether they represent politics, the economy or society at large, rather than law. Whether they may enable a better explanation of how law operates in society is questionable. But, a sociological investigation of jurisprudence as internal self-description using a constructivist epistemology is crucial if modern society is, as systems theory suggests, functionally differentiated. Under these conditions it would only be

---

[31] At this stage we do not wish to complicate this statement by raising Luhmann's challenge to constructivism (1990a), as his response to those who criticise autopoiesis as constructivist; see King and Thornhill, 2003, 21.

possible to understand law's role in society once one has understood how it constructs itself from its own elements (and, more than this, constructs its own understanding of society at the same time).

This sociology of jurisprudence, possibly unlike some other jurisprudence or analyses of jurisprudence, is not geared toward being useful for or in the legal system. It is geared toward empirical references rather than value or purpose based ones. Does a given jurisprudence—a particular theory within jurisprudence—constitute its object—law—from its own elements? Does it capture law's operations through self-observation and self-description? Does it capture law's information system, its communication system, its complexity and its evolution? How does it account for law's unity and its difference? These questions need to be answered in relation to different jurisprudence theories through empirical references, elucidating upon facts and concept-formation. What characterises law's unity is its internal self-references to itself, what characterises its difference are its internal self-references to that which it is not, to its environment, which can broadly be represented as society. Of course there is something that can be characterised as society, and something that can be characterised as law, but the relationship between the two, and an understanding of how the one acts on the other, is first dependent on a marking of their differences. Jurisprudence is a key player in such an exercise.

To treat jurisprudence as self-description gives it, as other theories in relation to other functioning subsystems, a particular task. This task, as emphasised by Luhmann, involves 'finding out *what is implied when a system promises to give an answer to every question and forces all the operations of the system to presuppose that there is such an answer.*'[32] What, within law, is the meaning of every question to which all the operations of the system presuppose that there is an answer? And, if we can understand what is meant by these questions, in what sense do we expect jurisprudence to imply that answers are available? If

---

[32] Luhmann, 2004, 429.

there are compulsory elements in systems, and the legal system in particular, then does it follow that jurisprudence as self-description is bound to recognise those elements? Within law, this question requires us to consider whether law, or at least every communication within law 'must be styled as leading to a decision'[33] whether based on 'good' reasons or not—namely, whether law involves compulsory decision-making, or its opposite, a prohibition on non-decision making.[34] Is it the case that once a question has been formulated as a legal question, a decision in response to that question is a necessary corollary, even though the information available to make such a decision makes it highly likely that the decision will be, and may well remain, contentious?

In the course of our discussion of different jurisprudence theories we address the question of whether, irrespective of the particular answers given, jurisprudential theories recognise that there must be an answer to the question as to the legality or illegality of any given action brought by parties recognised by the courts, or admitted by other legal personnel or other actors as raising legal (justiciable) questions. There are many issues here that might need to be clarified, for example the way in which law might find a way to exclude its decision making processes by rejecting the question as a legal question, thereby suggesting that it can be dealt with in some other forum. But, for the purpose of this introductory chapter, all that needs to be considered is how, to the extent that such compulsory decision making is an element that all the operations within the legal system imply, different theories as self-description accommodate this.

We will address this question, as much in the writing of Ronald Dworkin or other natural law theory, or Hans Kelsen and other positivist legal theory, as in the writing of what is known as Critical Legal Theory, which is explicitly hostile to

---

[33] Luhmann, 2004, 428.

[34] Although we introduce this question here in general terms, it recurs throughout this book—see, for example, ch 6 on the Critical Legal Theorists.

much of what Dworkin's and other central jurisprudence theory says. However, we elucidate on all modern theories for their ability to account for, and engage with, what the operations of the system presuppose an answer to. The most obvious jurisprudence to engage with this question is in the writings of Dworkin, in his criticism of Hart's reasoning about judicial discretion as operating somehow beyond the standards (rules) that represent law. For Dworkin there is, unquestionably, a legal answer, and perhaps a 'right' legal answer to any 'hard case'. But, within Hart's own analysis, there is also an answer which accepts that law must respond by reaching a decision, in Hart's case by claiming that judicial discretion is not antithetical to legal decision making, but rather that each legal rule has a penumbra of uncertainty that allows it to be adapted to produce a legal answer in all cases. It will not be so much the different answers that will engage our attention, but whether each theorist represents law as something that '*promises to give an answer to every question and forces all the operations of the system* [as each theorist represents those operations] *to presuppose that there is such an answer.*'[35] Namely, how well each theory attempts its self-description, capturing its own operations and conditions, and what foundation, or lack of it, each theory offers as a response to the task of self-description.

We can now refer to the title of this chapter, to locate jurisprudence sociologically, and hopefully anticipate that its meaning is clear—namely that what is meant is that theories in jurisprudence will be looked at using the tools of the sociology of systems theory. And, on the basis of that exercise, propositions about current jurisprudential theories will be advanced. Having stated what the exercise involves, and by now having probably indicated how complicated it is, we should continue by stating why it is being undertaken, and why it is so complicated.

Law and sociology have an unstable relationship, despite the extraordinary amount of interchange between them. The reasons for this have been elucidated on for well over a century,

---

[35] Luhmann, 2004, 429.

from the time of the earliest writings that are now understood as sociology. To give a typical example: in the book of essays *Sociology of Law*, a book significant for its input into sociology's revival of interest in law in the 1960s, and its not only continuing but burgeoning interest since then, the editor Vilhelm Aubert suggests that there is a 'basic tendency in the differences between the two disciplines . . . which are rooted in the different social functions of law and of sociology.'[36] So much ground has been travelled since that book was published, but the instability of the relationship remains. In the Introduction to the first edition of his book *The Sociology of Law: An Introduction*, Roger Cotterrell strongly espouses the need to overcome 'compartmentalism' and to develop sociological understanding of law, and within law, but nevertheless recognises that:

'. . . sociological study of law remains marginal to academic sociology (although it represents a field of rapidly increasing interest). At the same time it coexists uneasily with the established discipline of law (which is nevertheless changing in important respects to accommodate the new perspectives which social scientific research has introduced in legal study.'[37]

This hope, that law and sociology might become better integrated as disciplines, seems to have been disappointed.[38] Indeed, in a recent essay the same author indicates how, despite all the cross-fertilisation between the disciplines, legal theory has hardly come to terms with the range of approaches and debates that characterise sociology. The implication of this being that those engaged in legal theory know no more about sociology and even the sociology of law, than in the recent past.[39] Whereas there has been burgeoning interest of sociology in law and vice

[36] Aubert, 1969, 9.

[37] Cotterrell, 1984, 8.

[38] Or at least, the basic terms and methodology in which cooperation can be enhanced have remained controversial and disputed. See the debate between Cotterrell and Nelken: Cotterrell, 1998; Nelken, 1998; see also Banakar, 2000.

[39] Cotterrell, 2006; he does not, however, lose faith in how 'law's cocoon-like official existence' can be enhanced by sociology, and of the 'important lessons [that sociology offers] for legal theorists'.

versa to the extent that sociological theories of law or legal theories informed by particular sociologies abound, and new subject areas have emerged that represent an active interrelationship between these disciplines,[40] this interpenetration operates but, arguably, does not cooperate.[41] What characterises these relationships is instability, at the same time as greater interdependency. The complications of this first chapter, and the next, and the focus of the critical sociological appraisal in the next four chapters, as well what we discuss in the final chapter, will all be geared towards explaining this situation.

Before undertaking this task, one further question about the approach being adopted in this book needs to be addressed. We rely on Luhmann's theoretical position—his systems theory—which claims that it is only through communications that one can grasp the nature and operations of social phenomena.[42] Communication is the medium by which society and its functioning subsystems operate and interact. To address how communication does this requires observation on the processes involved. In engaging with that exercise, we are observing, and can only do so from a position. Equally, those who write jurisprudence use their observations and communications, from their positions. Thus jurisprudence does not have a fixed location, despite our attempt here to locate it sociologically. And our observations cannot locate jurisprudence within law since its meaning to itself within or in relation to legal practice is other than its meaning that a sociological study can observe from within sociology's own understandings. Thus, even though

---

[40] Such as law and regulation, and alternative dispute resolution.

[41] Thus, as a common example, the view of the editors in their 'Introduction' to a recent book of essays on Law and Social Theory states: 'Law and sociology have always had a close, if troubled, relationship as academic disciplines . . . despite some attempts to bring the two disciplines closer together, they remain frustratingly apart. Jurists complain that sociologists do not understand or respect the content of law, or seek to undermine law as a profession. Sociologists complain that "law in context" courses, and the research pursued by the Law and Society movement, are not sufficiently sociological.' Banakar and Travers, 2002, 1.

[42] We will elaborate further on this in ch 2.

sociology cannot locate jurisprudence in a way that is consistent with its own observations of its location, it can nevertheless observe on its location sociologically. And from this perspective, one can equally observe sociologically on jurisprudential theories, which is what we will be attempting throughout this book. However, to be consistent with the theory on which we are relying, we cannot claim to do so while at the same time observing ourselves undertaking this exercise. For us, we focus on a marked space, which is this sociology's depiction of jurisprudence, based on the distinction of what is, and what is not jurisprudence. There is however, as a consequence of this distinction, an unmarked space, which is whatever falls into the category of what is not jurisprudence, and one into which much[43] of our commentary falls. Or, to put this into more everyday language, if one is engaged in an exercise from a position one cannot at the same time observe what one is engaged in without adding an element which changes the perspective of one's observations; one's observations are now directed to one's position and how to communicate within it, rather than solely to the activity originally being observed and its communications. To move back to the theoretical expression of this: not to see is the condition for seeing. Thus, jurisprudence observes law and, as self-description, marks out, as part of those observations, what it thinks law involves. We observe jurisprudence. As second order observers we observe the observations on law of those engaged in jurisprudence. Third-order observers, critics of what we write, may engage with our observations, but they will be critics, or sociologists. What will be meaningful in their observations is how well or appropriately we have carried out our sociological task, while what is meaningful to us is how well or appropriately jurisprudence has carried out its self-description.

---

[43] Perhaps much, but certainly not all; we attempt to explore the possibilities for new questions within jurisprudence in a number of the chapters, but especially the final chapter.

2
Understanding Closure

In the course of its various explorations, descriptions and analyses, closure is a central concern of jurisprudence. What separates (closes off) law and the legal system from all the things that it is not? No theory, whether jurisprudential or sociological, asserts the causal independence of the legal system. A nuclear holocaust will take out the legal system alongside the political, economic and scientific systems, and even perhaps, humanity itself. And at a less dramatic level, any legal system will be affected by economic activity (everything from legal fees to the state of the housing market) and political activity (the legislative process and ensuing legislation, policies on legal services, etc). Basically, within society, the chains of cause and effect are infinite and endless and, with the understanding offered by chaos theory, we know that even the smallest change at one point in the world can have the most dramatic effect (the example of the butterfly whose flapping wings produce a hurricane, representing the extreme sensitivities within the world to its initial conditions).

The complexity of causality, whether within the physical world or society, does not prevent science from attempting to produce causal explanations of events. In the case of the sociology of law, these will include theories about the influences of events within the political or economic sphere upon the legal system, and vice versa. The concession that this is not a one way causal relationship, that any social activity that can influence law may also be open to the influence of law—that law is both constituted by social relations and itself constitutes social relations—leads to the claim that law is 'relatively autonomous'. This claim is an invitation to study the relationship between law and other aspects of society, rather than studying it in isolation, using a concept likely to assist that study. However, **by itself**, the admission that law is causally only relatively autonomous is simply a restatement of the complexities of causality. Everything that causes is itself an effect of causes, and, in that sense, everything on the planet, let alone further afield, is 'relatively autonomous'.

The ideas of closure that concern jurisprudence are not claims about causal independence, but are claims to do with identity. Of course, the two are linked. First, in order to make any argument as to the causal relationship between objects it is necessary to identify them. So one cannot talk of the content of law being determined by politics without implying the existence of two objects whose relationship is open to observation. Second, in the identification of objects one may describe features that have implications for any causal theory. So, for example, if law were identified by reference to a rule of recognition,[1] one would not expect norms that fall outside that rule to be part of law; which means in turn that if political norms are to produce changes in the legal system then, at least while the current rule of recognition operates, those who seek through political action to change legal structures need to have regard to the content of this composite rule. And, in combination with a theory of identity, this allows the concept of relative autonomy to do more than make a statement of the obvious. A statement that identifies the legal system may also indicate what relationships, including causal ones, are possible between law and other aspects of society.

Jurisprudence contains a rich collection of narratives on the identity of law. There are natural law theories that seek to account for law as the embodiment of some criteria of morality, through the use of practical reason, within the rules for human association. And positivist legal theories that persist in identifying law as a system of norms, but deny any necessary connection with morality or moral norms, and instead locate legal norms by reference to specific human (and hence posited) norm creating acts, or attitudes. And there are various realist

---

[1] As proposed by Hart in *The Concept of Law*, 1961.

legal theories that seek to describe law by reference to underlying facts rather than norms. Some examples of these theories will be considered in the chapters that follow. However, in this chapter we wish to set out the component parts of systems theory, and explain why this theory allows one to examine jurisprudential theories of law's distinct existence, nature and effects as 'self-descriptions'.

Luhmann's understanding of law as an autopoietic system of communication forms part of a sociological theory that identifies society as made up of systems of communication. This is not a claim that the only thing that exists in the universe is communications. But if the object of sociology is meaningful[2] human action, then this is manifested and structured through communications.[3] Luhmann's writings on law also form part of a wider account of the nature of modern society. Like Durkheim, Luhmann recognises that modern society involves a far greater differentiation than earlier societies. Whilst Durkheim saw this in terms of roles, or division of labour, and sought to account for the stability of modern society in terms of the interdependence generated by increased division of labour,[4] Luhmann identifies society with its communications, and the evolution of society in terms of the increased differentiation of those communications.[5] One of the most controversial claims of this

[2] See Luhmann, 1990b, ch 2 'Meaning as Sociology's Basic Concept'.

[3] The centrality of communication to sociological and historical analysis has recently been clarified by Thomas Luckmann, joint author of the influential 1960's work with PL Berger, *The Social Construction of Reality: a Treatise in The Sociology of Knowledge*, 1967. In a lecture at LSE, February 2005, Luckmann demonstrated recognition of the centrality of communication, which would have been controversial fifty years ago, but is now commonplace, namely: 'The human social world is mainly constructed in communicative interaction and all the world view that motivates and guides interaction is constructed in communicative processes.'

[4] See Durkheim, 1960; and, for a critical account, see Cotterrell, 1999, Part 3 'Legal Values and Social Complexity'.

[5] For a succinct statement of the relationship between the ideas of differentiation of Luhmann and Durkheim, see Teubner, Nobles and Schiff, 2002, 897–902.

theory is that, in modern society, subsystems of communication become autopoietic, as a result of achieving operative closure.

To understand the nature of this claim, it is useful to start by considering the role and nature of language. Autopoiesis, a term taken from biology and the study of cells,[6] is the description given to the process whereby something reproduces itself from itself, from its own elements.[7] In the case of language, it seems appropriate to understand it as autopoietic. In order to speak, we have to use language. We construct new meaningful utterances out of existing language. This does not ignore the fact that language is supported by, and stimulated by, all sorts of things other than language (feelings, biological processes, etc). But in order to speak, we have to form meaningful sentences. And our resource for doing this is language. This resource does not mean that language is static. It evolves. Variations are offered (eg new words and phrases) which, like all words, take their meanings from their relationship to existing words (eg the current use of 'wicked' to mean 'great'). We are aware that successful speech, including novel speech, requires a successful connection or relationship to existing language (grammar, syntax, etc) even though language is open to incremental change.

From this perspective on language, it is possible to say that society, understood as its communications, and taken as a totality (the social system of communication), is autopoietic. One can only create communications out of other communications. And the social system of communication exhibits closure. Of course, this does not mean causal closure. Communications use

---

[6] See Maturana and Varela, 1980.

[7] Teubner, 1993(a), 22–24, lists the key ingredients of the 'official' definition of autopoiesis, noting how it involves 'a particular combination of various mechanisms of self-reference. The self-production of elements can be regarded as only a minimum condition for autopoiesis.' After considering the possibility of how both 'hard' and 'soft' operations are involved in the self-reference 'hypercycle', which can be explored through 'second-order cybernetics', he is able to offer the following 'main features' of autopoiesis: '1. self-production of all the components of the system, 2. self-maintenance of the self-producing cycles by means of hypercyclical linking, 3. self-description as the regulation of self-production.'

up energy, and require the presence of atoms. But the fact that communications form part of the physical world does not alter the fact that communications are different from the medium that supports them. Closure arises because communications can only occur when the existing system of communication recognises some event as a further communication. Thus there is no atomic or chemical test for a communication, only the fact that it has occurred as a communication. Physical entities are preconditions for communications, and will have causal implications for the communications that occur, but they are not themselves communications, and cannot become such. And the making of communications will have consequences for that physical world (things will happen, including the using up of the energy required to make a communication, which would not have happened 'but-for' that communication). But not everything that is caused by a communication is itself a communication, as the only thing that one can add to a system of communication is a further communication. And the basis on which something can be recognised as a communication is found within the existing system of communications. All this allows us to describe the system of communications as autonomous from the physical world that supports it, and on which it comments.[8]

The closure of the social system of communication is an operative closure. First, because the closure is repeated each time that a communication occurs: each time a new communication is made (something is recognised as a communication), and secondly, because the closure is a product of operations. The structures of communication that restrict and facilitate what it means to communicate (and what each communication means) are themselves communications. This also explains the nature of the evolution of communications. Communications (operations) can lead to new bases for the making of novel communications.

The last few paragraphs represent a brief exegesis of systems theory as it applies to all of society's communications. The

---

[8] The intensity of contemporary comments/communications about the physical world is the subject of Luhmann's work *Ecological Communication*, 1989.

reason for setting out the theory at this level is that if one can understand the nature of closure and the resulting autonomy of general communication, it is easier and more straightforward to understand the particular claims of Luhmann's theory: that within modern society the process of autopoiesis is repeated at the level of subsystems.[9] Subsystems of communication, like the legal, political and economic systems, achieve their own operative closure. These separate systems identify, for themselves, which communications are communications within their own system, and which are not.

If you cannot accept that communications (as a totality) are something different from the physical world that supports them, and that it is the system of communication that establishes what can constitute a communication, then the theory is simply a non-starter for you.[10] But if you can accept the premise of this theory, then you will be led to some of its counter-intuitive conclusions (conclusions that are replicated when one considers the implications of subsystems evolving into autopoietic systems). The most important of these conclusions is that a system of communication establishes both itself, and its environment. Society, as a system of communication, communicates about the physical world, and communicates about itself (society) as something separate from that physical world. Thus, through its communications (operations) society as a system creates both itself (society) and its environment (the physical or 'other' worlds). 'Creates' here is not a causal claim, it is just an obser-

[9] These subsystems are functioning systems since, as we will demonstrate, they orientate themselves toward particular communicative functions underscored by their particular binary codes.

[10] If this is your view, you might like to take up the challenge of one clear and short chapter in which Luhmann (2002a) makes his case, which would allow you to address your concerns in response to it. At 160–61 Luhmann states: 'A system of communication is therefore a fully closed system that generates the components of which it consists through communication itself. In this sense, a system of communication is an autopoietic system that produces and reproduces through the system everything that functions for the system as a unit. It is self-evident that this can occur only within an environment and under conditions of dependency on limitations set by that environment.'

vation that society generates communications both about itself, and about what it is not, and both kinds of communications are separate from (closure and autonomy) the world (atomic, chemical, biological, etc) that we describe, within communications, as reality. And if one accepts the claim that not only is society (as a system of communication) autopoietic, but that its subsystems are also autopoietic, then this relationship with the physical world will be repeated at the subsystem level. Each subsystem (politics, law, media, economics, science, art, etc),[11] will identify the communications that belong to it. Each subsystem will communicate about itself, and what it describes as something other than itself: its environment. Only now, with the repetition of autopoiesis at the subsystem level, the environment that can be described is not only the physical world but also other subsystems of communication, as well as any communications that do not belong to any particular subsystem (general social communication). And if it can be shown that the basis on which the subsystems identify communications as belonging to themselves is not the same for each subsystem, then the 'realities' described through the communications of each subsystem (each respective description of the system and its environment) will not be the same.

For the general system of communication (which for Luhmann *is* society) to be successful, its closure cannot be total. This again is not a causal claim. The need for society to be open is a claim about the need for its communications to develop in ways that enable human beings to cope with the physical world. The physical world cannot communicate with the social world, or vice versa, although there may have been beliefs held, or even still held, that assume this possibility. Instead, society must communicate *about* the physical world[12] (and about itself, and its

[11] Luhmann describes the character of the communications relating to these functioning subsystems respectively in the following: politics, Luhmann, 2000b; law, Luhmann 2004; media, Luhmann, 2000c; economics, Luhmann, 1988a; science, Luhmann, 1990c; art, Luhmann, 2000a.

[12] And does so, of course, through communications that make up what is known as the natural sciences.

subjects) in a manner that allows society to continue. And we can see that such developments have taken place, and continue to occur. This openness to the physical world is what is termed cognition. Much theoretical writing is devoted to the location of this cognition and the conditions that make it possible. And much of that writing seeks to locate cognition within the experiences of individuals, most particularly by reference to the experience we understand as consciousness, and the entity that is referred to as the human mind. This location of cognition seems to accord with personal experience, even common sense. However, as part of this introduction to Luhmann's theory the reader will need to understand the argument that cognition does not exist (or at least only exist) at the level of individual human beings.[13] It is a feature of society. Society, as a system of communication, is also an observing system of communication.[14]

Here a legal example may assist. Consider the position of a judge called upon to make a decision. What forms the basis of her/his observations? Some theories will claim that judges make their decisions on the basis of their class, or the interests within society with which they identify—perhaps on the basis of personal experience. But such claims actually say almost nothing about how a judge comes to the point, literally the moment, when her/his decision needs to be made. She/he actually has to be a judge. She/he has to be in charge of a case, has to consider evidence, has to have regard to legal rules, etc, etc. The entities

[13] Severe criticism is raised against autopoietic theory, which relates to the difficulty that the theory seems to present to the way, if at all, that individual cognition and communication and that of systems can possibly interrelate in the terms expressed by the theory. Such a criticism is set out by Bankowski, 1996, and countered by Paterson, 1996.

[14] 'Within the communication system we call society, it is conventional to assume that humans communicate. Even clever analysts have been fooled by this convention. . . . Only communication can communicate. . . . The assumption that this occurs is nothing more than an observer's causal attribution. We have to start any clarification with the observer.' (Luhmann, 2002b, at 169). As an example of such a counter-intuitive theory as applied to what is usually understood as an experience of an intensely individual character, namely love, see Luhmann, 1986a.

that establish the point from which she/he must make her/his observation, and reach her/his decision, are communications. The judge is not observing (or at least not only observing) as a black or white, middle or working class, female or male person, with a happy or unhappy childhood, but is observing from a position, and context, created by the legal system. That system will identify what has to be decided and, which is really the same thing, what has to be looked for in order to decide the issue. Another judge (assuming, for example, that this one fell ill) who had to reach this decision, would also be making a decision from a point established through the system of communications we call the legal system. And if one can accept that each individual who was called upon to make this decision would be being asked to make the same decision,[15] then one can understand the claim that systems of communication do not only communicate about events, they establish the contexts in which observations on events occur. In this sense it is not human beings who observe, but systems that observe.[16] And the basis for that observation is not established by each individual for her or himself, but given to them by the system of communication in which she/he is participating.

So systems of communication are observing systems. And this process of observation is part of society's existence and its evolution. From positions (structures) established through communications, observations are made, that produce new communications. And some of these communications will produce new structures, that will allow new observations to occur. If one thinks about the endeavour that we call natural science, this

[15] Not in the sense that she/he would decide the same way, but that the legal system decides what decision needs to be made.

[16] Whilst recognising the importance of the distinction between internal and external observations, some critics of autopoietic social systems theory believe that to describe systems as 'thinking' and 'observing' reifies systems, and reduces the capacity of the theory to explain and offer accounts within sociology of law, and in particular, empirical sociology of law. This criticism is developed by writers such as Cotterrell, 2001, and Rottleuthner, 1989b; Paterson and Teubner, 1998, present the counter-argument, in relation to empirical sociology of law; while Teubner, 1989, presents the underlying epistemological rationale.

evolutionary process is quite familiar to us. Scientific findings, arising from scientific experiments, carried out according to scientific standards, produce new scientific knowledge, which forms the basis of new experiments and practices, etc. Thus, despite the fact that the physical world has no direct access to our communications, and we can only communicate about it, and in that sense society, as a system of communications, remains closed to the physical world, we have, through operations within communication, observed that world. Within communications we describe a physical world that exists outside of communications, and society as something separate from that physical world, and we establish a basis for the observation of that physical world, and evolve ever more complex communications about both that physical world and ourselves. (Observation is thus cognition both in the sense of seeing, and learning from seeing.)

At this point we have all the elements necessary to begin to consider the autopoiesis of subsystems. Luhmann claims that at a certain point in the evolution of society subsystems begin to exhibit the same characteristics as general communication, through a process of differentiation. Like society (the sum total of all communication[17]) subsystems remain operationally closed. Only a system of communication can identify something as a communication belonging to itself. Like society, each subsystem remains cognitively open. Each subsystem of communication establishes points from which to observe, and based on such observations, selects new communications. Like society, such observations are the basis for selections (decisions), and the communications that result can form new structures, which provide new contexts (ways of seeing).

Whilst the application of autopoiesis as a sociology will be novel to most readers, the kind of experience that autopoiesis seeks to explain is not. Many readers will be familiar with the

---

[17] For Luhmann it is the sum-total in the sense that it includes all the specialised communications of each subsystem of communication, as well as general social communication.

kind of transition that first year law students experience. Prior to studying law, persons who witness a road accident will think of helping the victim, and they might shout 'bastard' after a departing car that failed to stop, but they would not necessarily think of compensation, contributory negligence, and reckless driving. Similarly, one can make arguments about medical students. In their case a desire to help is replaced by the procedures for the examination of different kinds of trauma and injury. A systems theory understanding of this situation is that these different persons are embedded in, and carriers of, different systems of communication. But is this too extreme a view of what occurs in such a situation? Whilst we sometimes describe people as 'thinking like a lawyer', 'doctor', etc, we know that, on closer reflection, there is no purely legal, or medical, structures to thought. There are specialist terms, and specialist knowledge, but we can apply a common practical reasoning to different enterprises that allows us to understand their respective points or value. We can also use a common language and we are capable of explaining things to one another. So whilst it may be true that the physical world cannot address communications to human beings, this is not the case *between* human beings. How could a system of communication remain closed to another system of communication, at least where they are both using the same language? Reapplying the concept of autopoiesis at a subsystem level involves claiming that the respective systems select, by and for themselves, what constitutes a communication within their system. Only the legal system establishes what constitutes a legal communication, only the system of science establishes what constitutes a scientific communication, etc. But what would this mean, and how could it be achieved? What about communications that exist in more than one system, or perhaps in neither, as in the example of lawyers explaining things to doctors and vice versa, and on a more formal level, doctors giving medical evidence or lawyers informing doctors of their legal duties?

Luhmann claims that subsystems maintain their autonomy as systems through their different codes. The code of the legal system is legal/illegal. The code of the scientific system is true/false. Media apply the code information/not information (news/not news). Politics uses government/opposition.[18] Economics uses a distinction of 'payment/non-payment'.[19] Codes have to be distinguished from conditional programmes—the 'if clauses' of these respective systems. Systems may have quite elaborate conditions for the application of their code at any particular moment. And in building up these programmes they may make reference to the physical world, communication that does not operate within any particular system (general social communication), and each other (ie other subsystems of communication).

At first glance this seems a naïve and reductive answer to doubts that systems such as politics, economics and law could remain closed to each other (as closed as the physical world is to society as the totality of communications).[20] But if one can grasp the manner in which this closure operates, the separation of systems becomes clearer. Take a series of events such as a trial. This may involve all sorts of communications: economic, political, scientific, general, etc. How could the legal communications be separated from the others? The answer is the application of the code legal/illegal. The legal system will be repeatedly coding in terms of what is legal or illegal. There will be a lawful arrest, procedure that is legal, a conviction or not and, where conviction occurs the punishment of the defendant will be legal. Particular applications of the code at points in the system will be made by reference to communications about the legal system and its environment. And these communications (the conditional programmes for the particular coding) may

[18] See Luhmann, 1989, ch 13 'Politics' at 86.

[19] *Ibid*, ch 10 'Economy' at 52.

[20] And it is the criticism about reductionism that has commonly been levelled against autopoietic theory. See, for a powerful example: Rottleuthner, 1989a, especially 790–94. We believe that this criticism, as formulated against autopoietic systems theory, is unsuccessful, as we try to demonstrate in this chapter. Further, we return to reductionism in the final chapter and to what within jurisprudence is necessarily reductive.

include communications generated within other systems of communication. But the legal system will re-use such communications in a manner different from that in which they are used in the system that generated them. Most particularly, it will be using them to code in terms of legal/illegal rather than true/false, etc.

An example should help. When scientists give evidence at trial, they will talk of their findings and conclusions. And their evidence may assist in deciding whether to convict a defendant. But the conviction of the defendant will not establish the truth of the scientist's evidence (even if it is the only evidence on the only issue in the trial). And the scientist's tests cannot establish the legality of the conviction; only the decision of the jury will do for that. The conviction will be a conviction and the basis for the coding of the prisoner's punishment as legal, whether or not the scientist correctly or incorrectly applied the conditioning programmes and coding of science.[21] Thus, even if we think that the conditional programmes of the two systems (law and science) are identical at this point, the fact that they are conditions for the applications of different codes (legal/illegal and true/false) means that the communications of the scientist have different meaning for the two systems. (They exist as communications within two systems, rather than being an output of one and an input into the other).

When we look closer at what is going on in our example, we will see that more than the code is involved. The two programmes are not identical. The scientific meaning of the scientist's communication relates, for example, to tests, and how these were carried out. But science does not have cross-examination, it does not convict, it is not adversarial, it does not use the same widely (and wildly) different forms of proof to reach a single decision, the panel which accepts or rejects a scientist's tests is unlikely (within science) to be a group of twelve randomly selected members of the public, a scientific error will

[21] For a fuller account of how law constructs its own reality, see Luhmann, 1986(b).

not have to be corrected by an appeal court, and so on, and so on. While there is one set of tests, the conditional programmes for presentation of findings differs within the two systems. And the divergence between the two systems becomes even clearer if one examines what communications continue after the conviction. Within the legal system, having coded punishment as legal, one can continue to code the treatment of the prisoner (assaults, neglect, loss of remission, etc) as legal and illegal. The legal coding provides the basis for further ongoing communications, further coding. Within science, the prisoner's case notes might be written up as forensic science, and form the basis of some new innovation, or they may not. They are available (as memory) to form the basis for new scientific coding but there may be nothing in this event (the trial) to trigger any further scientific communications.

Viewed as an autopoietic system, law codes in terms of legal/illegal from points of observation established by the legal system itself. In establishing such points of observation the legal system is establishing points that are unique to it. No other system will have to reach a legal decision, making use of the same conditioning programmes. In our conviction example, the observation that constitutes a conviction is unique to the legal system. And the communications that are used by the legal system are used in different ways, and given different, (peculiarly legal) meanings, from those that occur in the system that generated them. Thus the focus on codes, rather than programming, is not as reductive as might at first appear. The claim is not that all legal communications contain the distinction legal/illegal. It is that all communications that are legal are leading towards or away from moments of application of the code. The points at which the code is applied are stable points for a system. Whether the coding applied is legal, or illegal, it provides a stable point from which to make new communications that also lead to the application of coding. Conversely, not every communication that uses the distinction legal/illegal is a legal communication. Some systems, such as the media, use legal communications as part of their conditioning programmes—in the media's case some legal cases are selected as 'news'. Thus coding, whilst simple, is not reductive. It stabilises the process of selection, allowing systems to develop as systems that have enormously diverse conditioning programmes. This complexity includes the potential for any system to re-use any other system's communications as part of its conditioning programmes, by selecting those communications in order to apply its own code. The only thing that a system cannot do, without losing its autonomy, is to apply another system's codes, as representing or uniting its operations, instead of its own.

The ability of codes to produce closure, and provide the basis for the connection between a system's communications is paradoxically because of their inherent meaninglessness. The distinction legal/illegal means nothing by itself. Consider: if I told you that an unknown state of affairs, X, was legal, what would this tell you except that it was not illegal? This is, of course, not usually apparent, because we have an enormously rich set of programmes (conditions) for the application of the code. But the richness of these programmes, the vast number of things that can in diverse areas (criminal, civil, public, private, substantive, procedural, regulation, human rights, etc, etc) result in the application of this code is possible because, inherently, the code is a distinction that has no meaning in and of itself. As such, there is also nothing in the code that prevents a system from evolving—from developing new programmes that rely upon, and generate, new meanings.

So, where does self-description fit into all of this? The answer lies in the nature of autopoiesis and, in particular, its contribution to evolution. Just as closure does not mean causal isolation, or a lack of cognition, it also does not mean that systems are static. They have evolved, and they continue to evolve. How can they evolve? Well, their evolution cannot take any form other than the one in which they exist: communications. To have novel kinds of communications, we have to have novel selections of things as communications. If we accept the existence of autopoietic subsystems, then, as with society as a whole, this selection is made by the subsystem identifying a novel kind of communication as part of itself. How does selection occur?—through making new communications. The possibilities of making new communications depend on what has already been established as a communication within a particular system. So memory is important here. And, in turn, writing (memory with less potential for forgetting)[22] produces a vastly greater store of communications from which to identify new communications.[23]

Within biological evolution, the existence and development of life does not depend upon cognition (observation). If it did, we would not have evolved from the primal swamp. But communication is a process that *does* involve observing, and the development of communication also involves observing. In order to make communications we not only communicate, but we also communicate about how we communicate. And in making communications about how we communicate including, at the most general level, communications about the totality of communication (society) and its relationship with all that is not communication (nature), we alter the possibilities of what, in future, will be communicated. And again, within subsystems, this process of observation is the basis of both stability and evolution.

Within the legal system, this process of observing, involves the repeated examination of earlier coding. Why was '*A*' legal, and '*B*' illegal? A communication explaining an earlier coding is also a communication available for the making of a future coding. This process produces, inevitably, distinctions. Distinctions, in turn, can be generalised into categories, building to the exercise well known to lawyers, the generation of doctrines. And, just as one can have, at the level of society, communications about both society and nature, one can have the equivalent within subsystems.

[22] 'As soon as writing was available, the system's memory lost its ease of forgetting, of not returning to an issue, or of remoulding a suitable past. Now the memory became hardened through writing and at the same time psychologically de-conditioned.' Luhmann, 2004, 138.

[23] The socio-psychological processes involved, with the development of written records of legal communication, are significant, but complicated; see Luhmann, 2004, 234–243.

Legal communications will include not only communications that apply the code, legal/illegal, and communications that account for earlier applications of that code (or, perhaps, earlier codes),[24] but communications that seek to describe the whole process of both coding and accounting for the application of the code. And, just as attempts to describe society within society's communications are autological (the communications describing society are themselves part of what they are attempting to describe) so too are legal communications attempting to describe the legal system. And just as communications about society appear to speak from some position outside of society but cannot, so too self-descriptions of the legal system (descriptions at the most general level of the processes whereby the legal system explains its own decisions to itself for the purposes of making further decisions) remain part of the system which has generated them, and which is also stabilised (but never determined) by them. These descriptions—the most general level of observation within systems—can be understood and known within the legal system as its jurisprudence.

Not all descriptions of the legal system are self-descriptions. It is possible to have scientific descriptions of the legal system (which treat it as an object of research, coding in terms of truth); and media descriptions of the legal system (identifying what is newsworthy) and ethical descriptions (identifying what is good). But these descriptions cannot escape using their own codes, and applying their own conditional programmes, as part of their observations. Such external descriptions reproduce, at a higher level of generality, the features identified earlier when discussing the differences between the operations of systems at lower levels. Consider again the example of the scientist and forensic evidence. The application of science within the trial cannot reproduce the meanings of the tests within science (or at least not

[24] Just as with the economic system where 'the binary coding of the economy through money and a change of the code having/not having to the code payment/non-payment led to the complete functional differentiation of the economic system' (Luhmann, 1989, 52), so the legal code might have changed from just/unjust, to legal/illegal as its functional differentiation evolved (see ch 3 below).

without abandoning the current construction of trial and the application of legal coding to the results of the tests). Similarly the application of law within science (the role of twelve jurors in establishing how and whether the tests contribute to truth) cannot be incorporated into science without changing the conditioning programmes of science, or the code applied. Considering these difficulties, at this level, points to the extraordinary (indeed impossible) task of describing the whole of one system using the conditioning programmes and codes of another.

It is fairly easy for an external system to generate a critique of the legal system at those points where the legal system re-uses its communications, and for such a critique to point to the inevitable differences between the manner in which its own communications operate within its own programmes, and their apparent misuse within law. Implicit or explicit within such critiques is the suggestion that the misuse by law of science, economics, politics, statistics, ethics, etc, etc, could be remedied by critique—ie that it represents a misunderstanding of the methodologies (programmes) of the external system that could be corrected by improved understanding. If the critique is understood as a reform proposal, then there will be some implicit or explicit suggestion that the legal system (perhaps after legislation) could incorporate the critique into its own operations. But the difficulties of accounting for one system using an external system multiply as the level of generality increases. Thus for example, a scientific critique of the whole of criminal procedure is likely to be less of a description (and more of a critique). Such a critique would need to treat criminal procedure as a whole-hearted pursuit of the factual truth of a person's guilt, which would therefore need to reject those aspects of procedure that law presents to itself as matters going to rights and justice independently of their contribution to truth. These rights, like failures to accurately reproduce scientific communications within individual trials, are likely to be observed within science as 'errors'.[25]

[25] For a recent discussion of this kind, in relation to the use of statistics in law, see the special issue of *Significance* 'Statistics and the Law' (Royal Statistical Society, 2005).

When one moves from attempts to superimpose the programmes of an external system on a location within the legal system to attempts to superimpose them upon the legal system as a unity, one experiences (from the described system's perspective) decreasing descriptive capacity (complaints of over-simplification, and extreme difficulty in re-using any part of the critique within law's own operations). Such external descriptions must necessarily jettison so much of law's own communications, including most particularly those communications that constitute observations (law's own accounts of how and why it labels events as legal or illegal). A central part of what such descriptions miss is the variety of sources from which law re-uses communications. For example, an attempt to describe the whole of law as a (flawed) application of economics (ie as a part of the economic system) not only fails to accord with the legal system's understanding of itself as a system of rights and entitlements undetermined by an individual's willingness to pay, but also fails to take account of law's construction of its conditional programmes through communications 'borrowed' from morality, politics, science, etc (all of which will also resist reduction to a calculus of social wealth).

By contrast to such external descriptions of the legal system, one encounters internal self-descriptions. Such descriptions take seriously and engage with law's operations. For a start, they will engage with law's own code, legal/illegal. Self-descriptions attempt to account for the application of the code legal/illegal without seeking to replace that code with a different one: true/false; government/opposition; good/not good. They accept that this is the code applied by the legal system through its own operations. Even natural law theory, for reasons discussed in the next chapter, does not confuse the unity that it seeks to describe with the application of a code outside of law. Thus, whilst modern natural law theories wish to show law's openness to morality, and accord morality a particular importance in establishing law's existence and identity, they do not seek to deny that identity follows coding, not morality. Law is law wherever events are coded legal/illegal. The view that a particular application of the code was, according to moral theory, unjust,[26] does not prevent that application of the code from forming part of a legal system: an unjust law is still a law.

Self-descriptions not only take the code of law seriously, and accept that it is the law and not another system that uniquely applies the code legal/illegal, they also take law's own account of its operations seriously. Self-descriptions cannot describe law entirely in terms of facts. They have to reproduce the legal system's own perception of itself as a structure of norms. This follows from the nature of the communications that are being described. Observation within the legal system of the applications of its own codes has generated communications that have a normative form. Law does not simply articulate an account of the application of its own code in terms of what was done, but what ought to have been done. The historical fact that this occurred has allowed law to develop a massive resistance to other systems—to be in some sense 'immune' to them. Thus while law may borrow from all sorts of systems in order to construct accounts of what it considers to be the relevant facts, it is never limited in its account of its own operations by reference to facts. There is always an additional element: the inclusion of 'oughts'. So, however law identifies and describes the facts of any previous coding, its account of that event always includes an assessment of whether the application of the code legal, or illegal, 'ought' to have been applied. The naked statement that, as a matter of fact, the code was applied in a particular way is not enough, within law, to generate new applications of the code. Observations stabilise future applications of the code when they contain the meaning that 'X ought to be coded' legal, or illegal.[27]

The immunising effect of the legal system's account of itself as a system of norms is two-fold. First, it changes the manner in

[26] See, for the moral code, Luhmann, 1992–1993.

[27] Luhmann characterises this as 'normative expectation' and makes a clear distinction between normative and cognitive expectation. The former is crucial for law since: 'support for the legal system in society as a whole depends largely on this mode of expecting.' (2004, 108, and see for a fuller account of this mode of expectation, ch 2/VI).

which law is required to alter its communications in response to communications about events that do not include 'ought propositions'. The communication that 'X ought to be coded illegal' does not need to be altered because X occurs, has occurred in the past, or is likely to occur in the future. Thus communications from science, or the media, that 'X happens' do not prevent regular meaningful legal communications that X ought to be coded illegal. This resistance to factual communications means that law does not have to 'learn' from disappointments. Law re-uses communications about facts for its conditional programmes ('if X has occurred code illegal'). And because its conditional programmes make use of such communications, changes in those communications (changes in the facts) can alter the code to be applied. But the legal system does not have to alter its conditional programmes just because of illegal events: 'X happens'. This is part of law's closure. Whilst it is open to its environment (by re-using communications from other systems) it establishes for itself both the communications about facts that it needs to re-use, and the conclusions on the coding to be applied. Observations on earlier coding, in the form: 'in the event of X code illegal' provide both forms of selection. This, in systems theory terms can be described as operative closure (a term common to all systems) or, using a term that attempts to get at the distinctive nature of law's communications: 'normative closure'. This selection of facts (for conditional programmes) whilst being resistant to facts (they do not alter the basis for selection) produces Luhmann's suggestive claim that law is 'normatively closed and, at the same time, cognitively open . . .'.[28]

The second manner in which the legal system is immunised from the rest of society by the normative form of its communications is by its ability to apply the code to itself. Not only can the legal system observe on its own earlier coding to account to

---

[28] Luhmann, 2004, 106. He goes on to say: 'This concise formula has met with considerable difficulties of understanding, especially in the context of a discussion on autonomy and causal dependencies on the environment.'

itself why it coded legal or illegal, but it can also revisit that coding to re-code it. A communication that seeks to account for earlier communications in the form 'in the event of X, the coding ought to be illegal' can be revisited, and reversed 'in the event of X, one ought to code legal'. This can happen anywhere in the system. One layperson's claim as to legality can be revisited, or a policeman's, or a court's, or on an appeal, and even the highest court in the system can revisit the communications of other courts and itself and re-apply the code. These possibilities mean that the system, whilst normatively closed (only the legal system can make the observations and the communications of those observations that alter the conditioning programmes that select the facts) can nevertheless evolve. But such evolution is not a direct input of communications from other systems. So law does not automatically evolve (either in the sense of a standard or a predictable reaction) whenever communications of fact alter. But changes in communications of fact do provide new opportunities for new coding, and for new observations on these and earlier coding.

Self-descriptions, unlike external descriptions, seek to describe law as a system of norms, which is law's own account to itself of its own communications. Whilst legal communications are both the re-used communications of fact and the norms applied to them (both of which are required for coding) the legal system identifies itself to itself as one half of these operations (the norms). Self-descriptions cannot seek to account for the legal system as a set of facts without losing the meanings generated within the system by the system. They cannot do this without losing what it is that they are seeking to generalise: the accounts generated within the legal system of the application of the distinction legal/illegal. If the normative meanings within those accounts are abandoned, then self-descriptions lose the very data that they are attempting to describe.[29]

[29] This is what Luhmann means by claiming that self-descriptions exhibit a *commitment* to law as a series of norms, and as a system uniquely employed to code the world in terms of the distinction legal/illegal. But this commitment to law as a series of norms is not a normative commitment. 'There is no exception

The apparent strength of self-descriptions (generalising from communications produced within the system) is also the source of some of their most problematic features. Whilst generalising from systems' own communications avoids the loss of meanings that results from attempts at external descriptions, it also reproduces the paradox that all system communications seek to unfold. The code of an autopoietic system is, in itself, a meaningless distinction. It is given meaning through the process of coding, and then observing on coding and describing that observation. But the communications that result from observation do not proceed on the basis that the distinction is meaningless, but quite the opposite, namely meaningful. Observations do not generate admissions that there were no reasons for the application of the code on the occasion being observed. Rather, they operate on the basis that reasons can be given, even if that reason is a communication that the code was wrongly applied on the earlier occasion. Observations that take the form: 'there was no reason for deciding how to apply the code on that occasion', block the further development of the system. The system can only evolve if observations and accounts represent a double denial. In order to evolve, the legal system cannot refuse to decide, or refuse to decide why it decided. Indeed, if one thinks of this in terms of evolution, starting with a distinction that has no inherent meaning, it is only by deciding and accounting for decisions even though there are no good reasons that enables the legal system to develop a vast amount of communications that do, in practice, provide good (re-usable) reasons for deciding. To put this colloquially, by coding when there are no good reasons for deciding one way or the other, and then giving reasons for those decisions, the legal system, like all other autopoietic systems, 'pulls itself up by its own bootstraps'. Which is just as

to the principle of the operative closure of the legal system. It is not a normative principle. There is no provision for the violation of this principle in the legal system. A communication is not unlawful, rather it is an impossible one, if it does not fit into the coding legal/illegal. The communication is simply not attributed to the legal system but is seen as a fact in its environment.' (Luhmann, 2004, 120).

well, because if it waited for a foundational value to establish, on all occasions, why anything should be coded legal as opposed to illegal it could not continue to code in the hugely variable circumstances encountered by the legal system within modern society. But and this is the drawback for self-descriptions—generalising from these accounts does not give a description of the unity of the system that acknowledges what such accounts, at every point in the system, constantly suppress: that there is no inherent basis for the application of the distinction. There are only communications that constantly reiterate, by their very existence, the assumption that the distinction is meaningful. The operations of law, endlessly repeated, generate values that any generalisation of such operations (communications at a more general level that seek to systematise communications at a lower level) simply cannot deny.[30] One such central value is the belief, endlessly demonstrated by law's operations, that it can account to itself for why it applies the code legal/illegal.

Not only do self-descriptions build on accounts provided in circumstances where there were no good reasons for deciding, or accounting for those decisions, in one way rather than another, but in so doing, self-descriptions can be productive for the system. By accounting for the unity of the system in a manner that denies the arbitrariness (in terms of foundational values but not in terms of re-usable communications) of the system, self-descriptions reinforce the system's perceptions of itself as a rationally organised system. Whatever such descriptions identify as the essential nature of the communications stabilising the application of the code (God, sources, constitutions, morality) will assist in that process of stabilisation. They are autological— they will form part of the communications that are available to account for the process of coding. But what they necessarily fail to describe adequately, is the arbitrariness of the process that generates re-usable (and therefore non-arbitrary) accounts for

---

[30] At this point we have returned to Luhmann's statement (2004, 429) introduced in ch 1, namely 'finding out *what is implied when a system promises to give an answer to every question and forces all the operations of the system to presuppose that there is such an answer.*'

the application of the code. This omission is what prevents self-descriptions from blocking further development (evolution). Whatever self-descriptions identify as essential to the process of coding can only stabilise, they cannot totally block. Because some decisions will be taken that are not referable to whatever self-descriptions identify as essential, then accounts of those decisions have the potential to require new self-descriptions. New communications will identify new structures as essential. As such, the evolution of self-descriptions is an inevitable accompaniment of the evolution of the legal system. And jurisprudence, as part of law's operations and an accompaniment to its practices, which incorporates its autological self-description, is also part of that evolution.

The final 'paradox' (from an external perspective) is that self-descriptions have to present part of the system as the unity of the system. This follows first from their autological nature. They are part of what they are seeking to describe. Secondly, this follows because the communications that they describe have already distinguished part of themselves as themselves, and another part as their environment. If all communications selected by the legal system for the purpose of coding are legal communications, then the ability of the legal system to identify itself with the 'legal' normative aspect of those communications—and its environment as the factual or 'other' normative aspect of those communications—is a description that has already excluded part of the unity that is going to be described. To these two reasons why self-descriptions present part of the legal system as the whole of the system, one can add a third. This third reason arises from the capacity to evolve generated by differentiation orientated around binary codes that have no inherent meaning, but rather rely on the communication of a distinction with no inherent limit to what might be coded as legal and illegal.[31] This is not to deny that the system, at any point in

---

[31] For example, it was no less difficult or easy for legal systems at earlier times to impose criminal liability on animals for their behaviour than today for corporations to be held criminally liable for crimes such as manslaughter.

its evolution, will face different degrees of difficulty in coding some things rather than others. But it does allow the legal system to utilise all kinds of communications to draw all kinds of distinctions from any number of points of observation within itself. And the task of reducing a unity that exists only in the presence of a common code (all communications selected by the legal system for the purposes of coding), to a statement of what is common to all the conditioning programmes that facilitate those communications, is inevitably a presentation of part of a unity as the whole unity.

However, to treat jurisprudence as self-description is in no sense to ignore law's current appearance as ubiquitous (whether viewed from an external or an internal perspective) in contemporary Western societies. Law occurs. In any twenty-four hour period billions of things happen that have legal significance. And such things have been happening for quite some time. However, by definition, law only exists in the present, even though it has existed in the past. In law's past it had forms, institutions and practices that are different from what they are today. And the obvious lesson that can be drawn from the differences in law between past, present and future is that it will evolve: that it has a different existence from its past and will have a different existence in the future. If one accepts these conditions, one must also accept the inevitable contingency of law. It has, and has always had, endless possibilities of being other than what it is now. But the nature of law's contingency[32] is not sufficient to prevent its existence. Indeed, recognition of the legal significance of social events takes place with sufficient stability and regularity, that not only can it become the subject of academic analysis and occupy an individual for years,[33] but—to repeat what is the character of

[32] Throughout this book we rely on the description of law as contingent. We do so without undertaking any analysis of the relevance of such a description within different strands of theoretical discourse. We simply use the word 'contingency' to represent a condition or situation that could be other than it is. For a discussion of the importance of contingency in generating Luhmann's systems theory, see Rasch, 2000.

[33] Or even a lifetime, as with Hans Kelsen and his Pure Theory!

the social reality that has to be described—incalculably numerous acts and decisions with acknowledged legal significance occur within fractions of each second. Jurisprudential theories as self-description of the nature of law, or law's unity, can be assessed by reference to their ability to account for law's vast but at the same time limited possibilities.

If one recognises the contingency of law, there immediately arises a problem in attempting to describe its unity. Law is never in a steady state. It constantly selects. Within the range of possibilities of what can have legal significance at any moment, there are selections of what that significance will be, and the range of possibilities of legal significance changes over time: law evolves. Jurisprudential theories that seek to describe or otherwise give a reason for the unity of law have to offer an explanation for this contingency and evolution. In so doing, they seek to identify structures that account for both its stability and change. However, many of their descriptions of these structures might be found wanting, in that they may appear too far removed from the actual happenings of law's operations. What then is the relationship between such 'texts of self-description' (jurisprudence) and law's operations? As explained in chapter 1, we assume that any developed sociological understanding of such happenings must take into account lawyers' self-understandings of what they do and what law is. And systems theory offers one possible route to such self-understanding (one that addresses the problem that discussion of 'justice' or 'due process and fairness', or other values that try to express law's unity might seem to bear only the most tangential relationship to concrete practices, and might arouse suspicions that what is being represented is primarily no more than some self-serving gloss adopted for professional interest purposes).

Systems theory offers a way to take practicing lawyers' self-understandings seriously and to investigate the relationship between these self-understandings and the self-descriptions offered within jurisprudence, while at the same time accounting for the detail and practical manifestation of law's operations. Both the evolution of legal doctrines (the generalisation of particular legal rules and decisions) and the even more general theories offered within jurisprudence, can be understood as attempts by both practicing lawyers as much as by legal theorists to disguise and avoid what appears as a tautology[34] at the heart of law's supposed or assumed unity.[35] A systems theory approach to this task would acknowledge and thereby respond to what amounts to the paradox[36] that results from law's autonomic form, namely the paradox consequential to the tautology that the law decides what is and can be law at any and every moment; it is the legal system itself that identifies its own boundaries. This way of thinking about the law starts with the simple logical tautology: the law is what the law says it is; the law determines itself—both what is legal and illegal. The theory works from the premise that there is nothing outside of law that can establish the identity and existence of law. But, despite that, the theory does not presume that systems operate with a self-conscious (or system self-conscious) awareness of such tautologies. Indeed, on the contrary, the need to make meaningful distinctions despite the absence of any value or interest that can determine what is legal, generates structures within law that hide

[34] We use the word tautology not to represent the fault of saying the same thing twice (what might be understood as a verbal tautology), but rather the idea of a statement that is necessarily true within itself (what might be understood as a logical tautology).

[35] To repeat a quotation from Luhmann (2004, 425) set out in ch 1: 'But it can be assumed that legal practice presupposes that the fundamental questions of the meaning of the system can be answered and it bases its decision-making on that in the form of a presupposition (rather than on information).'

[36] We recognise that this might appear to be a paradox, rather than actually be a paradox. But, as with many 'supposed' paradoxes (a statement that might be anathema to logicians) the puzzle represented by the paradox 'has been the occasion for major reconstruction at the foundation of thought.' (Quine, quoted in Clark, 2002, *ix*. See n 40 below for a fuller statement of Luhmann's characterisation of law's paradox.) For Luhmann (2004, 182), while 'The unity of a system operating a binary code can be described only as existing in the form of a paradox', this paradox is extremely productive: 'The paradox of the system—in law as, in a different way, in logic—is its blind spot, one that renders the operation of observing possible in the first place.'

and displace its tautological form.[37] And theories that take these structures seriously, most notably jurisprudential theories, will seek, and fail to find answers to the nature of law's existence and evolution that are not themselves tautological.[38] Systems theory, on the other hand, recognises and delves into law's autonomic character, and it does so by exploring the apparent paradox associated with law's tautology,[39] how it establishes itself and evolves through its own circular self-reference, its operative closure.[40]

[37] On the complications associated with the internal/external character of descriptions of self-descriptions of law (this sociology of jurisprudence), see Luhmann, 2004, 426–431.

[38] Thus, in discussing economic theories of law, as with other jurisprudential theories, Luhmann (2004, 64) states: 'Like all attempts at introducing the unity of law in any form (and, that is, through a relevant distinction) into law, this attempt also rests on the dissolution (unfolding, making invisible, civilizing, making asymmetrical) of a paradox.' Or, in one of Luhmann's most succinct statements (2004, 212): 'The unity of the binary code, therefore, can only be understood as a paradox . . . The paradox is rendered invisible through the process of its unfolding and determination.'

[39] 'There is no supreme norm which guarantees that coding represents the unity of the system within the system . . . Coding legal/illegal cannot be applied to itself without running into a paradox that blocks further observations.' (Luhmann, 2004, 101–102).

[40] In summary, we believe that as applied to law (and equivalently to other sub-systems) Luhmann uses the term paradox to describe the following propositions: 1. Only the law can decide what can be law. 2. Law is the application by law of a distinction particular to law: legal/illegal. 3. The distinction has no meaning outside of law, and no meaning inside of law other than the history of its application. 4. Whilst the law decides what is law (nothing else can) law cannot decide in a deterministic manner, as there is nothing that law can use to determine (code) the application of the distinction legal/illegal other than its own past applications. Thus 'One has to apply this distinction even though one can neither ask nor answer the question (because it would lead to a paradox) as to whether the distinction between legal and illegal itself is legal or illegal. The paradox itself turns unwittingly into a creative principle because one has to try so hard to avoid and to conceal it.' (Luhmann, 2004, 177). On the creative use of paradox within legal theory, see Luhmann, 1988b.

3

A Sociological Understanding of Natural Law and Common Law Theory: Constructing the Conditions for Legal Positivism

In this chapter we examine the relationship between legal positivist and natural law theories from the perspective of systems theory ie viewing these theories as self-descriptions: communications generated within the legal system that explain itself to itself. This approach examines developments in jurisprudence from the perspective of evolution within the legal system, rather than as a result of changes that occur in the rest of society. Such an exploration is a background to the main substantive chapters of this book, chapters 4, 5 and 6, which three chapters offer a systems theory critique of Dworkin's natural law theory, Kelsen's positivist legal theory, and the writings of critical legal theorists as a modern example of post-positivist, realist theory. Those three chapters represent a sociology of the three leading forms of modern jurisprudence, while this chapter will highlight the importance of treating jurisprudential theories as self-description. Through such treatment it will be shown how the classic natural law form has limited possibilities for accommodating a developing legal linguistics and structure whereby the legal system experiences itself as undergoing routine and frequent change. In response, the legal system's self-observation and self-description is reconstructed, with positivist theories of law being generated. Such generation, rather than being a reflection of a contrasting outlook, is rather part of law's internal evolution, a characteristic of its internal variety. However, this chapter will also explore the limitations of positivist legal theory as self-description and as an observation of law's changing practices.[1]

As shown in the introductory section to the previous chapter, the focus on internal developments within the legal system is not part of a claim that the legal system is causally independent of changes in the rest of society. However, the communications that the legal system selects, in order to explain its own operations to itself, facilitate and stabilise those operations. The basis of selection remains internal. Changes in communications generated outside the legal system, such as changes in the self-description of politics (in terms of God, or the common good) alter the possibilities of what can be selected for reuse by the legal system. But this is not an inevitable process. The legal system, like any of society's systems, does not necessarily 'learn' from what, with the benefit of hindsight,[2] seems to be a superior idea circulating within another system. So, for example, the legal system did not have to adjust its communications because the arguments of Hobbes, or Bentham, seemed, from contemporary points of observation, superior to those of Aquinas or Blackstone. Indeed, the teaching of natural law within a course on jurisprudence usually involves an historical

---

[1] Those changing practices are generally represented in phrases such as the 'positivity' or 'positivisation' of law. Positivity and positivisation are by no means elegant, or clear terms. In modern parlance they have been overtaken by use of the word 'juridification', the idea that more and more of the world is being appropriated into legal forms, being subjected to more specific legal provisions that are less obviously grounded in the simple distinction of just and unjust, but nonetheless grounded in the distinction of legal and illegal. This latter distinction communicates as easily about the 'administration of things' as it does about those matters to which moral reasoning can more obviously be applied. For a sustained statement about the limitations of 'positivity', see Luhmann, 2004, ch 2/I.

[2] From an internal perspective this might be hindsight—the system seeing its own past and as progress from that past. From an external perspective, a different system will simply note the differences between itself and the observed system thus, for example, the legal system might be analysed as having lagged behind.

account which demonstrates, from a post-enlightenment position, an astounding ability for legal systems to resist learning what seems to be the obvious fact that law is not the application of general principles of a common human good. It is this history that makes sense of Alf Ross' description of natural law theory as '. . . at the disposal of everyone. The ideology does not exist that cannot be defended by an appeal to the law of nature'.[3] Natural law has been used to justify the Greek polis, the Greek and Roman Empires, the medieval principality, and the French and American revolutions and their subsequent constitutions. But whilst, from the perspective of natural law as a scientific idea, this may represent a devastating critique (that which justifies everything, justifies nothing) the question that remains is why a theory that had served so many different legal regimes should ever have been abandoned? The answer suggested by this chapter is not an external one: the growth of scientific knowledge, or the relative percentage of the population with shared moral values or a belief in God. Nor is the answer provided by the growth of law as a profession, although this is part of the story. Lawyers, identified by themselves and others as a distinct group with highly artificial practices, were able to utilise natural law for centuries. Rather the changes that generated an evolution in jurisprudential ideas, viewed as self-description, were changes within the legal system itself. In particular, the enormous growth of legislation and its understanding as a source of law **from the beginning of the 19th century** made it no longer possible for the legal system to communicate about itself as a unity by reference to natural law theories.[4]

---

[3] Ross, 1958, 261.

[4] Maitland (1926, 382–4) points out the fact that notwithstanding the bulk of the statute-book in the eighteenth century, comparatively few acts of real legislation ('any alteration of the general rules of law') were passed before the first Reform Act of 1832, which produced radical and sweeping changes in laws, such as, for example, the Poor Law Reform Act of 1834. ' "Within these last two hundred and fifty years," Francis Stoughton Sullivan instructed the university students of Dublin in the 1760's, "the inhabitants of Europe . . . seem to have

Natural Law as the Continuity of Existing Law

The classical natural law theory of Thomas Aquinas[5] posits a hierarchical relationship between positive law and divine law or natural law. The borders of positive law are established by reference to what is unjust. What is unjust (incompatible with natural law or divine law) is outside positive law ('In so far as it deviates from reason it is called an unjust law, and has the quality not of law but of violence'[6]). Within natural law theory's debate with positivist legal theory its focus is upon the claim that an unjust law is not a law (and the challenge that this represents to a positivist account of law). As an analytic scheme, viewed from a modern perspective, this hierarchy of laws represents a possible restraint upon positive law, at least if one presupposes a consensus as to what constitutes injustice. However, as an analytic scheme this hierarchy is quite limited as a restraint, particularly outside the matters pertaining to heresy (which can be concretised through the procedures of the established Church), as it acknowledges that what constitutes the 'common good' is not capable of deduction, but must be established by reference to the particular circumstances of each community. Aquinas did not claim that the content of positive law could be identified by extrapolation from general moral principles. The lack of an objective standard for the rules of particular communities is part of what, within natural law theory, justified the need for rulers whose rules were binding by reason of their authority rather than their content. As such, subject only to a universal understanding as to what constituted heresy or injustice, Aquinas' natural law theory might, from a modern perspective, be seen as an endorse-

been seized with an epidemic madness of making new laws."' (Lieberman, 1989, 14). If our historical exploration were developed fully it would require a huge historical compass, which goes much further than the limited exploration that will be offered here. In his writings Luhmann has engaged in such exploration, and the references he uses in ch. 11 of *Law as a Social System* (2004) are directions for a fuller review of this large history.

5 See his '*Summa Theologica*' in Aquinas, 1959 edn.
6 *Ibid*, 121.

ment of the 'divine right' of rulers to introduce whatever rules they regard as expedient i.e. a scheme which authorises legislation, subject only to quite minimal restraints (by reference to a higher form of law) on introducing what could universally be judged to be unjust laws.[7]

Understanding natural law theory from such a modern perspective does not allow one to understand how it operated as a self-description of law. In turn, it does not provide an adequate understanding of how and why law changed from understanding itself in terms of natural law, to understanding itself by reference to the tenets of positivist legal theory. What gave Aquinas' natural law theory a purchase upon the everyday operations of law was not its general principles, but the nature of the order that it described. The local order that was experienced as natural, despite differences between communities, was a customary or traditional order. And the positive law, which differed from community to community, was a customary form of law that was both a creation of each community and something that constituted each community. As such, it both lacked a single author, and was not something that could be radically altered by any single ruler as she/he or it saw fit.[8] This is a type of law that operated as a considerable constraint against the introduction of what is understood today by the term legislation.[9] Tyranny (ruling without law) was not likely to be experienced as the introduction of laws that

[7] Similar observations apply when one considers the reforming capacity of the systems of equity that developed alongside more formal systems of law. Here 'justice' operated, as it still does today, as a 'formula for variety': an alternative to accepting the outcomes of formal systems of law is to appeal to justice. Again, from a modern perspective, this move seems basically without limit, or is only limited by the outer reaches of what can be thought just.

[8] '. . . medieval and early modern Europe managed without national legal systems.' (van Caenegem, 2002, 1).

[9] 'Bracton's *De Legibus Et Consuetudinibus Angliae* (Laws and Customs of England) of the mid-thirteenth century states: "Rex non debet esse sub homine sed sub deo et sub lege, quia lex facit regem . . . non est enim rex ubi dominatur voluntas et non lex." The King is under God and the law. He is no king when will and not law is the principle of his rule. Law is a rule of reason and not a mere command of a superior.' (Quote and translation from O'Sullivan, 1965, 125).

were universally agreed to be unjust, but as the introduction of laws that represented a radical breach with an existing local order.[10] In turn, the natural law that operated as a higher law than local positive law was not simply universal moral ideas on the nature of justice, but supra-community forms of law such as 'the law of the Church and the neo-Roman law of the universities (known as "the common, written laws" or the learned *ius commune)'.*[11] Thus, as a self-description, natural law did not refer to a relationship between abstract moral principles and the political authority of a ruler to legislate at will (a modern perspective on the clash between positivism and natural law) but a relationship principally constituted by two kinds of law: local custom and more universal forms of law (on the continent the *ius commune*).

Natural law theory as a self-description thus stabilised and facilitated many different legal operations. It identified what was customary as law, claiming authority for what was traditional by reference to ideas that conflate order and nature, yet allowed for the possibility that rulers could introduce new law when the common good required this. However, because the order, which was understood as positive law, was customary, the ability of rulers to introduce new laws was restrained. Rulers who attempted to introduce radical changes ran the risk of their communications not being recognised as contributions to the legal order i.e. of ruling without law.[12] On the continent, during the

[10] Postema (not, of course, presenting his analysis as an autopoietic analysis), in *Bentham and the Common Law Tradition* (1986) examines the plausibility of the claim that it is local orders, and not general moral principles, that provide workable conditions for natural law reasoning (see ch 4, 'Hume's Jurisprudence: Common Law Conventionalism'). Postema discusses how much greater are the possibilities of agreement on social contracts once one has a conventional order in place (which one can agree to maintain or exchange for chaos) rather than where one starts from some original position where society is yet to be created.

[11] 'Cross-fertilization was the order of the day, because the law was seen as a vast treasure house from which kings and nations could pick and choose what suited them.' (van Caenegem, 2002, 1–2).

[12] The positivist idea that a sovereign could be the source of all law runs counter to the idea of tyranny as a sovereign ruling without law. It is the latter idea that gave rise to documents in Europe, such as the English *Magna Carta*

medieval and early modern period, attempts to alter local customs in significant ways did not take the form of social policies enacted into law, but the displacement of local custom by the *ius commune*.[13] Such innovation was compatible with natural law theory, as the provisions of the *ius commune* could be presented as superior (closer to the reason associated with natural law) than local custom.[14] But whilst this form of law could be introduced through legislation, it was not legislative in form. The *ius commune* was a combination of canon law and the codification of Roman law by the Emperor Justinian: the *Corpus Iuris Civilis*. The latter underwent a process of elucidation and explanation in order to adapt it to local legal systems' needs. This was the sort of exegesis associated with scripture, and not the application of political authority to change law in response to perceived

Liberatum, 'Great Charter of Liberties' 1215 (see van Caenegem, 1995, 80), which documents formed the beginnings of the constitutional developments of legal restraints on sovereign power.

[13] Another example of the need to construct law from existing law (most of which was customary) rather than through legislation, simply imposed by superior force, is found in events following the Norman Conquest. William allowed his English subjects to continue to apply their Anglo-Saxon customs in disputes between themselves, but allowed his Norman subjects to apply their own customs in the administration of their own affairs. At the same time, he increased his power beyond that possible as a Norman duke by adopting the English customs that identified their leaders as kings. None of this 'pick and choose' situation represents legislation, as we would understand it today. See van Caenegem, 1973, 8–15.

[14] '. . . the civil lawyer is heir to a legal tradition in which law is seen as being a particular manifestation of a greater order of which it is a part not the whole. The law of a particular country, its civil law in a narrow sense, is only part of a greater legal order. The Roman jurists used the words *ius civile* for the proper law of a particular people, while recognising that some laws were common to all mankind. This latter body of law was at times described as the law of nations, the *ius gentium*, but at other times as being part of the law which was common to all creatures, the natural law or *ius naturale*. Christian thinkers saw this latter concept as being a part of the divine order, a manifestation in nature of the divine will, a God-given law which mere human legislation could not revoke and ought not to contravene.' (Watkin, 1999, 5).

social or political needs.[15] Thus both forms of law, custom and the exegesis of Roman law, could be located within natural law theory, and each required the development of law out of existing law (with change presented as continuity).[16]

Natural law, as jurisprudential self-description, is not the same thing as natural law as a political theory. As a political theory, natural law is ambiguous as between the right of those in authority to establish a local version of the common good, and the extent to which any local order partakes of the wider natural order and is thereby constrained by natural law. Rulers who wished to make radical changes and those who wished to maintain local practices could both appeal to natural law to justify their positions. But as jurisprudential self-description one needs to have regard to how the theory functioned in relation to the day-to-day operations of law. And here natural law ideas of order, nature and reason provided communications that allowed law to develop from local customs via a process that distinguished between what was local and what was universal, and established a hierarchy in favour of the latter. The idea that law was something more universal than local custom, and the identification of law with Roman law,[17] became incorporated into local law when students who had studied the *ius commune*

[15] 'Most of the work on the Roman Law portions of the Civil Law down to the end of the sixteenth century was really exegesis . . . [which] tries to relate [texts] to each other in terms of more general principles and doctrines, and then to find embedded in the mass of law certain concepts, which seem to be the true component parts of the legal machine.' (Lawson, 1955, 63–4). See also, van Caenegem, 2002, 33–5.

[16] Even the process of codification, which replaced much customary law and Roman law through legislative enactment, was open to natural law not simply because it was justified in terms of reason, but because the application of that reason took the form of the simplification and harmonisation of existing laws (Lawson, 1955, 76). Codification uses legislation to replace a disorganised scheme of law with a rationally organised one, on the assumption that this will have some permanence. This is a different experience of legislation from the modern one of prolific legislation in response to particular social problems.

[17] At later stages in European history, Roman law was seen as parochial, and continental jurists began to prioritise what was universal in their own local legal systems over 'foreign' Roman law.

at universities, particularly in Italy, returned to work in their local courts:

> The rediscovery of the [Justinian] Digest inspired several generations of scholars at Bologna to devote their energies to a complete understanding and mastery of what they perceived to be *the* legal text. The Digest, it was thought and accepted, manifested not just a legal system but legal perfection. . . . if there were repetitions, they were for a purpose; if there appeared to be contradictions or errors, such appearances were due to deficiencies in the reader and not the text. Greater understanding and more careful analysis it was believed would overcome such apparent blemishes.[18]

This approach to legal study involved the application of reason to rules, but not the application of abstract moral or religious principles directly onto the empirical situation. Everything had to be mediated through the text of the Digest. This study not only led to the incorporation of Roman law into continental legal systems, but the growth of juristic reasoning based upon text. Techniques were fashioned for jurists to develop the principles found in written laws to suit current social conditions. And this technique once employed in the study of Roman law, not only led to local laws being supplemented by Roman law, but to local laws similarly being reduced to writing and analysed and developed by what, within them, was considered principled and rational.[19] In this sense, it was not the adoption of Roman law per se, which generates the civilian tradition of what constitutes

---

[18] Watkin, 1999, 83. This approach to the Digest as a source of a universally valid and wholly consistent form of law led to the reconciliation of apparently contradictory provisions through various devices. A rule that was apparently in conflict might only have a local application, it might have a limited temporal application, it might apply to a different field of operation, or it might be an exception to a general rule (*ibid*, 85).

[19] See Watkin, 1999, 106–7. '[I]t is important to be clear that this reception did not involve the adoption of the *ius commune* in place of local or national laws. On the contrary, the *ius commune* constituted what has been described by one recent writer as "a secure point of reference"; it was the background to the operation of local statutes and customs, an interpretative framework within which sense could be made of these and a source of norms which could be called upon or dug into to fill in gaps in the individual legal systems.' (Ibbetson, 2001, 6).

law, but the methods and forms of reasoning that Roman law represented. This was a method that could not only be adapted from Roman law to local customary law, but also be used in later centuries to formulate civil codes that replaced forms of Roman law that were no longer considered appropriate to current conditions.

The extent to which the *ius commune* influenced the English common law is a matter of some controversy amongst legal historians.[20] But the processes involved in its formation and development still enabled natural law reasoning to play a role within law's everyday operations. 'In like manner [to the *ius commune*] the term common law came to mean in England the body of rational legal principles which were declared and administered by the King's Judges as opposed to the special customs or privileges of any county or borough. . . . Above all local customs rose the custom of the King's Courts: *tremendum regiae majestatis imperium*.'[21] This process of modernising and unifying law was articulated in terms of a higher law based on reason and nature:

> Against this law (of reason or of nature) prescription, statute nor custom may not prevail: and if any be brought in against it, they be not prescriptions, statutes, nor customs, but things void and against justice (Christopher St Germain, *Doctor and Student*).[22]

However, whilst there were undoubtedly civilian influences on the common law, and Roman law was one of the sources that could be referred to by judges when deciding difficult points of law, the different operations of the English legal system did not allow it to generate a self-description in the same terms as the civilian system. The unification of English law through a system of Kings' writs (rather than the adoption of a single authoritative text) gave rise to a self-description of law as a practical

[20] See Ibbetson, 2001.

[21] O'Sullivan, 1965, 119–120.

[22] O'Sullivan, 1965, 125. St Germain's dialogue was first published in Latin in 1523. It is one of the key sources of knowledge of late medieval and early modern English law. For a short summary, see McIlwain, 1910, 105–8.

means for providing remedies for pre-existing 'wrongs' drawing upon politics, morals and abstract notions of justice for solutions to cases. In this process law was a means to provide a just solution to any wrong, provided only that the dispute was presented in the appropriate manner. This understanding of justice identified it as the output of the formality and technicality of the common law system of specific pleading (a system in which any small mistake could compromise the action). 'Right' and 'wrong' were presumed to exist within society, but 'wrongs' could only be correctly 'seen', and remedies provided, if the issues were looked at though a lens fashioned by the extremely complex procedures of the common law.[23] Issues identified in this way were not to be resolved through the application of rules, but by a combination of maxims, eruditions, and principles.[24] As Plowden said:

> Maxims are the Foundations of the Law and the Conclusions of Reason, and therefore they ought not to be impugned, but always to be admitted; yet these maxims may by the Help of Reason, be compared together, and set one against another, (although they do not vary) where it may be distinguished by a Reason that a Thing is nearer to one Maxim than to another, or placed between two Maxims, nevertheless they ought never to be impeached or impugned, but always to be observed and held as firm Principles and Authorities of themselves.'[25]

The methods by which common law courts presented and resolved issues was understood as an application of reason, and as such it resembles the continental methods for developing law. But the reason in question was understood as 'artificial' reason, to distinguish it from the more general forms of reason associated

[23] See Lobban, 1991, especially ch 3 'The Logic of the Law'; Stoner, 1992, 18–22.

[24] Prior to its hardening in the 1770s, flexibility in the common law could also be achieved via an appeal to equity: see Lobban, 1991, 1; Lieberman, 1989 ch 3 'Equity, principle and precedent'.

[25] *The Commentaries or Reports of Edmund Plowden* (London, 1779) 27, quoted in Lobban, 1991, 7. The pre-echoes of Dworkin's arguments for right legal answers in hard cases are striking.

with the continental use of natural law theory. There was nothing equivalent to the Digest. Indeed, the common law, far from being understood as the principles implicit within a particular text was referred to as 'unwritten law',[26] on the basis that there was no text which contained everything of which it consisted. Nature, God, justice, public interest and convenience were sources of reasons for decisions (Coke said that there were 20 such sources.[27]) What prevented such an array of sources of law from undermining the law's ability to exist, and to be something other than the personal morality of particular judges, was the strict system of pleadings that carefully identified the issue that arose between plaintiff and defendant. In place of a text such as the Digest, English law had a system of pleadings that identified exactly what wrong a plaintiff alleged against a defendant, and indicated what evidence and arguments could be offered in support of this. Different pleadings (formerly writs) had a relationship to each other, especially in a context of precedent. What was identified as a relevant constituent of a specific cause of action provided a point of reference for other causes of action that appeared analogous, or distinguishable. Analogy is not a deductive process, and so in deciding a novel point (whether it was necessary to plead a particular fact for a particular cause of action in novel circumstances) the judges could have regard to their wide and (from an outside perspective) chaotic set of sources for deciding what was appropriate. But the use of such sources was always constrained by the need to show consistency with, or the ability convincingly to distinguish, what had already been decided, and what would remain. So, for example, once it was accepted that promises would not be enforced in the absence of consideration, it would have to be shown why consideration did not need to be pleaded when the contract which the plaintiff had relied up on was a bill of exchange.[28]

---

[26] Hale, for example, divided the law of England into the *lex scripta* (statutes) and the *lex non scripta*. The latter consisted of general customs (common law) and particular customs. See Simpson, 1986, 18–19.

[27] See Lobban, 1991, 59.

[28] See *Pillans v Van Mierop* (1765) 3 Burr 1663, discussed by Lobban, 1991, 108–111.

These kinds of legal operations could be articulated as 'artificial reason', and claimed to represent an acquired wisdom that was greater than that possible via an a priori application of general moral or ethical principles. But it was difficult for these operations to be described as a unity. The kinds of reasoning applied when decisions were taken to develop the law could be wide-ranging, and intellectual. But how could the qualities exhibited at each stage in this process of development be presented when one came to describe the system as a whole? One method, and the excerpt presented earlier from St. Germain is an example of this, is to ascribe some of the values utilised to make decisions to qualities of the whole system: reason, nature, custom, and God. However, whatever universal values were claimed to have gone into the production of the English legal system, unlike the civilian system, it could not claim to be a universal system of law, or even a local variant of such a universal system. Instead, it was driven to make its differences from the continent part of its own self-description, leading to an understanding of itself as appropriate to the particular society which it regulated: the English nation. Of course 'Englishness' may be as elusive as morality when it comes to definition. But English lawyers found its qualities within their own system. A system that communicates about itself as the application of reason in order to provide appropriate remedies for as many 'wrongs' as is practical does not understand itself to be actually deciding what is right and wrong, but as giving effect to ideas of what is unjust within the wider society. This exercise is amenable to natural law theorising, albeit not such as could be fitted into the categories of Roman law, or the general schemes of moral philosophy. (To remind the reader, the English system understood itself as procedural, with reason operating in order to consider whether particular remedies should be extended to cover new situations. The continental system understood itself as substantive (the *ius commune* was substantive, procedures remained local) and based on general principles. Such opposing legal traditions offer considerable resistance to attempts to reduce them to each other. Neither system is reducible to moral philosophy.)

The practices of the English legal system were presented (self-described), and understood by their participants, as the elaboration of the law in keeping with a natural order. The natural order celebrated within common law theory was a traditional order:

> For the *Common Law* of England is nothing else but the *Common Custome* of the Realm . . . it cannot be made or created either by Charter, or by Parliament . . . but being only matter of fact, and consisting in use and practice, it can be recorded and registered no-where but in the memory of the people.[29]

The process of elaborating on the common law had dual elements. As an elaboration of what already existed, it represented the continuation of custom. But the process of elaboration and identification also involved principles of reason, which maintained the contact between the common law and the sorts of general principles associated with natural law theory.[30] The extrapolation of what could be taken from existing procedure was identified by reference to arguments as to what was a rational, or fair, or just solution.[31] But what was fair and just was established by a contemplation of what had been found to be the existing law in cases that appeared similar to the case in question.[32] Whilst reason and general principles were understood to orientate the law, the law that resulted was not something capable of description through moral philosophy or theology. Such general schemes could not reproduce the particularity of adjudication, in which the decision to be made was presented to the judges as a case, and could only be orientated by reference to other cases. To return for a moment to systems theory, as set out in chapter 2, the observation of cases involved the utilisation of communications from natural law theory, but the point of observation (identifying what it meant to treat one legal case like another, remembering that cases involve parties, issues, rules,

---

[29] Sir John Davies, *Irish Reports*, quoted in Postema, 1986, 4.

[30] This dualism seems remarkably similar to Dworkin's idea of 'fit' within the conception of law as integrity (see ch 4 above).

[31] Postema, 1986, 7.

[32] Postema, 1986, 30–38.

procedures, remedies, and are restricted to arguments that don't occur outside the legal system) was unique to the legal system. To an external observer, the legal system's claim to be applying moral principles could appear quite bogus. Hobbes, for example, felt that the common lawyers' claim that the reason they found in the law could only be learned through a long period of initiation was simply ridiculous. He felt that common law reasoning was a pretentious and fictitious claim to expertise in rational thought, which any bystander could master in two months of legal training.[33]

The technicality and artificiality of common law did not prevent its participants from presenting its stability and developments as the working out of the implications of a traditional order. The claim that this legal order formed part of a wider social order was, historically at least, undoubtedly true. The evolution of law had been gradual; there had been no 'revolution' where the legal system perceived itself as breaking with what had gone before. The communications of the common law were connected to those of the past. Indeed, if such connections could not have been made, the legal system would not have evolved. This sense that the common law represented the continuation of what was just within an ancient order despite the obviousness of change is well captured by a metaphor used by Hale:

> [T]hey are the same English Laws now that they were six hundred years [ago] . . . the Argonauts ship was the same when it returned home, as it was when it went out, tho' in the long Voyage it had successive Amendments, and scarce came back with any of its former Materials.[34]

It was only the incremental nature of common law evolution that made its claim to be historically connected to a natural order plausible. This plausibility lay within law's operations. Arguments connecting decisions to what had gone before were not a historical or ideological gloss on the exercise of power, but

[33] Hobbes, *A Dialogue between a Philosopher and a Student of the Common Laws of England* (1971, edn) Dialogue 56; discussed by Postema, 1986, 47.

[34] Sir Matthew Hale, 1971 edn, 40; discussed by Postema, 1986, 6.

a constituent of what it meant to experience law. The tautology that exists at the heart of common law practices (that the law is the law) was unfolded (or denied) through the use of natural law theory. The common law was described as a repository of appropriate responses to the natural (national) order, which developed, incrementally, with that order.

This allowed the cases themselves to be communicated about as not being authorities in themselves, but only evidence of an order that existed outside of law, within society, or its history. To quote Blackstone: '*[T]he law*, and the *opinion of the judge*, are not always convertible terms, or one and the same thing; since it sometimes may happen that the judge may *mistake* the law.'[35] The common law legal system perceived itself as having originated as a response to a natural order, and having evolved, through reason, as that natural order evolved.

Autopoiesis and Natural Law Theory

The legal practices in relation to which natural law offered its self-description not only allowed for law to differ between communities, but allowed law to evolve. Justice, within systems theory's account of law, is a formula to increase law's variety.[36] The use of natural law, both on the continent and in England, facilitated law's evolution.[37] Classical natural law theory recognises the ability of rulers to determine the common good, treats human customs as part of a natural order, and at the same time identifies law with reason and treats this as a higher form of law than either statute or custom. But when natural law operates as a self-description, the reason to which it gives priority is not the a priori application of moral or ethical principles. To function as both a stabilising and an evolutionary communication reason

---

[35] Blackstone, *Commentaries*, vol 1, 1767, 71. Again, one is struck by the continuity between these sentiments and Dworkin's writings two centuries later.

[36] We develop this understanding of justice in ch 4; and see generally, Luhmann, 2004, ch 7 'Justice, A Formula for Contingency'.

[37] If one treated evolution as progress (which systems theory does not) one might talk of natural law as a self-description that facilitated law's modernisation.

operates as a basis for developing law from existing law. On the continent, this process took the form of incorporating the substance and more importantly the systematising methods of Roman law. Reason is the relationship between supposedly universal and exhaustive general laws. In England, law understands itself not as a system of rules, but as procedures providing remedies for existing wrongs. Reason is again the relationship between the laws, but in this system the application of reason is understood as the relationship between particular procedures. As a unity, the English system cannot present itself to itself as a systematic general system of rules, for it is no such thing.[38] Instead, it understands itself as the enforcement mechanism for a customary order, which order identifies the 'wrongs' that law remedies. The law develops as society develops, with new circumstances presenting novel 'wrongs' which require new remedies to be developed out of existing ones.

The identification of particular legal texts (on the continent the Digest and in England the writs and system of pleadings) as evidence of custom or reason, and the development of methods for the interpretation of those texts, leads to a situation in which the sense of what is just, or unjust is not the direct application of external influences upon law, but something which is constructed internally by the legal system for itself.[39] The laws are understood as justice, and the laws in turn give a sense of what

[38] Lobban, 1991, shows that Blackstone's contemporaries criticised his attempt to present the common law as a system of substantive rules, on the basis that this failed to describe the detailed system of pleadings that actually organised common law practice. Lobban himself believes that Blackstone set himself an impossible task (at 26, and see the whole of ch 2 'The Common Law and the Commentaries').

[39] Watkin argues that this development began with the move to feudalism, when law became territorial rather than tribal, and the judges who staffed the feudal lords' courts were no longer in a position to state the relevant customs from their knowledge alone. 'Here, for the first time, a measure of legal expertise became important, as customs were expected to be not just the practices of the community, but practices which were in accordance with divine law, the law of the Church and natural law, otherwise they were bad.' (Watkin, 1999, 77).

is a wholly unjust decision.[40] Through secondary observation (which takes as its premise that there **can be** consistent reasons for decisions—treating like cases alike) law necessarily insulates itself from the resolution of disputes by reference to the immediate application of the distribution of power between the parties appealing to law for a resolution of their disputes.[41] At the same time, it also insulates itself from the immediate application of widespread customary norms as to what is just and unjust. As law evolved it did not become a reflection of a wider society, but a highly technical and artificial version of that society.[42]

Law, which responds to change whilst lacking an understanding of itself that allows for radical legislation, must present its own evolution as a continuation of existing law. This leads to change as a process of extrapolation, of exception, with the possibility of such exceptions evolving into counter-rules, and in turn counter-exceptions. Thus while, if the law was truly incapable of change it would, over time, become increasingly experienced as injustice, its method of responding to injustice is also a means by which it becomes increasingly differentiated from other communications. Law becomes a system of communication whose complexity is accessible only to its initiates. And the order that law understands itself to represent has

[40] Within the common law, the sense that a law was against reason was often described as an 'inconvenience', which meant that it went against the rest of the common law as a whole. ('*Nihil quod est inconvenient est licitum* [nothing that is inconvenient is lawful]'.) This understanding of reason also limited what could be found to be unjust. One could not declare something contrary to reason if it would not cause 'inconvenience', be contrary to, too many other laws: 'It is better saith the Law to suffer a mischiefe (that is particular to one) then an inconuenience that may prejudice many.' (Stoner, 1992, 25, quoting Coke). Within these limits (or constituents) precedents against reason 'flatly absurd or unjust' do not bind (Stoner, 1992, 173).

[41] In the case of the *ius commune*, and later civil law traditions, this process is further removed by the development of law within universities (ie the systematic elaboration of the law by reference to perceived or expected problems rather than in the course of actual adjudication).

[42] 'The common lawyers saw society through the lens of law. In a sense, society *was* the structure of relations, customs, claims and obligations expressed in legal knowledge.' (Cotterrell, 2003, 32).

no separate existence outside the law itself. The order that law understands as reason or custom becomes its own internal arrangement or order.

Cotterrell, in *The Politics of Jurisprudence*, argues that the eclipse of natural law theory can be understood by reference to law's internal needs: 'The problem is that even if there *are* universal principles of natural law they may not offer a convincing guide or grounding for complex, highly technical and ever-changing modern law.'[43] Cotterrell identifies two changes in the nature of law that make it no longer possible for the legal system to guide its own operations by reference to natural law. The first is legal doctrine's ever-increasing technicality and complexity. This is partly the result of law's methods of compromise between conflicting interests being extended to cover more and more sectors of social life, and being invoked in support of more and more diverse interests within the regulated population. The other development is the deliberate use of law as a steering mechanism in society.[44] 'This presupposes that law can change rapidly and continuously but also that it does so not as a reflection of enduring principle but as a mechanism aimed at *creating* principles of social order . . . [that are] time bound; pragmatic principles for the moment and the context, quite unlike timeless principles of natural law'.[45]

We would agree with Cotterrell's broad thesis, but suggest that the key change that prevents legal systems from generating a self-description in terms of natural law is not so much the complexity or technicality of law, as the second development which he identifies (the deliberate use of law as a steering mechanism in society), and the consequent inability of law to

[43] 2003, 119.

[44] Both of these developments can be represented by the terms: positivity, positivisation and juridification, as characterised in n 1 above.

[45] Cotterrell, 2003, 119. Cotterrell continues, quoting Luhmann: 'it is increasingly questionable whether principles and ultimate perspectives [such as those of natural law] withdrawn from all variation and relativity' can 'provide an apt instrument for stabilisation and control' in modern societies.' (Luhmann, 1982, 103).

continue to guide its operations by reference to communications about its continuity (unchanging nature). Law's inability to use natural law theory is not simply the presence of rules that have little relationship to general principles to do with the right to life, or the rearing of children.[46] Nor is it due to the complexity of its communications, and their distant relationship from social mores or general social communication. Rather, it lies in the nature and manner of its creation. So long as the dominant route of legal evolution takes the form of connecting new legal communications to a store of existing communications that are understood to have a stable and consistent content, then positivist legal theory does not provide an adequate self-description of the law.[47] But when legislation became the dominant source of legal evolution,[48] then self-description evolves in turn from natural law to positivist legal theory.[49] Legislation, once it is understood within the legal system as a process that does not merely declare the law but changes it, requires interpretative processes that reflect this. Legislation, as a process that changes the law, needs to be interpreted as discontinuity, whilst earlier processes of development required a self-description that understood law as continuity. To understand how positivist legal theory became an accepted self-description of the legal system,

[46] The example used here is taken from Aquinas' precepts of natural law (Aquinas, 1959, 123).

[47] Indeed, custom and judicial precedent, forms of law and legal evolution that were so long presented through natural law theories, continue to provide the weak point in attempts to present the unity of the legal system solely in terms of source based theories.

[48] On the change in the frequency of legislation, which occurred from the 18th to the 19th centuries, see Lieberman, 1989, 13–20.

[49] 'They go too far who assert that Coke lacked the idea of legislation or new law; but it is clear from his writings that legislation comes about to fill in the gaps in the common law, not the reverse.' (Stoner, 1992, 61). For legislation to become the dominant source of legal evolution took time and required not only new operations, but also new self-observations and self-description: ' [T]he old idea that the common law rendered new legislation unnecessary died hard.' (Thomas, 1971, 45).

one needs to consider the generative effects of a constant outflow of particular legislation.[50]

When legislation had evolved to the point that it could no longer be interpreted within (and restrained by) communications that understood it as declaratory,[51] then an increasing number of legal communications had to take the form of an acknowledgment that the law changes. This does not in itself prevent claims that such new law is 'guided by' or 'an expression of' morality. But there is a fundamental difference between understanding something as a process of change guided by general principles that have universal application (making law), and understanding something as a continuation of what is rational within a concrete social (or legal) order (finding law).[52] Claims that legislation is guided by natural law principles may remain an indispensable part of politics (which government ever says that its legislative programme has been purchased by its sponsors?[53]) but they do not have the same existence as legal communications. As the level and variety of legislative output increased, it was no longer possible to maintain a self-description that law (as a unity) was either a system of reason (on the continent) or the consequence and application of reason (the common law).[54]

---

[50] In sheer volume, the legislation that an entire generation might produce relative to the law as a whole in the 16th and 17th century (for example, the 82 years of Coke's life) was small relative to the law as a whole: see Stoner, 1992, 61.

[51] The declaratory understanding of legislation was reinforced by the understanding of Parliament as a court which was supreme not in the sense that it could introduce whatever new law it wished, but in the sense that there was no appeal from its declarations. See Stoner, 1992, 37–38; see also McIlwain, 1910.

[52] See n 10 above.

[53] Even Hobbes, who argued that citizens surrendered all ability to question the reason for a sovereign's rules, believed that the sovereign's role was to govern his people for the common good. See his *Leviathan*, 1960 edn, *XXX*, 219; see also Postema, 1986, 57–58.

[54] Later in this chapter we trace this internal basis for the evolution from natural law to positivist legal theory within the English legal system. We do not, however, examine this process within continental systems.

The development of legislation does not logically or rationally require a positivist legal theory. Rather, law generates positivist legal theory through its own internal operations. Legislative operations do not need to be understood *within the legal system* as the continuation of something. Unlike changes produced within customary law (including common law), or Roman civil law, what is already in existence does not need to be examined for 'values' or 'principles' in order to develop the law as continuity despite apparent change. Nor is there any need for the legal system to examine claims by the legislature, as a political body, that what it enacts is pursuant to the common good. It requires no more, *within the legal system*, than an acknowledgment that what the legislator decides the law should be, **is** the law.

Of course, the fact that legislation created a situation in which a legal system **can** now carry out its operations without reference to morality does not mean that it should do so. Indeed, the presence of other logical possibilities is what allows the debate between natural law and positivist legal theories to continue (as a debate). But the sociological question that remains is whether natural law reasoning provides an adequate self-description for a legal system which experiences itself (communicates about itself to itself) as being in a constant state of change? The answer lies in the lack of communications within law capable of generating and sustaining such a self-description. One should not underestimate the importance of the historical fact that by the time legislation took its modern form the order that was understood within the natural law tradition as a natural social order was nothing more than the legal system itself. The legal system had a sense of itself, and its environment (society), that ordered its own evolution.[55] As such, the morality that it attributed to natural law was generated by its own communications. It was legal communications, communications about the correct way to apply and develop an increasingly technical set of posited laws,

[55] To re-use the same quotation from Cotterrell (n 42 above): 'The common lawyers saw society through the lens of law. In a sense, society *was* the structure of relations, customs, claims and obligations expressed in legal knowledge.'

which generated and sustained a self-description in terms of natural law. By contrast, the communications that accompany an acceptance that legislation affects legal change provide far less possibility for natural law reasoning within law's operations. Once law included prolific and particular legislation,[56] the existing law no longer provided a limit on what can be law. When natural law facilitated the identification of laws as unjust with a view to altering their operation within the legal system it was not enough to point to a contrast between a particular law and what general principles of morality might be taken to require.[57] One also had to identify how the law, that is to be impugned, contrasts with other law. This understanding, which allows the development of customary and traditional law—the need to treat like cases alike—requires a communication that explains why the law that is no longer law is different from other laws that continue to be law. But as legislation develops, and the possibility of using differences from existing law (novelty) as the basis for identifying something as unjust (irrational, or outside the established order) declines, so the capacity of legal communications to generate a self-description in terms of natural law decreases. Something that was an adequate self-description (generated by everyday operations throughout the legal system) becomes a far less satisfactory self-description. It links to, and is sustained by, fewer of the legal system's operations (some parts of the legal system continue to present and understand themselves as

---

[56] The changing nature of legislation in the 18th century was observed by contemporaries: 'The extreme particularity and limited provenance of so much of this law-making seemed to reduce the legislature, in Horace Walpoles's words, to "a mere quarter sessions, where nothing is transacted but turnpikes and poor rates."' (See Lieberman, 1989, 17).

[57] Thus, for example, of developments in Germany that followed the publication of Grotius' *De jure belli ac pacis*, Watson writes: '. . . natural law, as it entered the sphere of practical private law, would be tamed. Courts enforce existing and established law. To have any practical impact, natural law doctrines would have to appear consonant with the law as seen by the courts and as taught in the universities. With regard to the latter, books would emerge setting out Roman law, Romano-German law, and natural law together, or reconciling Roman law with natural law.' (Watson, 1981, 97).

continuity, but these make up less of the total body of legal operations). Under these conditions attempts to use natural law reasoning became a different experience. In claiming that something previously thought to be law is unjust and therefore not law, one is no longer pointing to a particular law and seeking to show why that law is different from other laws within the system. Instead, one is simply comparing a particular law with external communications from moral philosophy or politics and asking that the law in question be disapplied. With these developments, the separation thesis[58] argued for by positivist legal theory becomes the dominant self-description, not because of the inherent separation between human law and natural law, something derived from logic akin to the naturalistic fallacy, but because it does not describe the internal operations of law in a manner that can be generalised in order to stabilise day-to-day legal operations. The separation thesis 'proves' itself not logically or rationally, but sociologically. And the audience for that proof is not the political system (which continues to present itself as an instrument for achieving the common good) but the legal system itself, which ceases to make communications that no longer explain itself to itself.[59]

The Transition From Natural Law to Legal Positivism: The Example of the Common Law

The complex artificiality of the common law was presented, and understood, as an ancient order (the customs of the realm) evidenced by cases.[60] The perception of statutes as changing as opposed to declaring law occurred in the 17th century. Medieval

[58] On the separation thesis, see Alexy, 2002, ch 1 'The Basic Positions'; Hart, 1958.

[59] There is continuing scope for natural law reasoning to play a role with legislation that takes the form of codification, whereby a new legal order is available for development by reference to its inherent values. But sovereigns that successfully introduce legislation whenever it is their will so to do, appear to leave no basis other than their will for its interpretation.

[60] 'The only way to show that a given rule is a rule of Common Law is to show how it figures regularly in standard legal argument.' (Postema, 1986, 4).

jurisprudence held that statutes performed, in a more explicit and general way, the same task that occupied the judiciary: declaring law already existing in the traditional practices of the people.[61] Only a tiny part of private law was incorporated in statute until well into the 19th century.[62] During this period, and even into the 19th century, the system of common law proclaimed itself to be unchanging, whilst clearly undergoing steady and unceasing transformation. But the development of law as the working out of the implications of existing legal texts is a practice that presents change as the continuation of the present, so change is not *really* change.

During periods when natural law continued to provide law's self-description, one finds activities that seem, from a modern perspective, to be fictions. Take for example the understanding of statutes as merely declaratory instruments, even when those statutes represented major innovations in response to social problems.[63] Consider also the development of the English system of writs, which replaced feudal relationships based on personal service with a system of property rights.[64] But these fictions were a necessary part of a system that understood itself by reference to a self-description generated by common law adjudication. The common law dealt with the power of Parliament to require things contrary to the common law initially as a matter of jurisdiction. The Courts accepted that they had

[61] *Ibid*, 15.

[62] '. . . from the end of the thirteenth century to the beginning of the nineteenth, legislation played a tiny part in the development of private law.' (Milsom, 1985, 150).

[63] When statutes were not declaratory, they were considered 'remedial'. But remedy here does not mean social policy. They would remedy a 'mischief', a wrong that had not been remedied by the common law. As such, even when seen to change law, they were described in the same manner as that in which the common law described itself: as the provision of remedies for pre-existing wrongs. See Stoner, 1992, 215, our text at n 23 above, and n 68 below.

[64] Blackstone admitted that the notion that property had stayed the same was a legal fiction, but still sought to claim continuity, on the basis that new forms of property had been refashioned to achieve the same purposes as older forms. See Postema, 1986, 12.

no jurisdiction to question what Parliament introduced through statute,[65] but denied that such statues (until such time as they were integrated into the common law) were actually law.[66] The common lawyers at first treated statute as a source of error in the law, an intervention that deviated from the purity of the traditions and customs that judges sought to identify through their judgments. Sovereign will, as a basis of law making, was not felt likely to produce either justice or a coherent and rational scheme, which is how the common lawyers understood the common law. This theory could only be maintained while common law could present itself as the great 'substratum' of the law, into which all law, to be truly law, had to fit. The need for statutes to be integrated into the common law to be truly law resulted in statutes that deviated from the common law having a lesser status when first passed, more akin to regulation. Only when 'accepted' (integrated into legal argument within the common law) were they truly law.[67] But with the proliferation of statute law, particularly in areas of private law that was formerly reserved to the common law, it was not possible for statutes to be observed and communicated about within the legal system as temporary exceptions to the common law that awaited their full existence as law only at such time as they were integrated through legal judgments into this 'substratum'.[68]

[65] '. . . Hale is capable of giving credence to the idea of the legislative sovereignty of Parliament. For no court is competent to invalidate rules properly enacted by Parliament. Yet, for Hale, "Common Law and the Custom of the Realm . . . is the great Substratum" of the law.' (Postema, 1986, 26). See also Blackstone's *Commentaries,* vol 1, 1767, 244–5. This distinction (between having no jurisdiction to question something, and conceding that something is actually law) has been re-used by Dworkin some centuries later in *Taking Rights Seriously*, 1977.

[66] See Postema, 1986, 71. The French, during the period of absolute monarchy, treated laws introduced by the French King that were contrary to the *lois fondamentales* as binding during the King's reign, and abrogated on his death. (van Caenegem, 1995, 99).

[67] Postema, 1986, 26.

[68] Thus the ability of statute law to change law, and even the recognition of such by lawyers, did not lead immediately to a change in self-description. See Postema, 1986, 15–16, 26. Van Caenegem notes that even during the period in

Understanding developments within jurisprudence as changes produced by alterations in what needed to be described in legal practice leads one towards different perceptions of debates within jurisprudence. Both Austin and Bentham offer their theories of law as the will of a sovereign as superior accounts of the nature of law to those offered by the likes of Blackstone, who in his *Commentaries* on the common law presented the common law as an embodiment of natural law.[69] At this juncture jurisprudence offers two rival self-descriptions of the legal system.[70] Blackstone's *Commentaries* represent a self-description of law by reference to the operations of the common law. If common law had, at this time, remained the dominant mode of achieving legal change then Bentham's criticisms of the artificiality of the legal reasoning of 'judge and co' might have remained an external critique. But what Blackstone does not offer is a serviceable account of a legal system that has evolved to the point where large amounts of new law are generated through communications that acknowledge just that: that it is new law.

On Maine's reading of the history of the period, the conflict between the Common Law and positivist conceptions of law reflected rival

England closest to absolute monarchy, that of the Tudors, a period that saw 'massive law reform' in ordinary civil affairs, the 'common law remained the cornerstone of the legal system, in spite of the competition of statutes, Roman law and non-common law tribunals' (1995, 105 and 107). There may also be parallel developments on the continent. Consider Lawson's observation on the treatment of statutes that fell outside the traditional scope of the French Civil Code and earlier Roman law: '. . . the makers of a civil code do not usually wish to insert in their code anything that is not likely to stand for a very long time. Anything that is experimental must stay outside until it has, as it were, become naturalized; and often enough it stays outside for good.' (Lawson, 1955, 60–61).

[69] Blackstone, 1765–69. Lobban argues that Blackstone was criticised by much of the profession for seeking to present the unity of law as a matter of unifying principles. Many of his contemporaries preferred to conceive of the common law as a series of individual just solutions to the circumstances of particular cases (1991, especially ch 3 'The Logic of the Law').

[70] The differences between Blackstone and Bentham repeated many of the differences between Coke and Hobbes a century earlier (see Postema, 1986, 46–48, 314–317).

views of a practice in transition. Each had a right, to some extent, to claim that their own theory better captured the nature and foundations of legal practice. However, Common Law [theorists] sought to block the spread of what they regarded as distorting influence that threatened the integrity of that practice, while the positivists seized upon the new developments as the pivot around which to shape a new conception of the nature and point of that practice.[71]

Alongside the sociological explanation that systems theory offers for the rise of positivist legal theory and the decline of natural law theory, one should also consider how this theory might address the residual elements of natural law theorising that continues to occupy jurisprudence. The dominance of positivist theory—the acceptance that the law is the law even if it is unjust—continues to operate alongside theories that insist that the status of law, as law, is related to issues of ethics and morality. These residual elements take different forms. But their strength, as self-descriptions of law, lies in the difficulties faced by positivist theories in presenting themselves as an account of the unity of law. From the perspective of law's evolution, such difficulties should not be surprising. The operations that could be best generalised in terms of natural law theory did not disappear from the legal system just because legislation began to introduce operations that could not be accommodated within that theory. For while legislation at first supports and is in turn supported by a self-description of law in terms of the sovereign's will this theory provides no support to the processes of adjudication. An instruction to 'give effect to the sovereign's expressed will, and otherwise do what you think just, and wait to be reversed by litigation',[72] whatever its merits as a matter of polit-

[71] Postema, 1986, 329–330, commenting on Sir Henry Maine, 1875, Lecture XIII, 396–7.

[72] Hobbes had argued that when clear sovereign law ran out natural reason should guide the judge who must decide on the law (*Leviathan*, 1960 edn, XXVI 'Of Civil Laws', especially 172–3, 176–7, 183–4). By contrast Hale had argued that the common law does not run out, but is applied through analogies from what is clear to what is not (see Postema, 1986, 71). This opposition anticipates the Hart-Dworkin debate on the nature of judicial discretion.

ical theory, is not an adequate self-description for a legal system whose operations involve comparisons between cases (treating like cases alike) and not the *a priori* application of general moral or ethical principles.[73]

The self-description that facilitated the legal system's processing of legislation, the positivist idea that the legal system as a unity could be accounted for through ideas of authority rather than order, generated changes to the nature of adjudication. Immediately prior to the rise of positivist legal theory in the 19th century adjudication had been a process that communicated about itself in terms of the continuities of case law—and the need to re-direct that process in the face of perceived injustices—with an overarching narrative of natural law and links to an original social order. But with the shift in self-description generated by the changing practices associated with positivisation, the legal system altered the manner in which it communicated about the nature of adjudication. Legal decisions were no longer regarded as giving expression to an order lying outside law, but were regarded as partaking of the same kind of authority as legislation.[74] Cases, like legislation, simply decided what

---

[73] Bentham could not develop a positivist theory of adjudication. While his general theory of laws described law as the command of a sovereign, and therefore a social fact, adjudication outside of what the sovereign had clearly commanded could not be reduced by him to a fact, but remained a moral exercise. Bentham's own writings on adjudication supported the doctrine of stare decisis, but not in a manner that maintained a separation of law and morality. In his early writings on the common law he argued for a rigid doctrine of stare decisis, supplemented by the further development of case law through a process of analogising (treating like cases alike) on the basis that this arrangement would be most productive of utility. The most important element of this utility was the security of public expectations. In individual cases, benefits from possible increases in utility that fell outside this pattern would ordinarily outweigh the damage from disappointed expectations and loss of confidence in the system as a whole that would follow from abandoning the use of analogies. He later came to the view that judges should apply legislated codes, but have the ability to disapply them, or supplement them, when this maximised utility (see Postema, 1986, 197–217, 403–434).

[74] 'I cannot understand how any person who has considered the subject can suppose that society could possibly have gone on if judges had not legislated, or that there is any danger whatever in allowing them that power which they have

77

the law was to be. A complex doctrine of stare decisis evolved.[75] This connection between the eclipse of natural law theory as a self-description of legal practice, and the consequences for adjudication, is described by Postema thus:

> For once the traditional, declaratory theory of Common Law was seen to be a mask for the pervasive fact of judicial legislation—once it became second nature to call the rules of Common Law 'judge-made law'—a process which began in the eighteenth century culminating in the London Street Tramways decision in the 1890s—it was no longer possible to leave judges uncontrolled in the exercise of this legislative power. Thus, the strict doctrine of precedent was the natural product of the shift in view of the activity of judges under Common Law from that of Coke, Hale and Blackstone to that of Bentham and Austin.[76]

Postema's claim that judicial communications about the manner in which they undertook their task in developing the common law were a 'mask', suggests that there was something false or disingenuous in the writings of Hale, Coke and Blackstone, and that the judges either learned that their earlier understanding was mistaken, or became unable to continue with a knowing deception that had been discredited. But he also suggests that it was an outcome of a 'shift' of activity. Systems theory suggests what this 'shift' involved. The inability of the legal system to communicate about itself in terms of unchanging law that was required by developments in legislation made it difficult

in fact exercised, to make up for the negligence or incapacity of the avowed legislator.' (Austin, 1955/1832, 191). The argument that positivism treats all law as if it were statute ('more or less assimilates all law to statute law') is made by Simpson, 1986, 10–13.

[75] Stare decisis, and the complementary doctrine of a case's ratio decidendi, is the application of the understanding of law as legislation to judicial practice. This contrasts with the earlier self-description (which was never totally eclipsed) that the opinions of judges could only provide evidence of the law, a law that existed prior to their pronouncements and continued unaffected whenever their pronouncements could be shown to be mistaken. For a statement of this dualism within stare decisis, see Postema, 1987.

[76] Postema, 1986, 209–210.

for the judiciary to continue to articulate the common law in terms of a customary order which was only 'evidenced' in cases. In the absence of communications that the cases were not authorities, but only evidence of something else, the process of 'treating like cases alike' evolved into an understanding of cases as precedents, which did not refer to anything outside of themselves ie as authorities. As we shall see in the next section of this chapter, the need for judges to decide what the law is did not end with the move to stare decisis, nor did their inability to articulate such decisions in terms of 'making' law.[77]

Whilst legal positivism as a self-description reinforces certain developments within the legal system, it cannot account for all of them. It cannot adequately represent the unity of the system. One aspect of the legal system that legal positivism lacks is the escape clause offered by natural law: the ability to say that the law is the law, except when 'flatly absurd or unjust'.[78] This difficulty is compounded when one remembers that the role played by a sovereign's tacit will is not limited to case law. It is one thing to accept that a newly passed statute, which produces extremely harsh consequences, is the will of the sovereign, and by that fact, law. It is more difficult to accept that a statute of

[77] However, what the changing self-observation of judicial decisions produced, in turn, was a further development in the form of positivism able to operate as a self-description of the legal system. When judges articulated the common law in terms of reason, the alternative self-description, generated and sustained by legislation, was in terms of sovereign will. But when the common law evolved into an activity understood in terms of authority, then attempts to describe all of law's authority in terms of sovereignty proved inadequate. Positivist self-description evolved into accounts of law's unity in terms of author- itative sources which were not limited to sovereignty, but included the common law. The best example of this being Hart's introduction of secondary rules in *The Concept of Law*, developed in turn by Raz, in *The Concept of a Legal System*. We have not described this next development in detail because our use of his- tory in this chapter is intended to demonstrate the nature of self-description and its role within law's operations and evolution, not to write a complete history of law's self-description .

[78] According to Blackstone: 'precedents and rules must be followed, unless flatly absurd or unjust.' *Commentaries*, Vol 1, 1767, 70; see Lieberman, 1989, 86.

Henry VIII that now has harsh consequences is similarly so intended.[79] Some escape from such conclusions is provided by decisions similar in form to those used to justify the opposition between equity and the common law. Sufficiently unjust consequences can be presented as absurdities that the sovereign could not have willed.[80] But the circumstances, that lead to law adopting a positivist self-description inhibit the use of this technique. The very same variety of what can be coded legal or illegal that undermined law's self-description as natural law also serves to inhibit the ability to label a particular interpretation that is dictated by routine interpretative techniques as an 'absurdity'. That said, the ability of courts to reach such decisions, and the need for the courts to decide for themselves in what circumstances such decisions are justified, threatens (as a matter of description) to subvert the self-description of positivism, which presupposes a hierarchy between the courts and the legislature. So too does the inability of that hierarchy to determine how the courts should interpret statutes. The fact that statutes change the law is a given in a system that ceases (except in the most exceptional circumstances) to regard them as merely declaratory (leaving the law unchanged). But how they change the law requires a consideration of what the law was before, and regard to the structures established within the legal system (methods for statutory interpretation) that allow the legal system to identify what that change might be.

[79] This particular difficulty is cured by a doctrine of *desuetude*, as evolved on the continent. Practices with a comparable function existed within the English legal system, as part of the common law tradition. When statutes were viewed as contributions to the common law, they were open to erosion over time when overtaken by 'contrary usage'. When statutes became dominant, and positivist legal theory provided the system's self-description, this doctrine for the gradual abandonment of out-dated statutes was lost (see Postema, 1986, 24–25).

[80] In terms of approaches to the interpretation of statutes, this is represented in the 'golden rule', as an adjunct to the 'literal rule'; the idea that no literal interpretation should result in inferring to the intention of Parliament that it would intend an absurdity.

The continuing need for courts to adjudicate (decide how to apply the code legal/illegal) because of the indeterminacy of statutes, is simply part of the central paradox of the legal system: the basis for applying the code is observation on earlier applications of the code, and while the conditional programmes generated through such observation can stabilise the code's application, they can never determine, on all occasions, how it will be applied. The evolution of statutory interpretation to an acceptance that statutes change the law provides the legal system with a dynamic instrument of change, and improvement in the coupling of its operations with the rest of society, but it cannot remove this paradox. There will always be issues for which there are no good reasons for deciding a matter one way rather than another. And despite this, the courts will always have to decide, and these decisions will be the subject of observations and accounts. Positivist legal theory deals with this problem in terms of gaps in a system established by reference to the sovereign's will[81] or, in more developed versions of the theory, gaps in law established by reference to authoritative sources.[82] An insistence that law is the sovereign's will or—adopting the evolution of self-description that followed the development of stare decisis—that law is what has been decided according to decisions reached in accordance with a limited number of authoritative sources, points inevitably to the presence of some areas where decisions occur which are not the sovereign's will, or the result of legal materials identified by reference to sources.[83] However, while this escape clause exists within positivist legal theory, it is not reproduced within the communications of adjudication.

---

[81] As Postema (1986, 56) shows, even Hobbes had to acknowledge the need for courts to fill such gaps.

[82] Luhmann (2004, 123–5) feels that in more developed positivist legal theories sources are in turn displaced by internal criteria for validity. In Anglo-American jurisprudence, the best-known example of this would be Hart's rule of recognition (see his *Concept of Law* 1961, ch 6).

[83] These examples can be grouped together as representing forms of legal pluralism (see ch 1, n 8), an understanding of law that denies that there is one source of law, or even a pedigree test of what sources there might be.

Communications about what has been decided (stare decisis) stabilise adjudication, despite the absence of determinate tests of what has been decided (stare decisis and ratio decidendi cannot be exhaustedly defined). But the residual area of adjudication does not take the form of ad hoc and ad hominem arguments, or the communication by judges that X or Y is their personal 'political' or 'moral' preference. Instead, the legal system continues, as before, to develop what the law is, by reference to what the law is. In place of a process where law identifies a border, within itself, where what is communicated is not law (a point at which its participants begin to utilise communications from outside the legal system) we find that communication either side of what are claimed to be 'gaps' takes the same form. The process of observing earlier decisions to account for the application of the code legal/illegal, and the conditional programmes that this generates (which now includes a developed set of structures for the understanding of statutes and hierarchies of sources) is a process that does not exhibit the discontinuities that positivist legal theory might lead one to expect. There is no border, no clear point where legal communications cease and other kinds of communications start.

Positivist legal theory[84] operates on the assumption that the legal system can insulate itself from other kinds of communication, and thereby maintain its autonomy, provided that it can take communications from other systems into itself only at those points where it runs out of good reasons for deciding issues using materials already identified by authoritative sources.[85] Having decided a matter in this way (by reference to external communications or psychic factors) the curtain closes, and the decision of a legal organ thereafter stands in the place of that process as the reason why future decisions should be taken in the same way (treating like cases alike). However, if we start from the assumption that the code legal/illegal has no inherent meaning, and can only be guided by the way that it has been

[84] At least in the forms outlined by theorists such as HLA Hart and J Raz.

[85] That judges may use their discretion to decide 'penumbral' cases.

applied in the past, then the same material (past decisions, and accounts of past decisions) establishes both stable law and gaps and establishes the decisions that are possible, and even establishes the reasons that can be given for such decisions. Gaps represent choices between legal communications. Which of two or more sets of legal communications will be chosen to account for this particular decision? Both the choices, and the arguments to support them, will be legal communications. There will be a psychic factor in the choice, but this factor cannot be described in any way that expands upon the fact that it was a decision. 'Mr Justice X decided Y' is a communication that has been possible since the evolution of the courts. But 'Mr Justice X decided Y because he is a fascist, or because he has an infantile personality' is not a communication that the legal system can generate as an account of a decision. Nor, if the process of legal communication is to continue, can the decision be described within the legal system as: 'Mr. Justice X had no particular reason to decide Y but his decision nevertheless binds us'. Such an observation and account would block further legal evolution. If the answer to the question: 'Why was the code applied as it was in situation Y?' was 'For no particular reason', then the decision in Y provides no basis for further legal communications. It is only by observing upon a decision (however underdetermined by the legal system) to find a reason for that decision that one is able to identify something within that decision that can guide further applications of the code.[86] Whatever the 'psychic' realities, and however much particular decisions may be underdetermined by the legal system, the system can only continue by communicating as if court decisions could always be accounted for by reference to legal communications: as if there were always

---

[86] '. . . the workings of the judicial process [are] conducted upon the tacit assumption that the common law (we are not concerned here with statute) always provides an answer to the matter in issue, and one which is independent of the will of the court. Put differently, the conventions of legal argument embody a belief in the theoretical possibility of a comprehensive gapless rule of law. It is as if lawyers had all been convinced by Dworkin, though none of them have.' (Simpson, 1986, 9).

reasons for a decision one way rather than another.[87] Critics of common law reasoning, such as Bentham, have criticised common law adjudication, particularly the development of fictions, for its lack of honesty.[88] He felt that the common law hid the 'real' reasons for decisions.[89] But what systems theory suggests is that what cannot be communicated within a system cannot but remain 'hidden' from that system.

The inability of positivist legal theory to provide an adequate self-description of adjudication allows for other self-descriptions to operate alongside positivist ones. Various theories seek to account for the operations of the legal system that cannot be reduced to the application of the code by reference to authoritative sources. These include not only moral ones, but also various realist theories (see chapter 6 on the critical legal theorists).[90] In light of the central role of legislation in endlessly changing the law, self-descriptions in terms of a return to full natural law theorising, with law understood as the continuation of a natural order, cannot form a large part of law's operations. They remain utopian. Instead, contemporary natural law theories, as self-descriptions of the unity of law, combine elements of legal positivism with residual elements of natural law theory.

[87] 'Psychological systems observe the law but they do not produce it, otherwise law would be locked away deep in what Hegel called "the innermost dark thoughts of the mind." Therefore it is impossible to take psychological systems, consciousness, or even the whole human individual as a part or as an internal component of the legal system. The autopoiesis of law can only be realised through social operations.' (Luhmann, 2004, 84).

[88] 'As a system of general rules, the Common Law is a thing merely imaginary.' (Bentham, 1977, 119). Bentham suggested at one point that secondary observation (in his writings, the person who articulated what a case stood for as a general principle) was carried out as an act of legislation. And, if no person had particular authority to state what a case stood for, then the case simply failed to make law. Thus, without a system that clearly identified what constituted a binding precedent, the common law could not, according to him, really generate law. (Postema, 1986, 288).

[89] Postema, 1986, 272–4. In these pages Postema gives the main references to Bentham's vehement criticism of the 'mischief' of fictions in the common law.

[90] Although it is possible to treat such theories as representing external critique, our analysis in ch 6 treats them as internal, as examples of jurisprudence.

The process of interpretation, which identifies what has been decided (redundancy) and what choices are presented, is described within modern natural law as a dualism of morality and authoritative sources. As a self-description this is capable of forming part of law's operations (both its observations on those operations and its observations on those observations, namely both self-observation and, building on that self-observation, self-description). Moral communications, especially those relying on 'practical reason' are re-used, alongside communications about authoritative sources, to account for the application of the code (but so are accountancy and medical communications). Indeed, given the reservoir of natural law self-observation and self-description contained within the law when legal positivism became the dominant self-description, it would have been quite strange if the utilisation of existing legal materials in order to make legal communications had not contained re-usable moral communications. But what is most problematic about such self-descriptions is the need, in common with positivist legal theory, and full natural law theory, to externalise the basis for the use of such communications. The basis of natural law theory was located in a divine (secularised in the common law as a traditional) order of which positive law was a part. This allowed the tautology that the law decides what is law to exist as an operation, but not as a communication within the system.[91] Within positivist legal theories, communication of this tautology is avoided by the assumption that some exterior element (the will of a sovereign or the commitments of judges) provides the ultimate basis for deciding what is law. And a similar externalisation continues within modern natural law. As we shall see in the next chapter, which deals with this aspect of Dworkin's natural law theory, re-used moral communications are self-described as if morality, as a system, could structure the operations of law, as a system. But as we shall show in the next chapter, the points at which moral communications are re-used to account for the applications of the code that cannot be

---

[91] See the final paragraph of ch 2 above.

explained solely by reference to authoritative sources, cannot make those observations part of a moral system. They remain internal to the legal system, joined to other legal communications as part of a system that is coding in terms of legal/illegal.

The Transition From Natural Law to Legal Positivism: Other Examples

This chapter has provided a concrete example of jurisprudence as self-description in terms of the relationship between legislation and case law within the English common law system. We are aware that the continent has evolved differently, and has a different history. The continent has experienced more discontinuity, and natural law theory has been used to defend local systems of law as natural orders, to justify modernisation of those orders by reference to more universal forms of law such as Roman law, and in the 18th century, to justify major reforms by reference to the most general ideas of reason. At this stage, with regard to legal evolution on the continent, we can only offer this theory of the evolution of self-descriptions from natural law to legal positivism as a hypothesis. Jurisprudence as self-description requires one to look at the operations within the legal system that are structured and stabilised by general communications that present the legal system to itself. One needs to be sure that what one is observing are communications generated by the legal system about itself, and not communications developed within other systems, most importantly the political system, about the legal system.[92] Systems theory alerts us to the

[92] That is, one looks to see what actual operations, legal or political, utilise these communications. One also needs to be sensitive to what constitutes natural law at different stages of legal development. For example, natural law as a higher law than local law is a self-description that can account for the introduction of Roman law to supplement local customs at one stage of development, whilst the maintenance of such a Roman law system in the face of general ideas of reason can be described as resisting natural law at another stage: 'Although there had been a fierce and successful reaction against natural law as a philosophical basis for law, the natural law tendencies to generalise, to systematise, and to iron out any differences had persisted in full force'. Lawson, 1955, 41, speaking of the origins of the German Civil code.

possibility that the existence of natural law within a political system, to legitimate different forms of political authority, is not the same as its existence within a legal system, where it is applied, if at all, in communications that code initially in terms of what is just and unjust, and later, what is legal and illegal. The claim that legislation in 19th century England generated communications that prevented the legal system from continuing to communicate about itself using the ideas of order that had earlier orientated much of its communications is not a universal claim about legal development everywhere. Which operations, within continental legal systems, generated communications that allowed for self-description in terms of natural law theory, and how changes in those operations might have generated alternative self-descriptions, must be the subject of a separate enquiry.

Whilst this chapter has focused on the development of self-description in terms of the relationship between legislation and case law, systems theory also illuminates the relationship between both these operations and the introduction of constitutions. The self-description of law as natural law was utilised to introduce constitutional law as a higher form of law, most notably with the constitution introduced into the United States of America following the War of Independence. How, one might ask, does such a use of natural law differ from the claim by absolute monarchs to be giving effect to reason when they introduced large amounts of reforming legislation in the 18th century?[93] The answer lies, we suggest, as with the operations of common law, in the internal operations of the legal system and the communications that these generate. A constitution creates two kinds of law: changeable law and unchangeable law.[94] Natural law appears to point outwards, towards general moral principles, or, in the alternative, to the social order at the date of the constitution's introduction, to determine the content of that unchangeable law. But, as with the common law, the content of

[93] For example, the claim by Joseph II, that the 6000 ordinances that he introduced in his 10 year reign, in order to modernise administration, were a product of reason. See van Caenegem, 1995, 140.

[94] See Luhmann, 2004, 76–77, 130.

what is identified as unchangeable law has to be established in terms of what is already law.[95] Constitutional law is not an unchanging law; it develops. But it develops through forms of argumentation that seek to present change as continuity. And it develops in terms of what legal consequences (for changing law) follow from alterations to what is understood as unchanging law. Constitutional law thus allows the kinds of exegesis associated with customary (including common) law and Roman law to re-enter the legal system as a higher law than legislation. The processes whereby the law is developed as a continuation of what was already law, with a flexible capacity to develop and the ability to treat developments that become scandals as not law, is re-introduced to the legal system as constitutional law. Whilst one must not underestimate the human cost involved in the political revolutions that led to the introduction of constitutions, as an internal development of the legal system the 'revolution' is actually a continuity. Law continues to communicate about itself as an unbroken legal order by reference to the date of the constitution.[96] Understanding the legal system as a system, and considering the necessity for it to evolve (and the impossibility for all of the elements of a legal system to be invented from scratch, and then operate) points to the need for such continuities.[97] But the point to make here is that constitutional law no more requires or allows moral principles an *a priori* application within the operations of constitutional law than it does within customary law, or the common law. Nevertheless, the need to communicate about constitutional law as unchanging law generates

[95] For an observation on the parallels between common law attempts to identify certain laws as fundamental (and therefore unchanging) and constitutional law, and an argument for the continuity between common law practices and the American constitution, see Stoner, 1992, 65, and Part *IV*.

[96] In the case of French law, the division into the *droit nouveau* and the *ancien droit* (pre and post revolutionary law). But the *droit nouveau* took over a considerable mass of customary material. (See van Caenegem, 2002, 9).

[97] 'Even and especially when changes to law are concerned, what will be changed can be assumed to be known or to be determinable. The answer to the question as to what will be changed will never be: "Everything!" Not even in revolutions.' (Luhmann, 2004, 90–91).

operations, and in turn self-descriptions, that differ from those found within systems that simply rely on legislatures for their legal evolution. And the reason for such differences may not lie outside of these legal systems, in the communications about God or values that are available to be re-used in self-description, but in the operations that require such communications to be re-used in order to orientate legal operations. And this may explain why self-descriptions in terms of natural law theory have so much greater purchase within legal systems that have evolved constitutions. The operations that sustain them are the same ones that sustained natural law from the Middle Ages to the 18th century.

4

Law's Justice: Beyond Dworkin

In chapter 3, we described the evolution of law's self-description from natural law theory to that of legal positivism in terms of the changing nature of legal communications. As an evolution of self-description, there is no possibility that either could represent the totality of legal communications, for all the reasons set out in chapter 2. These self-descriptions are self-observations at a higher level of generality and thematisation, of communications that operate as structures within the legal system. Such structures stabilise the possibilities of legal communication. But stabilise does not mean 'freeze'. What stabilises also establishes possibilities for change, or variety. As such, it might be useful to think about such communications as 'orientating' legal communications. And orientation extends to evolution. So, to return to self-description, jurisprudence describes structures that both stabilise the legal system and allow it to change. And as autological, not only do jurisprudence texts describe communications that orientate other legal communications, but they too have an orientating capacity. This is a dynamic process, which does not allow foundations to determine possibilities.[1] There are simply endless connecting communications that, in the process of connecting, alter the possibilities of making further connections.

---

[1] As we saw in the history of the common law, the changing nature of the communications being described (the increase in legislation) reduced the ability to describe law's evolution by reference to values immanent within an unchanging law, which in turn altered communications about the nature of the common law (cases became authorities, and not evidence of law, and stricter versions of stare decisis developed).

Whilst positivist legal theories attempt to describe the unity of law in terms of authoritative sources, they cannot account for the whole of law in this way. In chapter 3 we suggested that the kinds of operations that generated natural law self-description did not immediately disappear from the legal system once legislation began to produce positivist self-descriptions. This might lead one to suppose that such operations—and communications about them—represent historical remnants that could be progressively removed from legal systems. But this would be an incorrect conclusion. There is no reason to expect the legal system ever to reduce itself solely to communications that can be identified as legal communications by reference to authoritative sources. In particular, the legal system, if it continues to evolve as it has in the past, cannot operate without communications that refer to 'justice'. Within Luhmann's theory, justice is described as a formula for contingency or variety and, as such, is central to the ability of legal systems to evolve.[2]

Similarly, Dworkin's conspectus of jurisprudential writings can be viewed as a sustained attempt to describe the unity of law in a manner that accounts for both its stability and its capacity to evolve by reference to ideas of justice. As such, it reproduces much of what, within Luhmann's theory, is described as a formula for contingency. However, whilst Luhmann's analysis of justice is in keeping with his claim that the legal system is closed, so that justice is produced by law's own operations and is not an input from outside, Dworkin identifies justice with communications from outside of the legal system. For Dworkin, law is both stabilised, and stimulated to evolve, through interpretative techniques that involve the utilisation of moral principles. Such interpretative techniques and their utilisation of moral principles offer themselves to his particular explanation of the legal system's autonomy. For while the legal system is open to communications generated within the political system through the legislative process, it can never become politics, as the interpretative techniques of judges require them to identify and apply

---

[2] See Luhmann, 2004, ch 5 'Justice, A Formula for Contingency'.

moral principles. Moral principles inform the interpretation of rules, operate within the gaps left unregulated by rules, and even overturn rules. Because, for Dworkin, politics does not involve the systematic application of moral principles, the two systems can never reduce to each other. These interpretative techniques ensure that judicial decisions are different from legislative operations.

Systems theory has its own explanation of the autonomy of law from politics, which we present in chapter 6. However, the particular aspect of Dworkin's writings that we wish to address in this chapter is his claim that law is both stabilised, and changed, through its incorporation of communications from outside of itself: moral principles. In systems theory terms, this represents a self-description that denies law's 'paradox', which we have set out in detail in the final paragraph of chapter 2: that the law itself decides what is law. Using systems theory we attempt here to demonstrate why Dworkin's account of the legal system provides an inadequate explanation of either its stability, or its capacity to change (which together constitute its evolution). While in the last part of this chapter we present Luhmann's own explanation of the nature and role of justice within the legal system.

Dworkin's Account of Law's Evolution

Dworkin's discussion of conventionalism, representing those conceptions or theories of law that try to account for law's identity by relying on a given pedigree test, is premised on the impossibility of law continuing to be what it has always been.[3] There must be a mechanism for change. Conventionalism fails to explain law's capacity to evolve. Mechanisms for change are

[3] 'We tested conventionalism against two perspectives on our practice: in cross-section, as an account of what particular judges do about particular cases, and over time, as a story about how legal culture develops and changes as a whole. Conventionalism failed from the latter perspective.' (Dworkin, 1986, 157). Others have, subject to redefining the character of conventionalism, reached the conclusion that it should not be rejected: see Simmonds, 1990.

obviously present in theories that represent law as an expression of the sovereign's will, since the sovereign body can change the law as much as it wishes. But such theories, by claiming that the sovereign is something that exists outside of law, and cannot be defined and limited by law, deny the existence and effects of constitutional law. The existence of a constitution prevents changes in the law from being exhaustively accounted for by reference to the operations of legislatures. Thus, for Dworkin, conventionalism as a conception of law that acknowledges constitutions as a source of law superior to legislation, cannot explain the evolution of the constitution, or the evolution of non-constitutional law that does not take the form of legislation.[4] But, having rejected conventionalism for failing to account for change, Dworkin rejects legal pragmatism for failing to account for what remains stable.[5] Pragmatism is what we might understand as politics in its most general sense. And in rejecting politics as the source of law's ability to change (a source that would include law making by judges as well as legislatures) Dworkin is also rejecting the claim that political consensus is the source of law's stability. For, if politics determines what changes in law, it must also determine what remains the same.[6] Dworkin's own answer to law's stability and change (its evolution) is law as integrity, a combination of things external and internal to the

[4] Dworkin, 1986, 139.

[5] *Ibid*, 159–64.

[6] Of course, attempts to export the source of law into politics presuppose that tautology will not simply reappear within politics. What, other than the political system, determines what has political significance within society? Dworkin seems to have some awareness of this when he re-exports this tautology into moral philosophy by attributing a doctrine of political responsibility to both political and legal actors, which doctrine restrains their actions by requiring consistency. Thus, in his early writing, he relies on the claim that 'Judges, like all political officials, are subject to the doctrine of political responsibility.' (Dworkin, 1977, 87). However, his attempts to identify what could stabilise politics are even less sociologically informed than those addressed to law. His definition of politics as policy resembles act utilitarianism without even the consistent commitment to general happiness: acts that maximise goals (see, as a stark example, *ibid*, 113–14).

legal system. Law as integrity,[7] a commitment to consistency and justice, allows law to be interpreted in a manner compatible with its history: law is stable, yet has the capacity to change. The capacity to change arises from the changing possibilities of attempts to justify existing legal material: statutes, the constitution, and legal decisions. The legal material is internal to law, but the plausibility of justification depends on developments outside of law, in particular, within political philosophy, rather than the political system.[8] As such, Dworkin is offering a selective account of the relationship between law and its environment, in which political philosophy operates as the basis of law's autonomy, since it both stabilises what will consistently be presented as a legal interpretation, and provides the basis for the evolution of such communications.[9]

Herculean Justice

The earlier writings of Dworkin[10] utilised the figure of Hercules, a personification of legal rationality, with infinite time and resources to devise a holistic theory of law, giving the best interpretation at every level of the legal system, and a right answer to

[7] The whole of *Law's Empire*, 1986, develops this interpretation. A short summary of the substantive argument of 'law as integrity' can be found at 216–24.

[8] There is however, although the account is never quite clear, an input from the political system *qua* system. Statutes represent material likely to be introduced for reasons which have no connection with the application of principles as they would be understood by a moral philosopher, but that can be used in the interpretive process as if they were.

[9] Dworkin's presentation of the doctrine of political responsibility within politics acknowledges the gap between philosophy and the likely behaviour of a senator in a manner likely to lead to idealism (senators do or ought to vote consistently), or cynicism (senators fail to take account of principles). As such it fails to reflect the manner in which principles operate constantly, within politics. Principles, it may be suggested, have a meaning within, and are constructed by, politics as a system—that is not the same as their construction within either moral philosophy or law.

[10] Dworkin's attempts to describe law by attributing the unity of law to the interpretive processes of judges, and insisting that these processes involve a significant use of both political and moral philosophy, have been subjected to numerous criticisms, particularly from analytical positivists like Raz. In response, Dworkin has repeatedly attempted to restate his position.

every difficult situation.[11] Crucial to the work of this figure, and reformulations of the theory, is the ability to declare earlier institutional history (earlier authoritative interpretations) to be mistakes.[12] This description of the judicial process provides no basis for the stability of the interpretation of legal materials other than the stability provided through political or moral philosophy. Legal materials have no authority in and of themselves, only that provided through the principles which justify their interpretation as authorities. Thus, in its most extreme formulation, Dworkin's attempt to defuse any tautology (or consequential paradox) in law (that law decides what is law) by attributing stability and change to a combination of matters that are internal and external to law, actually relies on external factors alone.

But, whilst avoiding paradox, the figure of Hercules provides a poor description of the practices of law, or at least one that might appeal to a sociologist concerned to accommodate the given world of law's vast numbers of operations within their descriptions. Although there are moments in the judicial process where thousands of hours go into a single judgment, and that judgment includes statements that appear to come from political or moral philosophy, any attempt to ascribe to these moments the unity of the legal system and its capacity for stability and change, is patently implausible. Decisions have to be made in an instant in huge numbers of situations. And the fact that these decisions are made, and closure achieved for so many legal questions all of the time, cannot be explained through the work of Hercules or Herculean actors. Later Dworkin modified his position, by arguing that Hercules is only an ideal figure, to which judges should (and if his theory is descriptively accurate, will) approximate. He also sought to reduce the burden of holistic reasoning by arguing that judges would seek to provide consistent explanations of local areas of doctrine, only moving outwards to check if their explanations of one area of doctrine were compatible with consistent explanations of surrounding

[11] Dworkin, 1977, 105–30.
[12] *Ibid*, 118–23.

areas of doctrine.[13] Provided surrounding areas confirmed the correctness of the principles and rights found to explain the original area of doctrine, there was no need to go further.[14] While these concessions increase the plausibility of his thesis in some respects, it still fails to account for the stability of law. Stability, with these concessions, is the restriction of contingency resulting from the consensus of political or moral justifications for the whole or significant parts of the legal system. Dworkin's theory cannot operate if it can be shown that not only are there contradictory rationales for particular areas of doctrine, but that such contradictions occur right across doctrine as a whole.[15]

Reconsidering Dworkin From a Systems Theory Perspective

The Local Nature of Connecting Legal Communications

Luhmann, in chapter 7 of *Law as a Social System* places judges in a central position in the legal system. But they are not in a hierarchical position; indeed, unlike Hercules, they do not determine the content of what can be legal. Judges, and their interpretive practices, are a structure within the legal system, which system comprises the totality of legal communications. Huge numbers of legal communications occur within the system. Membership of that system is established by the connection between legal communications, and what connects legal communications is their coding; they code the world into what is legal and what illegal.[16] And in this process of coding, the legal

---

[13] Dworkin, 1986, 245–50.

[14] *Ibid*, 250–254.

[15] As illustrated convincingly by the Critical Legal Theorists, see Collins, 2002, especially 287–320; and see ch 6 below.

[16] On the nature of this binary coding, its exclusion of third values (which would be included with the attempt to add any ingredient such as, even, legally significant/legally insignificant), its institutionalisation, and its ability to respond to its complex environment (society), see Luhmann, 2004, ch 4/*II*. The exclusion of third values has been strongly criticised (see Rottleuthner, 1989a), but that criticism rejected by Luhmann.

system establishes both itself, and its environment (what it considers it is not). This is not the work of a supra-individual like Hercules, or the distribution, within judges, of the ideal form of rationality he represents. It is, inevitably, the outcome of itself. The possibilities of what can be coded legal or illegal at any moment are the consequence at that moment of the state of the legal system. It is both total and local. Total, in the sense just stated—it is the outcome of all that currently exists. It is also local in that, at any moment, what a single legal communication can connect to is limited to material to which it has a limited proximity.

An example may assist in understanding how this way of viewing the legal system differs from Dworkin's analysis. Consider a demand to pay a parking fine. For Dworkin, using Hercules, the validity of this parking fine requires a systematic assessment of the totality of the legal system. The starting point for this assessment is pre-interpretive[17] (so we have an idea of what needs to be put into a best moral light prior to carrying out that assessment). In making that assessment we need to declare some part of our existing legal material to be mistakes at the outset, ie that these are not law after all. Under Dworkin's original formulation of his theory, our assessment needs to take account of every level in the legal system. Using his more modest theory, the assessment has a stopping point provided that the analysis of one area of doctrine can be confirmed by its ability to provide an equally appropriate explanation of surrounding areas of doctrine.

Within systems theory the account would be very different. There is no possibility, at one moment in the legal system, of connecting to every other part of that system. This does not alter the fact that the possibilities of connection at any moment are a consequence of the state of the legal system at that moment. But actual connections are, invariably, local. In the case of our parking fine, the first order of connection (or communication, which is the form of this connection) is that it conveys information on

[17] Dworkin, 1986, 65–6.

legality and illegality: your parking was illegal. Thus it is coding, rather than the view of a hypothetical supra-individual on the validity of the fine, that makes this a legal communication. All such coding can be re-coded, as a result of secondary observation. We can make communications about the validity of the parking fine. This re-coding does not make the original meaning of the parking fine anything other than a legal communication, even if a person making such a re-coding might describe the earlier coding as 'not law'. However, such re-coding, applied within structures such as a judiciary, will stabilise communications about parking fines. This is because the communications of judges have, within our legal system, evolved into a significant (but not determinant) structure for making communications about the application of the code. It is conceivable that a parking fine arises in situations that generate a massive judgment by the highest court in the land on a major constitutional issue. Such a judgment may be the consequence of connections between a large number of earlier legal communications but, however large, it cannot be a consequence of connection between all of the legal system. There is not the time, the connections are not established by logic but from the fact of connection (as in all successful uses of language) so they lie outside the capacity of even a supra-human individual and, in any case, by the time such connections could be made things have moved on (there are millions more communications). So the best that can be achieved, even in significant legal cases, is widespread connections. And these secondary observations do not determine the existence, as legal statements, of even the first order communication. Courts are structures, and structures stabilise the making of communications within and by a system, but they must not be understood as the unity of that system, or the cause of its unity. Courts are important for stabilising the making of communications about what is legal and illegal, but the unity of the legal system lies in the composite of the identity of such communications, not just in the communications of courts, and certainly not in the hypothetical possibilities of a supra-individual judge such as Hercules.

So far our systems theory analysis may be considered to do no more than present a criticism that can be made in far more straightforward terms: Dworkin attempts to present the interpretive practices of judges, which can only be one aspect of the legal system, as if they were the whole.[18] But the theory has more potential yet. Let us consider the debate between Dworkin and the positivists on the nature of the material used by judges to make their decisions. For Dworkin moral philosophy, because judges use it in the form of principles, *is* part of law.[19] For positivists such as Raz, moral philosophy is not law just because judges use it to make decisions. If it were, then science, aesthetics, even language would be law, because they share this feature of being used by judges to make decisions. Dworkin can only justify the use of moral philosophy as something legal if the manner in which that philosophy is used is peculiar to law. For the positivists, the legal part of a judge's decision is established by reference to authoritative sources. It is these sources that restrict what can be considered as part of a legal decision. In this way the reasoning processes of judges are only peculiar to law because law has institutional means of treating matters as having been decided.[20]

---

[18] See for example Raz's defence of Hart as set out in Raz, 1986.

[19] Kelsen (1991, ch 28) recognised the errors of this position in his debate with Esser who, in 1956, had offered a transformation theory that claimed that law is established through the input of moral principles. Kelsen argued that any claim that law transformed morality into itself was a confusion resulting from a mistaken metaphor. Craftsmen transform their material (wood, etc) into objects. Law cannot transform moral principles into legal principles. Law can only select principles, and the basis of selection remains with the law. Kelsen's critique of 'principles' as law was, of course, formulated without reference to Dworkin's analysis of principles. But as a critique of 'principles' Kelsen's work has much in common with the systems theory approach presented here, with one key difference, namely Kelsen's reliance on acts of will (and their objective meaning) as law forming acts (see ch 5 below).

[20] Principally it relies on the programmes associated with '*res judicata*' and equality (see later discussion of equality, as a legal communication).

Dworkin v The Positivists

Systems theory throws light on this debate between Dworkin and the positivists. It starts, in keeping with its central assumption of closure, from the premise that the law decides what can be law. This is further explored through the logic of forms.[21] The distinction between legal and illegal is simply a distinction. This can be understood through our by now familiar question: 'If I told you that an unknown fact "X" was legal, what would this tell you other than that it was not illegal, and vice versa?' If 'legal' cannot universally be equated with a third value, such as 'good' or 'politically acceptable', etc, then it can only be a distinction. As a distinction, there is nothing to distinguish what is put on either side of the distinction: the legal is illegal, and vice versa.[22] The legal system avoids or unfolds this 'paradox' through its logical tautology: the law decides what is legal and what is illegal. And it does so endlessly. In so doing it builds up structures, which constitute its conditioning programmes: 'in the case of X, Y is legal.' These structures can (only 'can', it is all contingent) include courts: 'If a person appointed as a high court judge decides this matter in this way, it is legal'.[23] These courts have a central role within the legal system as they have a duty to decide (they cannot decide not to decide). And this role makes the unfolding of the paradox of law central to their operation;[24] there is no third value that decides what is legal or

[21] See Luhmann, 2004, ch 4. In presenting his arguments he relies in particular on Brown, *Laws of Form*, 1969.

[22] See Luhmann, 2004, ch 4, at 175–77.

[23] Such a communication is, of course, closely analogous to Hart's characterisation of a rule of adjudication: see Hart, 1961, 94–6.

[24] To clarify the importance of paradox in relation to the duty of courts to decide, see Luhmann, 2004, 292–3. 'The paradox, however, is the holy shrine of the system. It is a deity in many forms: as *unitas multiplex* and as re-entry of the form into the form, as the sameness of difference, as the determinacy of indeterminacy, as self-legitimation. The unity of the system can be expressed in the system as distinctions, which turn into guiding distinctions in this function because they hide from view what they reveal. . . . courts are in charge of the task of unfolding the paradox of the legal system—as is required by and, at the same time, veiled by the prohibition of the denial of justice . . .' (292).

illegal. What the courts do is decide, and in so deciding they carry out secondary observation: they observe what has been decided before. In this role, they cannot avoid hard cases: whatever has been decided will not decide all that could be decided. It also means that there is no single way (no single structure) for describing how courts decide: the duty to decide forces courts to find reasons for deciding. And there is no way of deciding how 'successful' such reasons are except for the fact of their (or something they lead to) being re-used. This has a stabilising bias. The reasons, which are more obviously appropriate to justify decisions, are those that have been used before. These are reasons that are likely to provide stable structures for dealing with contingency. Positivists present this stabilising bias as the whole process. Thus judicial decisions are seen as authoritative sources, for one of the most common bases for justifying a decision is to claim that judges have decided this way before. Other sources, which provide structures to stabilise, and thus unfold the paradox that lies behind the legal/illegal distinction, include the constitution (particularly in the USA) and the sovereignty of parliament (particularly in the UK).

The debate between Dworkin and positivists can be reconsidered from the perspective of the duty to decide.[25] Whatever structures are developed to avoid the paradox of law's tautology will inevitably be used in some situations where they are not as successful as others. For example, the doctrine of sovereignty of parliament suffers not only from its patent fictional quality when considered by reference to the complexities of the political system (it is a construct of the legal system),[26] but its use within the legal system generates cases where it adds little (to secondary observers) to the fact that the relevant court decided the matter. The damage to the legal system's stability done by such cases is

[25] Or, as Luhmann describes it, 'the prohibition of the denial of justice': 2004, ch 7/IV.

[26] Hence the usual critique within jurisprudence of Austin's notion of sovereignty as descriptively inaccurate (see Hart, 1961, ch IV). Of course Austin simplifies two sovereignties, and then conflates them. His account does not adequately describe the role of legislatures within politics, or law.

further reduced, however, if in such situations decisions are treated as good reasons to decide the same way in future. But this means that the assumed hierarchy of parliament and courts is also paradoxical because, in these situations, the will of parliament is only expressed though fidelity to the decisions of the courts.[27]

With respect to decisions in situations as described above, positivists and Dworkin are trying to establish rival hierarchies for the structures that stabilise legal communications and determine their evolution. For positivists such as Hart and Raz, the reasons that 'best' explain legal decisions are the sources of law. The paradox of law's tautology—that law decides what is law—is avoided or defused by them through treating judicial commitment to these sources as a social fact established and maintained outside of the legal system. For Dworkin, the inability of such structures to explain all of the decisions made by courts leads him to look for alternative bases for stability and change. He finds these in moral philosophy, and moral principles. For him, principles establish the weight to be given to authoritative sources, and the decision to be reached when such sources do not by themselves indicate a particular result. Because authoritative sources are not always good reasons for decisions, principles (which operate most clearly when authoritative sources most clearly do not) are considered by him to be the superior structure. In addition, because his principles are weighted (at least partially) through their connection to morality, the stability and change of the legal system does not depend entirely on what is already law. The tautology is defused.[28]

---

[27] Thus, within this description, lies an explanation for the interminable debates about the relationship between courts and legislative bodies between jurisprudential theories. See, as a straightforward example, Hart's denunciation of the overly court centred approach of American Realists, in Hart, 1961, ch 7, and his 'Postscript' reply to his critics, in Hart, 1994. See, for a more extensive argument, Coleman, 2001a; see also essays in Coleman, 2001b.

[28] But defusing tautology by attributing the unity of law to inputs from outside, such as morality, has a cost in terms of failing to recognise the identity of law as something different from its inputs: see n 19 above.

Systems theory treats both Dworkin and positivists as operating at a third level of observation, the level of self-description.[29] The need to decide without any third value determining what is legal or illegal generates, at the first level, decisions. Secondary observation of such decisions generates structures that stabilise those decisions. At a third level, observations of those structures lead to attempts to present particular structures in a hierarchical manner, as if they represented or accounted for the unity and totality of the legal system: self-descriptions (the substance of so much jurisprudence).

Systems theory leads one to accept that all self-descriptions are partial, because the structures that they seek to arrange in hierarchical order cannot, in practice, maintain a hierarchical order. This occurs most fundamentally at the level of language: structures, which order communications, are generated by communications, so that what they order can change them. Within the Dworkin-positivist debate, the structures that are given central focus are those that stabilise judicial decisions. But attempts to present a constant hierarchy of structures that stabilise legal communications are doomed to failure. Just as parliamentary sovereignty exists alongside the courts duty to decide what is law (constantly threatening to reduce the hierarchy of parliament and politics over the courts and law to a rhetorical device), so too, principles constantly threaten to subvert the supremacy of rules and authoritative sources.

Adjudicating on Dworkin and The Positivists

The debate between Dworkin and his positivist critics has resulted in concessions on both sides that considerably narrow the differences between them. Hart's formulation of law as a matter of rules, and Dworkin's criticism of his omission of principles, has led Raz to concede that the legal system is made up of standards that consist of both, and that even the rule of recognition is not simply a rule but consists of 'all of the customary

---

[29] For a succinct statement about 'self-description', see Nobles and Schiff, 2004a, 12–13 and 44–8.

rules and principles of the law enforcing agencies [that identify] . . . all the laws recognized by them.'[30] But important differences remain. Dworkin denies the possibility of a general explanation of what counts as adequate institutional support for a legal principle: there is no measure or yardstick for the amount of institutional recognition required for a principle used by or presented to a court to count as a legal principle. Dworkin maintains the claim that one looks outside the legal system, to moral philosophy, to account for the legal system's ability to find weight in principles rather than in some empirical relationship such as the frequency of their citation or implied use by courts. For Raz, the inability to provide a general explanation of what counts as adequate institutional support would dissolve the border between law and non-law standards, and with it, the distinctive feature that distinguishes a legal system from the wider social system. He looks for an adequate explanation of the concept of a customary norm, so that one can make a complete statement of judicial custom and thus have a complete criterion of identity.[31]

While this exchange has sharpened our awareness of the many different kinds of standards used by judges when adjudicating on legal issues, the protagonists still leave us with two different ways to defuse the tautology that systems theory accepts. For Dworkin, law is not simply determined by law because there is a residual element of moral philosophy, or justice, which provides the relative commitment to stability and change. For Raz, the standards that are law do not determine themselves, because there is a sociological condition, the customary norms of judges as a group, which provide this commitment. Systems theory offers an alternative to both positions.

The ability of judges to find standards or reasons to determine every issue that comes before them is a process limited by the

[30] Raz, 1972, 853.

[31] *Ibid*, 854. However, at a later stage, Raz (1986, 1105), concedes that the standards binding upon judges may be supplemented by standards that they can only reach through processes that are so indeterminate that they could best be described as exercises of discretion.

same process by which all communications are made: the ability to communicate is determined by the system to which any new communication seeks to connect. These are not processes for which one can substitute any other factor and have it stand in place of the process of communication. So the psychological or normative commitments of the participants (judicial customs) do not determine the possibilities of communication. It is the existing state of communication that determines what can be connected. Thus, (as we believe Fish would acknowledge)[32] communicating law requires the participants to have regard to the existing structures of communication. In the case of law, at this moment, in most legal systems, these are constitutions, cases, and statutes: forms that generate and support innumerable rules and principles. These structures are used in making communications not simply because the participants are committed to them in a normative sense, but because utilising them to make communications increases the chances of successful[33] communication. Change is restricted by the same factors that encourage stability. Jettisoning an important structure (such as parliamentary sovereignty) is not difficult because of an internal (psychological) or external (universal moral value) commitment to democracy. It is first and foremost difficult because massive amounts of law would not be possible. An all out attack on this structure would require vast numbers of laws to be re-configured. Whatever the weaknesses of this structure, and however many times its nakedness is exposed, its abandonment would require a substitute structure that allowed similar communications to be made. From the point of view of the courts, one would need a structure that has a similar ability to provide reasons for decisions. To express this in systems theory terms: evolution requires the variation of an element, which results in the selection of a structure that is capable of stable reproduction. Variations that do not amount to new structures do not lead to

[32] Fish, 1982, 551–67.

[33] Success here only refers to the likelihood of increasing the stability of such communications, and thus having the practical effect of reinforcing normative expectations.

evolution, and new structures that do not stabilise and reproduce themselves also do not result in evolution.[34]

The judiciary appear to function as a subsystem of the legal system, carrying out secondary observation of legal communications and developing structures that stabilise the application of the code legal/illegal. They put into operation a value that is commonly thought to be external to the legal system: equality. The value remains internal because the equality required is to 'treat like cases alike'. This is an *eigenvalue*—a value that has no existence outside of the operations that express it. Judges observe what has been coded, and seek to account for that coding. These accounts have the possibility, if reproduced, of becoming structures. Consistent accounts of coding are (in *whatever* form they develop) treating like cases alike. Equality is consistency, and consistency is the only equality the law intrinsically expresses. This process is partial, and local, but has the capacity to be dynamic. The configurations of what can be compared are not given from outside the legal system but from within. Only the legal system can construct a 'case' that needs to be compared with another 'case'. This means that the issue decided by a judicial decision is never the issue that would arise if a decision were taken in another area of social life. (The legality of a particular abortion never determines, even to an incremental degree, the moral right to life).

The dynamics of this basis for decisions cannot be captured by a meta-structure, such as a criterion of identity. Fortunately this does not have the outcome, as Raz supposes, of a conflation of legal and non-legal standards that results in the legal system having no separate identity from the rest of society. The separation is simply not reducible to a philosophical distinction between the standards appropriate to law and elsewhere. The uniqueness of law is found in what it does and how it does it. It codes in terms of what is legal as opposed to, and dependent on, what is illegal, and it constructs, through its own programmes,

---

[34] For more detail see Luhmann, 2004, ch 6 'The Evolution of Law', and particularly Part I.

what (such as cases) it codes. To take Dworkin's own iconic example of the decision in *Riggs v Palmer*,[35] the application of a standard such as 'no one shall be permitted . . . to take advantage of his own wrong'[36] does not result in the dissolution of law into morality for so many reasons. First, the standard is being used to apply a label that is not moral: to decide what is legal. Second, the 'wrongdoing' and the 'benefit' will be identified through legal categories (in the case of *Riggs v Palmer* that of being convicted of murder and inheriting through a properly executed will). Third, the arrival of this issue for decision is a moment established by the legal system through writs, conviction, evidence, judgment and appeals. Fourth, the legal system has developed structures (precedent) that routinely replace reasons for decisions with decisions as reasons for decisions. In consequence of all of this, how (except within an exercise in self-description) could the selection of this moral communication for re-use by the legal system be treated as the superiority of moral values over legal ones, or the collapse of legal standards into social ones?

The morality identified by Dworkin within legal reasoning is not the morality of moral philosophy, or the principles of political theory. Justice, as the treating of like cases alike, is a mechanism for the evolution of law. The general norm to 'be just' is simply the process of justification involved in secondary observation. The evolutionary capacity of this process can generate rules, exceptions, and principles. What has been decided can be described in terms of rules. Distinctions based on rules allow for further distinctions in terms of exceptions. Distinctions that cannot be accommodated through rules and exceptions (and exceptions as rules with exceptions in turn) can be articulated in terms of principles: matters that need to be considered prior to the application of the code. Such non-rule restrictions on the basis for decisions can be termed 'discretion'. And the existence of such discretion, constructed through standards of

---

[35] 115 NY 506.

[36] The principle that Dworkin, 1977, 23, relies on to develop his argument.

what needs to be considered in order to decide, does not result in either subjectivity (a judge can communicate as law whatever she/he wants law to be) or morality. Discretion, and the standards which restrict its exercise, do not lie outside the legal system. Rather, they are structures for generating a more complex legal system with more capacity to precipitate productive interactions with other functioning subsystems of society than could ever be achieved through rules alone.

The values generated by this process of secondary observation are not the input of morality into the legal system from outside. This is not an input-output relationship.[37] Justice, understood by the legal system as something beyond and outside of itself, is more than the application of rules, because legal decisions are more than the application of rules. It is something always beyond what currently exists. But this 'justice' is a value whose existence still lies in the operations of the legal system: the search for reasons for decisions, most particularly located within the courts that have the duty to decide (and cannot deny justice). This search is not resolvable in terms of a rational schema, and certainly not one that would be recognised by moral philosophy. The process of secondary observation undertaken by courts assesses the 'equality' of its own deliberations by asking what are the consequences in terms of the re-configurations of legal relationships, of alternative descriptions of what has already been decided. These re-configurations are accessible to the legal imagination. One can say 'If you decide this case in this way, you would have to decide all these other cases in a similar/different way.' In some cases, the equality represented by treating like cases alike can be understood as the application of rules. But in other situations, it can result in comparisons between areas of doctrine, requiring for example, the treatment of 'residence' for political rights to be the same, or different (for a reason) as that for housing rights. Here, provided that the difficulties for communication created by such 'equalities' can

---

[37] Such a statement goes to the biological foundations of autopoietic systems theory, see Maturana and Varela, 1980 and 1988.

be stabilised, one has a fruitful basis from which to reach new legal conclusions: make novel legal communications.

Another reason why judicial reasoning cannot be described solely by reference to moral values is that the values utilised in secondary observation are not only moral ones. The rules and principles generated by secondary observation are conditional programmes for the application of the code legal/illegal. At the moments of their generation they allow all kinds of values generated within other systems to form part of what is regarded as equal or unequal about different constellations of legal relationships. For example, in criminal law the legal system can assess the consequences of different combinations of defence rights for the likelihood that evidence will reveal the truth of what has occurred. But this momentary consideration of matters pertaining to truth will not make the criminal justice process into an expression of scientific, or other expressions, of the values of truth. And in contract law, a decision on the concept of duress may make reference to 'fair competition', but this will not make contract law an expression of morality (fairness) or economics (competition). Nor will law be troubled by philosophical arguments on the incommensurability of fairness and competition, or of either with truth.[38]

While conditioning programmes may be constructed by reference to every kind of value communicated within society, they never impose a value that determines, for the system as a whole, what is legal and illegal. Not only are too many values utilised for them ever to be reduced to a single value (or rationalised within one meta-moral schema), but also no value utilised within a conditional programme is applied in the same manner as it exists in the system from which it originated. To re-use one of the above examples, law has regard to fairness and competition only for the purposes of deciding whether a contract should be coded as legal or illegal ie to determine what other legal communications can be generated in turn. The alternative possibilities remain legal, even

[38] This aspect of legal reasoning has been recognised by Sunstein, who refers to it as 'incompletely theorised agreements'; see Sunstein, 1996, ch 2.

though the legal system has constructed something outside itself (fairness and competition) for the purposes of determining which coding on this occasion is a more consistent application of its coding: legal/illegal.

Systems theory allows us to agree with Raz that by demonstrating that judges have regard to morality in their decisions, Dworkin has not shown that morality is part of law. However, within systems theory, this is not achieved by taking particular structures, such as sources, or the ability of law to limit what counts as a reason for a decision, and treating these as the basis of the unity of law while casting morality and other 'values' into the category of non-law. Law not only constructs itself, but also constructs its environment. Law constructs the things that it identifies as different from itself. Thus references to morality in law are legal, even on those occasions when their use cannot be accounted for through a theory of sources, or an adequate comprehensive statement of judicial custom. They are legal, not because they are identified as such by legal sources, but because they are selected by the law, from the system where they occur in a manner that gives them a quite different meaning from that given by their original generating system. Morality within law is not morality, just as truth within law is not scientific or any other expression of truth. Law selects and reconstructs communications from other systems as it endlessly develops programmes that apply the code legal/illegal.

Moral communications are only one of the communications that law can select as something different from itself in order to explain, to itself, how it decides what is to be legal and illegal. It can also use economic, political and other communications. However, law appears to have more to do with morality than other aspects of society and its functioning subsystems because the function of law (the major consequence of its operations) is the stabilisation of normative expectations.[39] This is a consequence of the operations (secondary observation) that provide structures to stabilise the application of the code. And

---

[39] See particularly, Luhmann, 2004, ch 2/*VI*.

this stabiliszation (consistency) is primarily organised by reference to justice as equality. It is this commitment to consistency (justice as equality) that Dworkin attempts to capture within his writings. But his attempt to attribute it to moral or political philosophy, and to attribute the evolution of law to a process of constant approximation to such moral or political philosophy is sociologically inadequate. The use of morality in law requires a description of the processes by which law identifies itself and its environment through a fact/norm distinction, and controls for itself the processes by which this border is constantly developed and articulated. Law (the existing state of the legal system) controls not only what counts as a relevant fact (selected by law's norms) but also when and how communications about values can be utilised by law for the application of the code legal/illegal. But the overlapping use of terminology and syntax from science, religion, accountancy, economics, politics or morality cannot retain the meaning of such communications within their own systems. And it is in this sense that, ultimately, law remains tautological: it is the legal system that determines what is and can be law. As such, systems theory's answer to the 'great jurisprudential debate' between natural law and legal positivist theories is a quiet and subtle answer. Law borrows whatever it attributes as law from whatever environmental sources it understands as part of its own communications. There is no answer to the source or determinacy of law except that which operates within law. There is no structure outside of law that determines the possibilities of what can be law, since law cannot be external to itself.

Luhmann's Account of Justice—a Formula for Variety

Justice as a formula for variety plays a role within the legal system that, within other systems, is played by other such formulas (eg allocation in response to 'scarcity' within the economic system). Such formulas refer to the potential within all systems, for things to be different: contingency. This possibility exists at many levels. Individual decisions applying a system's code can always be different. Observations on decisions can treat them as mistakes or not, and in each case produce accounts. Such accounts build into a system's conditional programmes: 'if x apply the code legal'. And the processes that build conditional programmes can also change them. Justice, as a formula for variety, is not something that is present when systems change and absent when they remain the same, but something that is present on both occasions. This is not just because what remains the same could always be different, and whilst everything can always be different it can also (and more commonly) stay the same. It is because the same formula is applied on both occasions: treat like cases alike. Justice as this formula is not a value *applied* to legal operations. Rather, it is the value exhibited by a legal operation simply by the fact of that operation having occurred (what Luhmann, taking the term from mathematical operations, calls an *eigenvalue*).

Secondary observation inevitably involves treating like cases alike, since observation involves the application of a distinction (why x is like or not like y). In the case of law this formula invariably has a particularly apt application, since what requires to be treated alike is habitually a 'case'. This is particularly so within the courts, which observe on their own earlier decisions, and do so in the context of a matter that has been brought to them for decisions via pleadings, evidence, earlier decisions, appeals, etc.

The importance of this formula within the legal system is apparent when one contemplates the vast and complex set of conditional programmes that have been developed within a modern legal system. Justice, as the treating of like cases alike (secondary observation), has not only developed a huge number of substantive rules, but a vast number of procedural ones as well. On the one hand these observations have generated accounts of legal decisions that increase the precision of what might occur in response to any set of facts (communications that the law selects for re-use by reference to its norms). On the other, they represent further decisions that can be made on the application of the code legal/illegal—all of which, as decisions, are not determined and could be different. Justice, as the endless application of the formula 'treat like cases alike' is the potential for difference represented by and within the system. However spectacular and public a crime and the capture of a criminal, justice does not allow the perpetrator to be immediately punished. Arrest and trial are necessary precursors to verdict and punishment. One has to entertain the possibility that the outcome (verdict and sentence) could be different. This possibility not only extends to the decisions needed to be made by reference to law's current conditioning programmes, but to the knowledge that those programmes will, at some point in the future, be different from what they are now, and that the nature and timing of that difference cannot be known, for certain, in the present. Thus justice, as this formula, produces contradictory expectations. On the one hand it generates structures that stabilise the application of the code legal/illegal and on the other it allows for fresh observations that change structures. For example, appeals both generate communications that tell lawyers what their client needs to do to achieve particular results, and communications that undo what lawyers believed their clients needed to do.

We can see from this why justice cannot be excluded from the legal system and conversely, the difficulties of a self-description that attempts to present the system as a body of rules, or even as standards identified by pre-existing authoritative standards (rules and principles). To describe law as the application of standards does not do justice (excuse the pun) to the dynamic nature of this process. Every decision within the legal system involves the requirement to 'treat like cases alike'. But the range of what can be considered to be 'alike' can only be constructed at the point of each observation. Thus, to the extent that law operates routinely and predictably, this is made possible by routine repetition of what, at that point, counts as 'alike' (it is local). And, as pointed out in chapter 2, the extent to which such stability is the consequence of identical psychic experiences (common chemical or neurological reactions to particular communications) cannot be known to the system. So the 'alikeness' of cases can only take the form of accounts that the system can generate as part of its observations of itself. (Legal communications will create a decision to be decided, and legal communications will account for that decision in preparation for any further legal decision that needs to be made in response to that earlier decision). The need to provide accounts that 'treat like cases alike' applies to both routine decisions that repeat what is common and expected, and to novel decisions that generate new accounts. A new account will have to show why and how cases treated in this new way are like other cases: what it means to treat like cases alike in the presence of this decision. Novelty is not the same as unrestricted invention. An account of this decision will still exhibit the quality of justice as an *eigenvalue*. Like cases will still be treated alike. Any new account of this decision will need to show why the previous identification of cases as alike was incorrect, and why the new selection of cases, which are to be treated like each other, is appropriate.

Justice as an eigenvalue

Justice as treating like cases alike (an *eigenvalue*) is not a commitment to something outside of the legal system, either in the sense of something located within another system, or an attitude or emotion generated within legal actors. Thus whilst it is a form of consistency, it is not a commitment to consistency (or a desire to secure the legitimacy that might follow from consistency). Treating like cases alike is simply what it means to undertake observation on decisions. Observation that continues the legal system consists of legal communications. (Using legal communications to observe on decisions within the legal system is system self-observation). Take the example of a judge. If this judge announced that the law was whatever she/he wanted it to be then she/he would not be able to account for the decision she/he was being asked to take. To understand her/himself as a judge, the issue to be decided, and the persons before her/him as parties, she/he needs to utilise vast numbers of existing accounts of prior legal decisions. In order to locate the decision that needs to be made she/he cannot but continue the process of treating like cases alike and, having located her/his decision, any account that she/he (or later observers who use legal communications in order to observe on her/his decision) gives for this decision must also treat like cases alike.

If observations that leave law unchanged, and those that make changes, are both conducted according to the rubric 'treat like cases alike', then this formula does not explain when change will occur and when it will not. Is there then a third value that determines when one occurs rather than another? And could this value possibly be a form of justice that has more substantive content than the need to identify like cases? Not if this amounts to a value that, on all occasions, determines how to apply the code legal/illegal. Accounts (observations) on the application of the code will utilise reasons going to authority (legislative intention, stare decisis, contractual intention) as well as reasons going to the policies and principles that might be taken to inform such authoritative sources with regard to the matter in issue. These reasons for decisions are the legal system's conditioning programmes. There is no single value that operates to determine the content of all these conditioning programmes. That said, there *is* a norm that operates on all occasions in the development of these diverse conditioning programmes. This is described by Luhmann as a general norm to 'be just'. Rather like Kelsen's infamous *grundnorm*, this is a norm without content. The norm operates as a requirement to perpetually find reasons for legal decisions. Given the paradox that underlies all of law's operations (that the code legal/illegal is a distinction which has no inherent meaning), the requirement to find reasons for the application of the code is a norm requiring the 'dance' to continue. Further reasons will continue to avoid recognition of this paradox. In terms of the theory, the paradox continues to be 'unfolded'. This requirement to 'be just' may well be experienced as a norm in the sense that there is a general expectation amongst those engaged in making or receiving legal communications that reasons *will* be provided. But it is again an *eigenvalue*—something generated by law's own operations. The alternative to continuing the processes of secondary observation (observing on law's operations and accounting for them according to the formula treat like cases alike) is not to do so—to stop. There is no reason within law why law should continue reproducing itself through its communications. But what we do know is that *if* law is to continue reproducing itself then it has to find reasons for its decisions even when there are no 'good' reasons for deciding in one particular way rather than another. On every occasion that law generates reasons for decisions, it executes the norm to 'be just'. And in so doing, it recreates the expectation that it will 'be just' in future.[40]

Let us pause here to consider the potential for variety described so far. The constant elaboration of reasons for decisions produces ever more conditioning programmes. This proliferation of conditioning programmes produces different configurations of relationships within the system. This in turn provides a basis to re-examine cases that were considered to be alike when previous reasons were provided. So, for example, rules of residence for the purposes of a right to vote may be disturbed by developments within family or housing law that take a different view of the nature of residence. More generally, rules announced in one episode of litigation are constantly re-examined in new litigation: is there a material difference, or not? Lawyers constantly generate new transactions that they hope to show are like previous transactions that have been dealt with in a manner favourable to their clients. When one remembers the billions of legal decisions that occur within a relatively short space of time within a single national legal system, all organised

---

[40] If the general norm to 'be just' is an *eigenvalue* within law, is it also a norm, with effects upon law, within politics, economics and morality? As such, does this generate norms requiring reasons—such that the giving of reasons is moral, efficient and democratic? As these reasons within law are simply the continuation of secondary observation, talking of an outside norm that requires them to continue is really no more than the expectation within these other systems that *law* will continue. This is the most general form of structural coupling (see ch 7)—politics, economics and morality carry out their operations in the expectation that the legal system will continue to exist.

through communications that constantly treat like cases alike, the potential for this process to produce change as well as stability becomes easier to understand.

Up to this point, our description of justice may have suggested that it has no connection with anything outside of law. This impression needs to be corrected, but in a way that reiterates the limited manner in which law, or any other functioning subsystem, is able to engage with its environment. The need to treat like cases alike is a requirement for the legal system to constantly check back and forth between its programmes and its environment. To remind you of the nature of closure, as explained in chapter 2, law's environment is a construct of itself. Only law, through its norms, can select what communications from other systems will be re-used in order to provide law with its facts. But, having constructed its environment in this manner (remembering that law can no more have immediate access to its environment than it can automatically 'know' the guilt of those accused of even the most public and spectacular of criminal acts)[41] it can then assess the justice of its own norms by reference to the manner in which these identified facts will be coded. In selecting what cases are to be treated alike, the legal system has regard to how its environment will be coded. And in looking at alternative versions of like cases, the legal system identifies different ways in which its environment will be coded. Just as law can select facts (re-use communications generated by other systems) appropriate to its norms (conditioning programmes), so too it can select different facts through alterations to its norms. And this allows it to compare two states of its own environment, both of which it has created for itself through its own selections. And in choosing between these two states, both of which are created by norms that involve treating like cases alike (albeit different cases in each instance) it follows the general norm to 'be just'.[42] The choice is not an instrumental one,

---

[41] We have, in another publication, described this as law's 'truth deficit': Nobles and Schiff, 2006.

[42] This is not, for reasons that will be developed at length in ch 6, simply the application of politics, or even political policies, within law.

if that is understood to mean the legal system's active participation in another system, or the ability to comprehend the implications of its own coding for the possibilities of communicating further communication within that system. Whilst the reconfiguration of legal relationships that will follow a new selection of cases to be treated as alike can be known with some certainty, the legal system cannot know how its re-coding will affect the ongoing communications of external systems. Law can decide what is legal, but it cannot decided how its coding will affect the application of the code payment/non payment in the economic system, or the political system's ability to code in terms of government/opposition.

The formula for variety allows for the possibility of an alternative to repeating past observations, but the need for reconfiguration is always an additional cost, in terms of the resources required to make legal communications, compared simply to repeating what is already available to be re-used. And the ongoing consequences (in terms of communications) of such reconfigurations can never be fully known in advance, either within the legal system or within its environment. The system can look back at its own earlier communications and identify decisions that have enormous importance in terms of changing structures: *Henningsen v Bloomfield Motors, Inc* in the US, and *Donoghue v Stevenson* in the UK, are two such moments. But those involved in making such decisions cannot know in advance whether the choices made will be reproduced within the legal system. Only if the system can use a decision to form a new consistent relationship with its environment, a new basis for treating like cases alike, can that decision operate as a structure that stabilises legal communications. Those that fail to do so may operate as 'irritations' generating further communications, such as additional litigation, or they may be ignored. We know that decisions like *Henningsen* and *Donoghue* offered new bases for the orientation of litigation arising from personal injury not because individuals chose to make those decisions, but because the legal system has constantly re-selected those decisions as a basis for making legal communications about personal injuries.

Some part of the trajectories represented by alternative legal relationships can form part of the arguments offered at any moment of choosing, but only hindsight can trace what actual trajectories later occurred.

But with all these caveats, how are these choices made? What does it mean, in conditions of contingency (which extend to every part of the legal system in the long term) to 'be just'? As described in chapter 3, the processes, which have resulted in a change in law's self-description from one based on ideas of reason to one organised around ideas of authority, place additional constraints upon any claim to justice. The more particular legislation that is passed, the harder it is to point to any uniform basis by which to identify the likeness of particular cases as 'unjust', and therefore not really law. But the legal system does not need a uniform basis of justice in order to operate this general norm. All that is required, or involved, is the impression of injustice of particular regulations as they operate at one particular point in the system.[43] Choosing between alternatives generated by the legal system, whether those alternatives are different ways of dealing with a situation that appears wholly novel, or choices between re-using or not re-using earlier structures for deciding, can be made on the basis of *avoiding injustice*.

One particularly apposite example of this aspect of justice is provided by the decision in *Riggs v Palmer*. The issue in the case was whether Elmer Palmer was entitled to inherit under the testator's will, given that he had been convicted of the murder of the testator (his grandfather). The legal communications that constructed the moment of, and issue for, decision included statutory provisions for a valid will—which had been met in the case. Should Elmer inherit in these circumstances? Of course the justice of a will, whether the person who is going to inherit deserves to do so, is reduced by the legal system to the question of whether the passing over of property to them will be legal. And this question, in turn, is only answered through the application of justice if one accepts that giving effect to an intention constructed by the legal system (that of the testator, as identified through the provisions of the statute) is necessarily just. Of course one of the consequences of testamentary provisions within legal systems, both private and statutory, is that the question of what is just is generally made irrelevant. The existing structures provide a legal answer to a legal question. But *Riggs v Palmer* is not an ordinary case. Elmer is not an undeserving beneficiary because he is lazy whilst other family members are hard working, or already has more money than he needs whilst others are poor. Or even, just because he is a murderer. He has been convicted of murdering the testator. Can the established structure (the intention of the testator as set out in the will) determine this decision? Perhaps, but the decision also provides a moment when justice can (not must—it is not inevitable) provide a formula for variety. Giving effect to the intention of the testator as set out in the will is a structure that stabilises the making of many communications by screening out an enormous number of facts (communications) as not being relevant to (selected by) the legal system. Announcing that wills must always be just is a communication that could not be taken up by the legal system without enormous cost to that system in terms of its ability routinely to apply the code legal/illegal. Simply continuing with the existing structure is definitely possible for the legal system. But this option, as with all other moments when the system re-uses its existing structures, provides no basis for the legal system to consider any alternative configurations of legal relationships than those already available. But examining the application of existing structures in this situation by reference to the avoidance of injustice does provide a basis for selection that, unlike the pursuit of justice, will not destabilise the routine disposal of testamentary cases. For the dissenting judges (Gray and Danforth) the fact of murder was not a reason for exception, nor was the identity of the victim. For the majority the fact of murder was not alone a relevant factor, but the identity of the victim was. Choosing between an interpretation (observation) of testamentary provisions that prevented inheritance by the convicted murderer of a testator, and one that did not, the majority chose the latter as, for them, it avoided injustice.

Let us pause here. How much has been conceded? Why can't a general norm that impels injustice to be avoided operate as an obligation to do justice, and thus generate and sustain a self-description of the legal system in terms of natural law? To put this another way, why can't a general norm that requires injustice to be avoided progressively cleanse the legal system of all unjust elements, with the result that the system works itself into the embodiment of some moral scheme? To understand why this does not occur one needs to understand the residual nature of this operation. The structures that stabilise legal operations, which now include many communications organised around ideas of authority (what positivist theories call sources of law), are understood within the system as justice: treating like cases alike. To give effect to the need to avoid injustice one needs to show why structures that ordinarily constitute justice do not do so in the particular case. The role played by the norm to 'be just' in unsettling established complex and technical programmes for the application of the code legal/illegal is 'exceptional'. It is this sense of the exceptional that makes it impossible to remove the formula from the system, yet prevents its operation from overwhelming the system. However much the structures of law routinely orientate communications for the application of the code, they will not do so on all occasions. There always remains the possibility of an 'exception.' Indeed the strength of natural law theories that seek to challenge the attempt of positivist theories to present authoritative structures as the whole of the law is the answer to the question: 'Is there any conditioning programme in the form "if X then apply the code legal" to which there could not be an exception?'[44] However settled and routine the selection of a particular communication (parliamentary sovereignty, binding precedent), and however much the complexity and particularity of law's conditional programmes seems to squeeze out the possibilities of applying communications generated

[44] A point made by MacCormick, 1986, 69–73.

within religious or ethical systems, there remains the possibility of exceptions. Positivist theories admit to exceptions in the form of 'gaps'—issues identified by legal norms but not resolved by them. And in these 'gaps' communications taken from ethics and religious systems can be re-used to account for a decision. But the norm to 'be just' also generates exceptions even where communications are available within law that could resolve an issue, and where legal relationships may even have to be reconfigured in order for the issue to be resolved differently. The legal system can tolerate such operations, provided that they remain exceptional. The distinction, normal/exceptional, blocks the operations that would follow from a repeated use of justice as a basis for the application of the code. What is exceptional can either remain so, in the form of one-off decisions that are incapable of providing accounts. Or, if generalised, immediately reaffirm the normal basis for the observation of decisions: that like cases will be treated alike. Thus, to the extent that ideas of substantive justice can ever operate within law, they do so only as exceptions, followed by business as usual: treat like cases alike. As such, rather than providing moments that can join together—working through the system to provide ever greater congruence between the legal system and ethical, religious or even political systems—they operate only as part of the legal system's formula for variety. They contribute to the system's ability to evolve, and they assist the system's endless attempts to produce consistent dualist relationships between its norms and the facts that those norms select. But they do not result in a system whose evolution can be described as directed by, or becoming ever closer to, other communications of ethical, religious or political systems.

Within the legal system, the general norm to 'be just', to treat like cases alike and to avoid the appearance of injustice, is the only way in which the system can have a basis of selection that can maintain its relationship with its environment. The legal system cannot routinely know whether it is effective as a policy tool. Nor can it routinely know its status as a cost to—or a facilitator of—business. But what it can do is compare states of its environment as selected by alternative configurations of legal relationships, and seek to be just in two senses: treat like cases alike, and avoid the appearance of injustice.

Although from a sociological point of view, justice as a formula for variety is not a process whereby the legal system becomes increasingly more just, so that the formula for variety generates what might optimistically be termed 'progress'—this contrasts with the legal system's internal understanding of itself. The legal system understands everything that it does as justice, and some of what it does as justice, as progress. When a legal system goes through its procedures instead of immediately applying sanctions to persons accused (however plausibly) of crimes, it understands itself as a system involved in the delivery of justice. When the legal system applies rules in a routine fashion, treating like cases alike, it considers itself to be dispensing justice.[45] And when the legal system perceives an unjust relationship between the states of its environment and its norms, and attempts to respond to these situations by offering new accounts of its decisions, it still considers itself to be dispensing justice. This is what Luhmann means when he claims that justice represents the unity of the system within the system. The legal system understands everything that it does as justice.

To summarise. Systems theory envisages a dynamic process involving endless observations on decisions that seek to account for the application of the code by reference to a schema of treating like cases alike. As the conditional programmes of law become ever more technical and particular, and the number of points of observation proliferates, the capacity to develop variations in accounts also proliferates. Thus treating like cases alike, whilst it stabilises the process of coding, also has the capacity to destabilise it. This capacity to destabilise is presented in decisions for which there are no good reasons ('gaps'). Such decisions are nevertheless made, and accounts of those decisions

---

[45] See the dissenting opinion of Gray J in *Riggs v Palmer* (discussed in the next chapter, in the text at n 52) in which he clearly articulates his decision as one dispensing justice, or at least avoiding the injustice of double punishments.

generated. Such decisions do not continue to operate as gaps, or even filled gaps, but provide new material that has to be accounted for, and which can therefore destabilise existing accounts of previous decisions. The process of checking the likeness of cases utilises legal norms, but is not restricted to them. Norms select facts, and choices of norms select choices of states of the system's environment. Thus the likeness of cases involves a dualism of norms and facts, such that changes in the communications generated outside of the system that are available to be re-used by the system also alter perceptions within the system as to what cases are like other cases. This too allows a process of treating like cases alike to generate variety. At a residual level, justice operates as a mechanism whereby the legal system can check its relationship with its own environment.[46] And it is not necessary for every actor who takes a particular decision to reach the same conclusion as to the injustice of a particular outcome.

[46] The legal system's version of what Rawls describes as 'reflective equilibrium': for a succinct statement of this, see Reiner, 2002, 727, reflecting on much of Rawls' *A Theory of Justice*, 1973.

5

Law's Closure: Beyond Kelsen

As part of the conclusion that we offered in the last chapter to the 'great jurisprudential debate' between natural law and positivist legal theories, we stated that 'law cannot be external to itself', for, as we attempted to demonstrate 'there is no structure outside of law that determines the possibilities of what can be law.' But, if that is so, then in what sense is law internal, or closed? Systems theory offers a dual account of what is involved: it claims that law constructs both itself and *its* environment, and this dual account is part of the claim that the legal system, along with the political and economic systems, is 'closed'. Namely, that the legal system constructs both itself, and how it communicates about other systems and society—which is a different construction from those other systems' construction of themselves, the legal system, and society, etc. This seems to many to be a counter-intuitive claim, which appears to have led some critics to reject systems theory, and at the same time deterred novices from tackling what gives the impression of being a complex and difficult theory.[1] After all, since law is so obviously related to so much of the rest of society, even to the point of having fields of law organised around particular social activities (family law, housing law, banking law, etc), what is the point of tackling a theory that proclaims something that seems so clearly to be

---

[1] 'What is irritating about the concept of autopoiesis, which leads to extensive critical discussion, is that the revolutionary effect of the concept is inversely related to its explanatory power. The concept merely states that the elements and structures of a system exist only as long as it manages to maintain its autopoiesis. The concept does not say anything about the kind of structures that are developed in cooperation with the structural couplings between system and environment.' (Luhmann, 2004, 81).

wrong? However, as we illustrated in chapter 2, Luhmann did not simply say that law was closed. He said that it was 'normatively closed' (which we described as its being 'operationally closed') but 'cognitively open'.[2]

Some version of normative closure is a claim common to many positivist legal theories as diverse as those of Raz, Hart, or Kelsen.[3] According to these theories legal norms certainly cannot be identified as moral norms per se, but nor are they social norms per se, rather they are, according to these theories, either particular kinds of rules or norms, or particular kinds of social rules or social norms. Luhmann's theory differs from these other positivist legal theories in two very important ways. First, it has a different account of how law achieves normative or operational closure. Second, it is a theory that explains how that normative closure does not lead to the isolation of law from the rest of society, but forms the basis of law's interaction with it. Law's normative closure is the basis for its construction of its own environment and thus its engagement with society that, in turn, it constructs for itself.[4]

In this chapter we explore the writings of the jurisprudential theorist most closely associated with the idea of law's closure, namely the positivist theorist Hans Kelsen. We show how his account of the basis of law's separation might be improved on by comparing it with Luhmann's analysis.[5] We propose to

[2] Luhmann recognised that such a 'concise formulation has met with considerable difficulties of understanding . . .' (2004, 106–7). This 'concise formulation' is however crucial to his analysis.

[3] Another way of describing such closure, as representing positivist legal theories, is to formulate the character of law's 'autonomy'. For classic essays orientated around a sophisticated understanding of law's autonomy, see George, 1996.

[4] Useful background to, and explanation of, such 'constructivist epistemology' can be found in Teubner, 1989.

[5] The relationship between an autopoietic understanding of law and Kelsen's theory has been particularly noted, among others, by Ewald: 'Autopoiesis is indisputably the daughter of Kelsen's Pure Theory. Kelsen's reversal is familiar: whereas hitherto the philosophy of law sought outside positive law, and mostly at its foundation, for the principle of its legality and validity (the one entailing

utilise, in particular, Kelsen's later and less well-known book, *General Theory of Norms*.[6] A link between Kelsen, as a jurisprudential writer, and Luhmann, as a sociologist, is their common commitment to the scientific study of law, which requires a theory capable of adequately describing its object.[7] This enterprise is necessary to the sociology of law, but it is also fraught with difficulties. To study law's relationships with and within society implies the existence of an object, law, which has an identity that can be described with sufficient accuracy to allow analysis of its relationships with morals, politics, social interests, etc. However, every attempt to establish that identity, and to delineate law's boundaries (law's closure) runs the risk of denying law's connections with other social processes.[8] But the alternative, to claim that law simply *is* politics, economics, social interests, or 'nothing special', leaves us without an object capable of sustaining any sociology. Since both Kelsen's and Luhmann's theories claim that law is a closed system (of norms and communications respectively) exploring their contrasts and similarities might allow us to explore the nature of such closure and its relevance to sociological analysis.

---

the other), Kelsen, in an inaugural gesture unheard of in legal tradition posited that legality (and the validity) of the legal system could be based only on its own positiveness. . . . The law, Kelsen posits, is founded on nothing other than its own positivity . . . Autopoiesis is fundamentally following up Kelsen's gesture.' (Ewald, 1988, 36, at 39–40). Luhmann does not agree with the breadth of Ewald's 'daughter' hypothesis, as can be evidenced by the various critical comments he makes about Kelsen's Pure Theory in *Law as a Social System*.

[6] Kelsen, 1991. His better known work is *The Pure Theory of Law*, 1967, which English title represents his overall theory, and the many books and articles in which his theory was formulated over a period of nearly seventy years during the twentieth century. For an introduction, see Schiff, 2002.

[7] '. . . an adequate sociological theory of law . . . should not lose sight of its object.' Luhmann, 2004, 60.

[8] For example, Kelsen's attempt to identify what constitutes law's separate existence has prompted many of those who have studied his work in English to agree with Laski's dismissive assessment of it as one in which 'neither ethical nor sociological considerations could penetrate . . . its substance is an exercise in logic and not in life'. Laski, 1967, *vi*.

What needs to be borne in mind in approaching this task is that both theories, whether they are described as jurisprudential, scientific or sociological theories of law are engaged, according to their authors, in examining law as 'serviceable for the cognition of social life'.[9] In other words, these theorists clearly believed that their descriptions and/or analysis were not some arid exercise[10] but one that engaged the way in which law operates in society. Thus, as Luhmann states quite categorically: 'Nobody would deny the importance of law in society'.[11] Since most of this chapter examines Kelsen's theory from a sociological perspective in the sense of analysing its contribution to a sociology of law, readers who have followed the argument set out in the previous chapters will ask the question: how is Kelsen's theory related to Luhmann's claim that jurisprudence is self-description? This question is discussed in a postscript to this chapter, and is re-visited in Chapter 7.

Law As Norm (in Kelsen's Later Writing)

Kelsen's best known work is *Pure Theory of Law*. Less well known is his collection of essays gathered together as *General Theory of Norms*, published in German in 1979, but not published in English until 1991.[12] This latter work represents a sustained attempt to describe the nature of legal norms, and one that endeavours to tackle many of the criticisms levelled at his earlier work. Most significantly Kelsen denied that what makes a norm legal is its logical relationship to other norms.[13] The

[9] Kelsen, 1945, 4.

[10] We return to law's potential aridity in the final chapter of this book.

[11] Luhmann, 2004, *vii*.

[12] Some 18 years after Kelsen's death.

[13] As Hartney puts it: '. . . he gave up the position that he had long held concerning the applicability of logic to norms. This . . . led him to expand his Pure Theory of Law into a "general theory of norms".' (Kelsen, 1991, *ix*) Apparently Kelsen adopted this position first in 1965 in 'Law and Logic' (Kelsen, 1973). As not everyone would agree with this observation by Hartney, we wish to make it clear that we are content to explore this 'improved' position whether or not he had already expounded it within his earlier writings.

relationship of validity, which characterises the relationship between norms, is not one of logical inference.[14] One cannot deduce the validity of a more specific norm, either legal or moral, from a more general one.[15] The key to legal validity is not logic, but actual acts occurring within society. The acts in question are acts of will. Persons actually have to will behaviour for that behaviour to occur. And further, if no one willed behaviour to occur, then there could be no norm in respect of that behaviour, for a norm depends on an act of will (whatever supposedly legal or moral documents might say).[16]

The level and nature of the 'realism' involved in this understanding of norms may not be fully appreciated by most of those who base their understanding of Kelsen on his earlier works. Neither a general norm, such as 'don't steal', nor a more directed one, such as 'a person who steals should be sentenced to five years in prison', are in themselves valid norms. For Kelsen, the behaviour that can be the object of a valid norm is extremely specific.[17] A valid norm cannot be directed, other

[14] It is probable that, in reaching this position in *General Theory of Norms*, Kelsen has moved from a Kantian 'normative' to a more descriptive positivistic idea of validity (see Bulygin, 1998). This issue strays beyond those that we attempt to consider here.

[15] This stance is urged throughout *General Theory of Norms*. To give one example from the final chapter, 61 'Is There a Specifically "Juristic" Logic?' at 269: '. . . the validity of this individual norm *cannot* be obtained by way of a logical inference . . . the validity of every positive norm, and hence of the individual norm representing the judicial decision, is conditional upon an act of will whose meaning it is, and this act of will cannot be produced by way of logical inference (ie a thought-process).'

[16] The most sustained statement of this position can be found in ch 58 'The Application of the Rule of Inference to Norms' (226–251). However, it appears throughout *General Theory of Norms* (although not necessarily as a consistent and clear statement, see Hartney's Introduction, xlii–lii). See also the criticism of 'the weakness of Kelsen's views about the relation between logic and norms' as set out in Celano, 1998, especially at 359.

[17] Thus 'Immediate observance or violation is possible only with a categorically valid individual norm, and not with a general norm (whether categorically or hypothetically valid). For behaviour which can be characterized as observance or violation of a norm is possible only after the condition abstractly specified in the general norm is concretely realized.' (Kelsen, 1991, ch 12, at 46).

than 'conditionally' towards general classes of acts, rather than immediately toward particular acts: '. . . a general hypothetical norm can be valid only mediately, that is, through the *intermediary* of the validity of the corresponding individual categorical norm in which the behaviour abstractly decreed to be obligatory in the general hypothetical norm is concretely decreed to be obligatory.'[18] The acts that are involved in norms have actually to have happened. Thus a norm directing judges to apply a sanction in all cases of stealing is not an act of willing in response to particular human behaviour, as the behaviour that is the condition of the act of willing has not yet occurred. Norms do not exist as hypothetical acts of willing, only actual acts of willing. When someone is convicted of stealing, the judge who sentences that person to imprisonment is actually willing that a particular individual should suffer imprisonment. The actuality is twofold. The judge is not thinking about what might happen if conviction should occur. Nor is she/he willing in some abstract way in respect of all classes of acts that would fall within a definition of a particular crime, or all crimes in general. In this situation, specific behaviour has occurred that results in an act of will that other specific behaviour ought to occur.[19]

A thought experiment might assist here. If a sociologist were to count up the sum total of all norms by reference to this definition, she/he would be identifying every occasion when an individual's behaviour is subject to an act of will, by her/himself or another

---

[18] Kelsen, 1991, ch 13, at 50.

[19] Kelsen calls this process one of 'individualization', and describes it as a 'dynamic process'. (1991, ch 13, at 50). In this process Kelsen is able to describe the much discussed, and controversial, relationship between validity and effectiveness. 'This general norm is effective when it is applied by and large, that is, when by and large the competent courts, once they have found a concrete state of affairs specified abstractly in the general norm, posit an individual norm which decrees to be obligatory a concrete coercive act subsumable under the state of affairs specified abstractly in the general norm, and furthermore when this individual norm is observed, that is, the coercive act is executed.' (*Ibid*, ch 34, at 141).

individual,[20] whose meaning is that he she ought to do something. So, if a foreign tourist drove past a 'No Entry' sign without understanding it, the sociologist would record this as 'zero norm'. If the tourist recognised the meaning of the sign, and applied it to her/himself (stopping) the sociologist would record 'one norm'. If the tourist understood the sign, but drove on, the sociologist would record 'zero norm'. If a pedestrian crossed in front of the tourist, willing the tourist to stop at the sign, the sociologist would record 'one norm'. If the pedestrian sees the sign, but does not will the tourist to stop at the sign, there is 'zero norm'.

In the situations recorded as 'zero norm', the no entry sign has not formed part of norms directed at the behaviour that has actually occurred, and other behaviour that ought (which includes empowered as well as required) to occur. The tourist failed to stop. If the sociologist noted that a bystander felt entitled to show anger or disapproval, she/he would record 'one norm' (a norm directed by the bystander to her/himself in relation to the behaviour of the tourist). If a policeman observed the incident, and arrested the tourist, the sociologist would also record 'one norm'. If the bystander called on the policeman to arrest the tourist, this would be another norm.

What do we learn from such a thought experiment? Norms only exist in the concrete acts of thinking of actual individuals willing behaviour to happen. If no one wills such behaviour (if there is no subjective volition) there is no norm. If there is mere cognition, namely the recognition that others will particular behaviour, this is not itself a norm. Once one understands individual norms as requiring actual acts of willing, one understands that law cannot be reduced to an exercise in logic.[21]

---

[20] We do not feel it is necessary, for the purposes of this thought experiment, to explore the nature of 'willing', either psychologically or philosophically, in order to ask whether an individual can or cannot 'will' their own behaviour.

[21] One does not have direct access to acts of willing, although we do have indications that what is occurring is an act of willing, evidenced by particular kinds of behaviour and speech. We may experience willing ourselves to do things, and understand situations as others willing us to do things. Interpretation is an inevitable part of this process of norm identification.

This concrete and dynamic understanding of the validity of norms (whose existence lies in acts, not in the logical application of general norms) poses the question: which of these acts of thinking, these concrete norms, are part of the legal order? If one thought that Kelsen saw law as a logical structure, one would expect him to see legal norms as those that bore a logical relationship to the constitution. But in *General Theory of Norms* Kelsen makes it clear that the process that establishes orders of norms is not one of logical inference, but of one of recognition. A concrete individual norm cannot exist without the individual whose act of will has the meaning of an 'ought' recognising that the occurrence of this act of will is authorised by a general norm.[22] The need for this recognition is a logical necessity, but the occurrence of such recognition is not the application of logic. Thus, for example, an egoistic individual could validate concrete norms through acts of will (telling others or her/himself what she/he ought to do), coupled with a general norm: 'I ought to be obeyed'.

The need for a norm to exist prior to an act (including an act of will) for that act to have normative significance is a logical necessity.[23] But the actual norms recognised by individuals, when they undertake acts of will, need have no logical relationship to the concrete norms that they create. So, mad solipsists can create unique concrete norms, and valid norms can be created on the basis of incorrect beliefs as to the existence of prior norms, or poor reasoning as to their scope and application. Recognition is an actual act, but in the end (and in the case of

[22] 'This presupposes the recognition of the general hypothetical norm by the individual positing the individual categorical norm. To that extent, we must agree with the frequently advanced *Recognition Theory* according to which the validity of a moral or legal order depends on its recognition by the individuals subject to it.' (Kelsen, 1991, ch 13, at 50).

[23] For without it, as Kelsen would say, there is no 'objective' meaning, observance or violation: 'A command is objectively observed or violated if the behaviour it prescribes actually takes place or does not take place (if the person to whom something is commanded actually performs or does not perform the behaviour in question, if his behaviour agrees or does not agree with the command), whether or not he is aware of the command.' (Kelsen, 1991, ch 15, at 57).

an egoist very soon after the beginning) the logical need for general norms as pre-conditions to concrete norms takes the form of a basic norm, which simply takes the form: you (the addressee) ought to do what has been posited.

The logical part of all this is that implicit in all individual norms are prior, more general, norms—that these have to exist prior to those individual norms to give those individual subjective acts of will an objective normative meaning—and that this process suffers from an infinite regress which will always (although in some cases quicker than others) run out, so that ultimately authority is something which can have no foundation in reality (actual acts of will directed concretely to actual behaviour). The sociological part of this is that all norms share this structure, so if we are going to find out which norms are part of a legal order we have to see what acts of recognition actually occur. When individuals carry out acts of will that have norms as their meaning, what normative resources do they use (or recognise) to give this meaning to their individual norms?

Logic offers one method concerning how one 'ought' to reason, and can inform how one 'ought' to undertake the task of identifying prior norms that can give normative meaning to individual acts of will. But recognition is a relationship based not on logic, but meaning. This is not the place to explore the feasibility of a private language, but if such a thing could occur, then an individual's subjective act of will would only have a normative meaning by reference to her/his own unique system of prior norms. However, for their acts of will to have an objective meaning their acts of recognition must then be capable of being recognised by others. Individual norms have an objective meaning when others recognise that the individual act of will is authorised by the same general norms as the author of the individual act of will relied on.

In order to understand the nature of the sociological task in identifying law, which is being implicitly proposed by Kelsen, it is important to understand how pluralistic the position to which Kelsen has taken us in *General Theory of Norms* is. The world is buzzing with subjective individual acts of will, directed by individuals to themselves and others, willing them to do things. Little is screened out, at least in a modern world, by the search for shared meanings in their array of forms: consequential reasoning, different ideas of family and kinship, moral indeterminacy, friendship, loyalty to colleagues or institutions, causes, animal rights, professional codes and practices, etc. Alongside a vast set of resources for giving objective meaning to subjective acts of will, there is complexity and specificity of situations in the modern world. For much of the time, shared recognition of norms is limited to recognising that one is being willed to do things by another who understands their act of will as an norm. Often we experience only individual norms and basic norms (understanding that the person who addresses a normative claim to us believes that her/his command is constitutionally authorised).

Is there anything that can be said about this norm creating activity, other than by way of investigation of what is recognised by particular individuals at the moment when they posit individual concrete norms? Indeed, can we really undertake the task of describing each individual's normative understanding if there are no shared general norms? And if the resources that individuals use to give normative meanings to their particular acts of will are shared, can they be systematised? Can the hermeneutic understandings of individuals be organised and described in statements that can have the qualities of falsity and truth? Kelsen certainly thought so, and saw the work of identifying these resources as a form of science. Moral science identifies the resources available to make concrete moral norms, and legal science identifies the resources available to make concrete legal norms.

At this point, Kelsen's theory ceases to be pluralistic, and understandably so. Could one systematise the resources used by lay individuals to claim legal normativity for their acts of will anymore than one could systematise popular conceptions of science and present this as scientific knowledge?[24] Take the

---

[24] 'And just as the scientific view of the physical world differs from a naïve everyday view, the view of jurisprudence differs from the picture which the layman may hold of the immediately given positive law.' Kelsen, quoted by Weinberger, 1986, 189–90.

common popular belief that all contracts have to be in writing. Is this statement really true? Is it true if believed? And are lay statements of science similarly true if believed? To organise legal knowledge, Kelsen focused on bodies which themselves utilise legal knowledge in a systematic manner: legal organs (most notably courts and administrative or executive bodies). The operations of these bodies form the basis of law's closure. And it is, as we shall see, not a logical but a sociological closure.

Kelsen never abandoned the centrality of coercive orders: the primary norm is the norm stipulating the application of a sanction.[25] This is the authorisation by a legal organ for a sanction to be applied; the most concrete existence a legal norm could have. At this point coercion is imminent, and the legal organ has established all the conditions required for the application of that sanction.[26] For Kelsen, the existence of this norm, the act of will requiring the application of a particular (and not a hypothetical) sanction, is what it means to experience valid law.[27] The separation of the legal system from other experience is achieved only in these moments, and exists in each of these moments.[28] Other legal norms are only experienced concretely in these moments; otherwise they are experienced only hypothetically.

To understand the nature of the closure identified by Kelsen, consider the authorisation of an individual fine, or custodial

[25] Kelsen, 1945: 'Law is the primary norm, which stipulates the sanction . . .' (61); '. . . the only genuine legal norm is the sanctioning norm.' (63).

[26] If the order is that sanctions are empowered (rather than required) the concrete individual norm need generate no further norm, even if nothing happens (non-observance is not the condition of the application of another norm).

[27] 'The immediate addressees of general hypothetical legal norms are the individuals who are empowered—and in certain circumstances, also obligated—to order concretely and to execute the coercive acts which serve as sanctions.' (Kelsen, 1991, ch 14, at 52).

[28] In describing the identity of legal systems over time, Moreso and Navarro (1998, 277) offer a comparable formulation: 'Legal systems are *momentary* normative systems, and each time a norm is issued or derogated by a competent authority, the result is a different legal system. Legal orders are *sequences* of legal systems.'

sentence. This is an act of will whose meaning is that the fine, or imprisonment of identified individuals, ought to occur. What gives it this meaning? Kelsen's answer is the norms recognised by the individual judge and by others as being capable of generating that meaning. One of these 'others' is the court bailiff.[29] For her/him, the sanction is valid because it is the order of the court (*res judicata*). That is enough—we have a valid law. For the bailiff, the order of the court is the only 'constitution' (authorising norm) she/he requires for her/his manhandling of the defendant to be valid. What then is the status of the general norms used by the judge in the making of her/his order? If she/he has recognised norms that another court (or the same judge on a later occasion) would not recognise as authorising the order made, then the defendant may obtain a new order for her/his release, or the repayment of her/his fine. This is a new individual norm.[30] It, too, is valid. Each of these court orders has indirectly been validated by general norms. In the first case, the norm validating indirectly the order of the court is the norm validating *res judicata* (orders of a body established by general legal norms as a court of law ought to be obeyed). In the second case this norm is again indirectly validated, alongside

[29] 'In modern legal orders where law is created and applied by organs functioning on the basis of a division of labour—legislative organs and law-implementing organs (courts and administrative agencies)—the performing of a coercive act occurs in two stages. . . . And if the organ to which this individual norm is addressed fails to execute the coercive act, it is only the individual norm posited by the court which is violated immediately.' (Kelsen, ch 14, at 52–3).

[30] Kelsen refers to this as a 'derogating norm'. And, crucially, 'There is no conflict between a norm and the derogating norm which repeals its validity, since the former ceases to be valid when the latter becomes valid.' However, prior to such a derogating norm 'When we have a conflict of norms, both norms are valid; otherwise, there would be no conflict. Neither of the conflicting norms repeals the validity of the other.' (Kelsen, 1991, ch 57, at 213). The status of derogating norms in Kelsen's writings has always been contentious, in particular whether principles of logical contradiction apply to them: see Paulson, 1986.

whichever norms were recognised by the second court to reach the conclusion that the first order should be revoked.[31]

To understand the dynamic nature of this analysis, it is useful to compare it with that of Hart.[32] For Kelsen, there is no single rule of recognition that establishes what can count as a rule of the system. The constitution is simply authorising norms. The content of that constitution is established in the moment of the creation of each individual norm, by reference to what is 'recognised' in order to give that individual norm its normative meaning. There is no logical relationship dictating the content of the individual norms, only the ability to use general norms to create the understanding that sanctions are authorised. The use of general norms is expected to be capable of being systematised, and this assumption forms the basis for the practice that Kelsen calls legal science. And logic indicates some of the limits of such systematisation. In particular, one can only point to pre-existing norms to authorise later norms, and those norms must be posited (if only through custom), so all legal scientists will operate on the basis of some historical cut-off (an historically first constitution). But this does not entail that all persons need to agree on the nature and date of that historical constitution. As the example of the bailiff indicates, agreement on the existence of norms low down in the system, such as *res judicata*, can generate a lot of authorisation.

Because validity is an existence based on the recognition of general norms as justifying individual norms, there is no need to claim that general norms cannot be contradictory or leave gaps. At the level that worries many legal academics, the law can exist

---

[31] Note that, because of the concrete nature of individuated legal norms (see n 26 above), if the second court describes the first order as 'invalid' this does not alter the fact that it has existed as a valid norm: it was created by an act of will with an ought meaning shared by the bailiff. Of course, it is highly unlikely that the judge in the first case recognised norms that no other person would recognise as legal norms. It is far more likely that he recognised norms that others would also recognise as legal, but would disagree that they were sufficient to justify the imposition of the sanction.

[32] See Hart, 1961, especially ch 6.

with large numbers of contradictions and many gaps. General norms will exist that justify the imposition of sanctions in circumstance X, alongside general norms that provide for sanctions not to exist in circumstance X, leading lots of legal scientists to state that they do not know which norms will be recognised in a concrete case. But there is no contradiction or gap at the level of law's most concrete operations. The legal organ charged with deciding whether to apply sanctions must decide whether an order to apply sanctions would, or would not, be authorised. It cannot decide that they are authorised, and at one and the same time decide that they are not authorised.[33] At this moment law has no contradictions and no gaps.[34] The claim that 'that which is prohibited cannot be permitted' only necessarily applies at the level of individual norms. If the legal organ orders the application of the sanction, then the secondary meaning of this order is that the behaviour identified by the legal organ as a condition of that order was prohibited. If the legal organ decides that no sanction is authorised, then no prohibited behaviour has occurred.[35]

Such closure as law achieves occurs operationally, not logically. But do the operations of law, in the form of individual sanctioning norms, create a legal system that is separate and different from other aspects of society, most notably political, moral or other social systems? What is there in the theory that leads us to believe that legal organs will not recognise political, moral and social norms when authorising sanctions? And if they do so, how can knowledge of the norms available to authorise sanctions represent a particularly legal knowledge? Kelsen, like Hart, offers us

[33] To be more precise, a legal organ cannot posit an act of will whose meaning is that the sanctions ought to be applied and simultaneously posit an act of will whose meaning is that the sanctions ought not to be applied.

[34] 'In this sense, we can speak of the *closure of the legal order*. Hence there are no "gaps" in the law, if by this we mean that some human behaviour is not legally regulated and that valid law is therefore not applicable to this behaviour. This is never the case . . .' (Kelsen, 1991, ch 31, at 131).

[35] The secondary meanings are not as clear and non-contradictory as the primary meanings. Failing to find legally prohibited behaviour could mean that the behaviour never happened, or that it is not thought to be prohibited.

the idea of the legal official. For Hart, the relevant legal officials are the judges, and the unity of the system is based on the common standards applied by judges in deciding what standards can constitute law. For Kelsen, the relevant body is the legal organ, which must decide if the conditions apply justifying the sanction. Like Hart's officials, legal organs are established self-referentially: only by the recognition of general norms can persons who authorise sanctions claim to be organs authorised to apply sanctions.[36] But, unlike Hart's officials, these organs do not have to have a common single standard uniting their understanding of what can be recognised as general norms justifying sanctions. It is important for the norms of the system to establish with sufficient 'effectiveness'[37] the identity of organs with authority to decide whether sanctions are authorised. But the process of recognition engaged in by those legal organs does not need to amount to a common standard that can be articulated by outside observers. There can be inconsistencies and contradictions in general norms, even those that operate at the greatest level of abstraction. Such inconsistencies and contradictions will restrict what can be stated objectively about the use of such norms, and thus limit the content of legal science. But they do not prevent the legal system from operating as a single system. What can be systematised through the recognition of general norms, and what

[36] In the case of Hart, rules of adjudication, recognised by legal officials are rules designating them as legal officials with authority to adjudicate, and thus establishing them as legal officials (1961, ch 6). For Kelsen, see the text at n 29 above.

[37] In *General Theory of Norms* (1991, ch 34 'Effectiveness, Validity, Positivity' 138–41, at 139–40) Kelsen does not alter his controversial formulation of the relationship between the validity and effectiveness of a legal norm. 'Thus the effectiveness of a norm commanding a certain behaviour is dependent on the effectiveness of the sanction-decreeing norm, the primary norm . . . the effectiveness of a norm does not mean that it is always observed and applied without exception; it means only that it is observed and applied *by and large* . . . even though validity and effectiveness are completely different, there nevertheless exists an essential relation between the two. Effectiveness is a condition for validity to the extent that a single norm and a whole normative order lose their validity—cease to be valid—if they lose their effectiveness or the possibility of effectiveness.'

can be in turn be stated systematically as legal knowledge, is first established operationally and self-referentially as decisions by legal organs to apply sanctions. Thus Kelsen's theory, unlike Hart's, does not presuppose an overarching standard common to judges as to what can be recognised as a rule of law, or (what often amounts to the same thing) the peculiar basis or foundation of legal reasoning.[38]

Within Kelsen's theory, the unity and closure of the legal system is established operationally—through its application of primary norms. What makes these norms legal rather than moral is that legal organs establish them. Provided one accepts that legal organs can be established that can decide on the authority of sanctions without reference to moral norms, then law has no necessary connection with morality. The content of law (what is recognised by legal organs in the process of positing individual norms) is not necessarily what is good, either by reference to critical theories of morality or social mores. The closure here is not only normative but also factual. The fact conditions of individual legal norms are those established by legal organs.[39] The authority to apply legal sanctions requires recognition of general

[38] The claim that objective legal knowledge exists only to the extent that legal organs, which authorise sanctions, recognise the same general norms is not a claim that those organs share a common standard as to what can count as law within the system taken as a whole. Inferior courts can have different reasons for believing that the same general norms are law, just as supreme courts can give different interpretations from case to case as to what the constitution requires. As the constitutional law of many countries demonstrates (as well as numerous and inconsistent attempts to state the content of the rule of recognition) legal orders can exist where one can state the law on numerous important topics with considerable certainty, despite a great deal of disagreement as to what can constitute a legal standard.

[39] Kelsen clarifies this with precision: 'Indeed, there are not two conditions, the existence of the fact of theft and the act of fact-finding; rather it is the latter which is *the* condition to which the general norm attaches the sanction. For it is not the fact of theft, or generally speaking the fact of the delict in itself, to which the general norm attaches the sanction, but rather the finding of fact by the law-applying organ.' (1991, ch 30 'Law as a Standard of Value and Law as 'Teaching'—The Significance of the Judge's Finding of Fact' 128–130, at 129).

norms, which go to procedures for finding facts as well as responses to those facts.

Whilst general legal norms, whether substantive or procedural, can have the same content as moral norms, the legal system remains closed due to the basis for their recognition. Moral norms can only enter into law through their recognition by legal organs, and there is nothing in the definition of a legal organ (a body authorised to apply sanctions) that ensures that the content of general legal norms will be moral.[40] The morality of any general legal norm is always contingent, just as the content of any general legal norm is always contingent; it just depends on what the organs identified by law to apply sanctions recognise.

The above re-statement of Kelsen has tried to demonstrate the sociological basis of his theory.[41] Law's unity and separateness can be described by reference to the most concrete moment of its existence: the authorisation by legal organs of specific sanctions whose application is 'imminent' for identified individuals. General legal norms have an existence as valid norms only when they are recognised at such moments. Kelsen is taking an operation: the authorisation of the application of a sanction, and seeing in that operation the reproduction of the unity of law and its separation from other aspects of society. Many of the criticisms levied at this theory are, we believe, mistaken. It is not a top-down theory, in which superior norms fix the content and meaning of inferior ones, along the lines of Hart's 'rule of recognition'. Nor would it be correct to describe it as a bottom-up

[40] See Kelsen, 1991, ch 28, 'Legal Norms and Legal Principles: Esser's Transformation Theory'.

[41] It is, one might playfully suggest, a theory that American Legal Realists might have used to inform their own methodologies, if they had only understood it better. Despite being playful, this suggestion can be given support. In analysing some of the critical contentions of Kelsen's *Pure Theory of Law* (which analysis is even more pertinent to *General Theory of Norms*) Hart claimed that: 'On a narrow interpretation, recognition by a court as a criterion of membership could mean that a rule could not be said to belong to a legal system until it had been actually applied by a court disposing of a case. This interpretation would come nearer to Gray's theory and to the doctrine ascribed to some later American Legal Realists . . .' (Hart, 1983a, at 340).

theory. Whilst the validity of general legal norms exists only in their recognition in the act of positing individual norms, the general norms have to pre-exist that positing for the meaning content of the individual norm to occur. Thus the creation of general norms provides the resources for this meaning content, resulting in interdependency between abstract and concrete norms, and the bodies that posit each of them.

Other criticisms of the theory are more justified. There is a price to be paid, in terms of the theory's descriptive potential, in seeking to identify two kinds of operations and thus to present these as the basis of law's unity and separation. Lay meanings, and legal advice, are demoted to the secondary meanings of primary norms. Soft law, without sanctions, is not valid law. The separateness of law is established by reference to a process of recognition, but the basis of its inter-connectedness with other areas of social life is reduced to what norms are recognised by particular institutions (legal organs) at the moment of sanctioning.

Luhmann's Improvements

Kelsen's theory, although to some extent 'serviceable for the cognition of social life',[42] nevertheless provides an inadequate account of the separation of law from other aspects of social life. Luhmann's theory offers a more complete separation, but one that also offers greater potential for understanding law's connectedness with the rest of society (both more closure, and more openness). We can introduce these improvements by reference to a debate generated by Kelsen and Hart, around the concept known as soft positivism. If law is what is recognised by Kelsen's legal organs or Hart's officials, then it may be true that there is no necessity for these institutions to recognise moral standards—but is there any reason why they could not, in appropriate circumstances, recognise moral standards, and why this does not make law, or at least those areas of law where such adoption occurs, moral?

---

[42] Kelsen, 1945, 4, repeating n 9 above.

In Kelsen's theory, recognition connects general norms to the application of physical sanctions by authorised persons. On some occasions, Kelsen defined the application of physical sanctions by others as something legal, insisting that moral systems are not directed toward the other-attribution of liability to physical sanctions, but toward the self-attribution of psychic sanctions.[43] This linkage with the real world threatens to subvert law's closure, for as soon as any persons can point to general norms to justify their application of physical sanctions, one is forced to accept that they are legal officials, or else to prioritise those institutions that seem to apply physical sanctions on the majority of occasions (law thus representing 'a monopoly of force of the legal community').[44] Raz seeks to avoid the contingent openness of law to morality by insisting that the legal materials that can authorise must have resolved issues with greater certainty than would occur by reference to moral values.[45] Luhmann has a more categorical answer, but one that at the same time leaves law far more flexible and open than either Kelsen's or Raz's theories do. For Luhmann, the differences between systems are maintained not by their programmes (in the case of law its rules, or particular values, or institutions or officials, or kinds of reasoning, etc) but by their coding. For law, the coding is legal/illegal, for morality, it would be good/bad, with politics, the code is government/opposition.[46]

[43] Kelsen, 1967, 35. Usually he describes this in terms of the difference between 'Transcendental and Socially Immanent Sanctions' (*ibid*, 28–30).

[44] Kelsen, 1967, 35. This obviously applies within the nation state, but also within international law, which despite its evolving nature, nevertheless has some of the characteristics of primitive legal orders that rely on the 'technique of self-help' (*ibid*, 323).

[45] Hence his analysis of the principal distinctions between rules and principles ('Rules prescribe relatively specific acts; principles prescribe highly unspecific actions.' Raz, 1972, 838), and between the deliberative and executive stages of practical reason (Raz, 1994, especially ch 9, 199–208).

[46] 'The schema government/opposition becomes the "form", the "code" of the political system in the sense that the form has an internal side and the code has a positive, connective side, "where the action is". . . . The legal system handles alternatives quite differently. They are and they remain scattered and dependent on individual cases and rules, and there is not the slightest hint of any

From this starting point, one can offer a significantly different explanation of the relationship between morality and law, and one that is socially relevant. Law can incorporate any amount of seemingly moral material—without that material being moral when used by law—because morality and law exist as the application of different codes. To understand this claim, and how it relates to the position reached by Kelsen, one needs to appreciate the anti-foundational nature of Luhmann's stance. Legal/illegal, good/bad, government/opposition are all distinctions. They do not mean anything in themselves. Nevertheless they cannot be exchanged for each other. Again, remember the thought experiment implied by this statement as to the emptiness of the distinction legal/illegal: If I told you that a fact X (say a particular behaviour) was legal, what would that tell you other than that X was not illegal? The meaning of legal and illegal is not established by the distinction itself, but by its application on past occasions, and by observations on the basis for those past applications. By observing on the application of a code that has been applied on billions of occasions, law has generated a vast, rich, and technical set of conditional programmes[47] to guide future applications of its code. Thus the content of what is likely to be coded legal as opposed to illegal is not given by the distinction, but by observations upon past applications of the coding. And while structures arise that stabilise the application of this code (doctrines about the constitution, legislature, secondary legislation, legal procedures, legal values, etc) these are themselves created by the application of coding, and can never determine the possibilities of further evolution.[48]

"consolidated opposition". And even if it did exist, it would not be recognized as a form of law but as a form of politics.' (Luhmann, 2004, 367).

[47] See Luhmann, 2004, ch 4 'Coding and Programming' and in particular section *IV* in which conditional programmes (programmes of the legal system are always *conditional programmes*) are distinguished from purpose-specific programmes, which 'do not allow for the setting of adequate limits to the facts that must be considered in a legal process' (at 196).

[48] Thus, Luhmann argues, in language reminiscent of Kelsen: 'It is incontestable that valid law cannot be understood as a logically closed system because no logical system can give reasons for the absence of contradictions in its own

This anti-foundational view of law (everything is contingent, and what currently exists has been established through past applications of the code) applies also to morality and politics. In the discourse of what is now described as postmodern society, there are no things or values that are inherently good or bad. There are only the past applications of the code good/bad, which have generated conditioning programmes (observed and described as intuitions, self-evident values, consequences, family values, consent, moral agency, etc) that in turn stabilise (in the sense of restricting what is likely to be coded as good rather than bad) the application of this code.

Whatever the possibilities of shared meanings between law and morality in the past, law has evolved to a point where the meaning of what within morality has been coded by reference to good/bad[49] *cannot* be incorporated within law *and* retain the same meaning. You will recall the example made famous by Ronald Dworkin, that we used in chapter 4 to illustrate this. In *Riggs v Palmer*, Elmer Palmer was denied his inheritance under the will of his grandfather whom he had murdered, by a court that applied the maxim 'No one shall be permitted to profit . . . or to take advantage of his own wrong'.[50] Dworkin sees this, in a particular form, as the incorporation of moral principles within law. But this maxim, in that case, was used to decide whether the denial of the inheritance would be legal or illegal, not

---

system. The answer to this problem of incompleteness, however, is not given by an external guarantee of validity but by the ongoing production of legal texts, which identify what is valid law and what is not. The "rationality" of the system, then, is not given by a goodness which is secured by principles, but by the question, which arises in every situation, whether or not the valid law should be changed in relation to the references which have become a problem.' But, he then adds: 'Therefore, the validity of law is founded not on unity but on difference. It cannot be seen, it cannot be "found"—it is the ongoing reproduction of law's difference.' (2004, ch 6 'The Evolution of Law' at 262).

[49] For an analysis of what, within Luhmann's systems theory, is the difficult distinction that moral communications systematically make between good and bad, see 'The Code of the Moral' (Luhmann, 1992–93).

[50] Dworkin, 1977, 23; for his later discussion of the case, see Dworkin, 1986, 15–20.

whether it would be wrong. It was also being used to adjudicate on a situation that had already been organised into categories that have no equivalent in morality: a person convicted of murder (with its legal definition) after a legal trial (jury, rules of evidence, procedure, etc) identified as the beneficiary of a legally valid will. Adjudication on this issue occurs in the context of an appeal from an earlier court decision, a position that can only be reached by going through legal procedures. This decision established a precedent (convicted murderers cannot inherit from those they murder), which precedent prevents the next court from having to decide the same issue again. We cannot know if the defendant would benefit personally from his wrong (as opposed to his relatives) without finding out whether this defendant was ever likely to be released from prison (a fact not discussed in the case, and one unlikely to affect the application of this precedent to States with, as opposed to without, the death penalty).[51] The dissent also borrowed what might be called a 'moral' principle: arguing that denying this inheritance was a form of double punishment.[52] This argument is also a construction within law: punishment following crime being equated with denial of inheritance. The majority did not have to weigh

[51] Even the dispute and the remedy were legal rather than moral. This testator had left property to his grandson rather than his daughters, with provision for the daughters to inherit only if the grandson died before his majority *without heirs*. This points to a dynastic ambition. While it may be true that this testator would not have left property to the grandson had he known of his murderous intent, it is pretty clear who his preferred alternative beneficiary might have been: his grandson's heir, as that person would have perpetuated the family name. This probability formed no part of the case, for all sorts of good legal reasons (not least, the absence of a plaintiff interested in making this argument). The moral and political issues not discussed in this case are considerable: family as dynasty and lineage does not allow patricide to redirect inheritance towards daughters, family as mutually loving individuals with reciprocal obligations clearly does.

[52] '. . . to concede the appellant's views would involve the imposition of an additional punishment or penalty upon the respondent. What power or warrant have the courts to add to the respondent's penalties by depriving him of property? The law has punished him for his crime . . .' Gray, J, *Riggs* v *Palmer* (1889) 22 NE 188, at 193.

this supposedly conflicting moral principle against their own, they simply dissolved it using a different legal argument: failing to qualify for an inheritance is not the same thing as being deprived of property. To sum this all up, while the most fundamental reason why a moral principle cannot have a moral meaning in this situation is that it is being used to apply a different code than that used by the moral system (from which it came)— a consequence of using morality in this way is that one can do things that would be wholly inappropriate if this principle was being applied within the system from which it came. The moral philosopher would have so many caveats (was the murder really a bad deed, and not a mercy killing? Is he really the perpetrator? Who would actually enjoy the property which the defendant is going to inherit? Which moral principle has greater weight? Etc).

Understanding this form of closure gives substance to Kelsen's insistence that moral principles cannot exist as such within the legal system, but only through their recognition by legal organs. The self-referential nature of this recognition (and the closure that results) is acknowledged in part by Kelsen by using the term 'legal organ'. But closure is not simply a consequence of having individual sanctioning norms applied by legal organs. The facts that are relevant to law's conditioning programmes are established by law's norms, including its procedural norms (which include norms establishing the bodies who will decide what facts exist in particular cases). The parties (defendants, executors, beneficiaries, etc) are legal categories. The sources of law's norms are established through law. And, most importantly of all, law's coding is unique to law.

Within Luhmann's system, coding replaces normative meaning as the basis for linking communications.[53] This not only begins to explain why the recognition of norms by courts

[53] Luhmann describes law as normative, as operating as a set of normative expectations that are resistant to counter-factual disappointments ('The breaking of norms alone does not lead to any adaptive learning that could change norms' Luhmann, 2004, 109). But, those norms and normative expectations are founded on law's code, legal/illegal, through which its norms are communicated.

cannot turn legal norms into moral norms, it also allows Luhmann's theory to be far more pluralistic than Kelsen's in what can be acknowledged as legal. Legal communications apply the distinction legal/illegal. They link together when the application of the code within one communication forms the basis for the application of the code within another. This allows lay views as to what is legal and illegal to form part of the legal system. For example, the lay view that oral contracts are not legal is not only a coding, but also one that forms the basis of other coding: many lay people believe that it would not be legal if one tried to sue on an oral contract. These views can generate more formal legal communications: is the lay view that an oral contract is not really legal a reason for treating their oral agreements as legally binding, or for treating oral contracts as situations where no legal relationships are intended? (Recoding of legal as illegal and vice versa continues the connections between legal communications, whether this occurs in appeals from trial courts, or court decisions from lay views). If we can include coding by laypersons, then we can include coding by legal advisers. And if the relevant operation is coding, then law is not limited to the normative meaning of sanctions, but can include legal coding which generates such diverse meanings as ultra vires acts, valid wills, etc.

For Kelsen, valid law exists only in the connections established at the most concrete moments of the legal system: when the application of sanctions is imminent. Outside of such moments, general norms have only a hypothetical existence. Legal science concerns itself with the systematisation of the systematic use of general norms, which occurs (to the extent that it does occur) at such moments. For Luhmann, this focus takes one part of the legal system and presents it as the whole. Like Kelsen, Luhmann sees validity as a process of connection. But it is not limited to the connections that legal organs make between imminent sanctions and general norms. Validity is the connections made between all legal communications (all communications that code in terms of the distinction: legal/illegal). Valid legal communications (within the theory) apply this distinction successfully, and can only do so by making connections with other communications where this distinction has been applied.

For Kelsen, general norms are the resources that allow individual norms to have their meaning. For Luhmann, the resources for making legal communications, which apply the distinction legal/illegal, are not limited to general norms recognised by courts, but extend to all communications where such distinctions have been applied. Kelsen uses the operation of recognition, but Luhmann has the far wider operation of observation. The distinction legal/illegal is applied, and then observed. Observation of the application of the distinction involves identifying features of a situation that account for the manner in which the distinction was applied. An institution that has become central to the generation of accounts (usually expressed as doctrine) of the application of this distinction is courts.[54] Courts have a duty to decide whether something is legal or illegal. The moments of such duties echo Kelsen's individuated norms, in that the court cannot be contradictory at such moments (the decision must apply one side of the legal/illegal distinction or the other, but not both simultaneously, or a third value, or amount to a refusal to apply the distinction). Having to decide[55] generates the basis for further observation and further accounts of the application of the

[54] Thus Luhmann analyses the courts as at the centre of the legal system, see generally Luhmann, 2004, ch 7 'The Position of Courts in the Legal System'. 'In light of our actual experience it is apparent that only courts have the task of supervising the consistency of legal decisions. This occurs in the mode of second-order observation, that is, in the mode of an observation of legal decisions (for example, those of statute, in contracts, or in judicial decisions) that in turn are observed in the law. The technical term for this is interpretation.' (Luhmann, 2004, 297).

[55] Luhmann, 2004, discusses this issue by analysing the nature of decision ('. . . a decision is always a matter of an alternative, which consists of two and frequently more paths that can be chosen', at 282) and the duty of courts, unlike political or other actors, to decide ('Contracts need not be concluded and statutes need not be passed (unless specified otherwise in the constitution), but courts have to decide every case submitted to them. The corresponding norm is called—and the double negation of this formulation demonstrates its logic-the prohibition of the denial of justice.' at 284).

distinction. This is, as Kelsen described, a dynamic process, based on operations and not on logic. It is a process that will reveal contradictory general norms, and gaps between them. Law (in the courts, as everywhere else) remains underdetermined.

For Luhmann, the underdetermined nature of law can never end, and causes the courts (who must decide) to provide both a mechanism for stabilising legal communications and a mechanism for change and evolution. The duty to decide means that courts have to decide when they have no good reason for deciding one way or another.[56] The application of distinctions in such situations, and the account of such applications, has the capacity to challenge existing accounts of prior applications: law evolves. The resources that are available to stabilise law (accounts for the application of the distinction legal/illegal) are also the resources available for its evolution. Thus for Luhmann, as for Kelsen, there is no inherent difference between applying law, and changing law.[57]

The closure achieved by both Kelsen and Luhmann is not a causal closure. Kelsen claimed that law was the meaning content that arose when sanctions were understood as authorised, and the secondary meanings that could be generated thereby. This is not a claim that the content of law, the positing of general norms whose recognition gives meaning to individual norms,

[56] Luhmann, 2004, considers this dilemma in a discussion of what has become known as 'hard cases'. 'These are cases, then, in which the knowledge of uncontested and valid law is not enough to state the facts of who is in a legal position and who is in an illegal position. *Nevertheless courts have to decide these cases as well.* This means: courts have to develop rules of decision-making for their decision and for its justification, which may be contested and which may remain so contested. Courts cannot refer to uncontested and valid law but have to create, postulate, and assume such a law, without being in a position to guarantee that the programme for the decision-making in this case will be valid beyond deciding this particular case.' (287).

[57] However, with Luhmann, this insight is taken much further, being discussed in relation to a temporal dimension, in which constructions in the present are directed toward the future through 'the past of a future present'. In this regard he quotes Eisenberg: 'The function of resolving disputes faces toward the parties and the past. The function of enriching the supply of legal rules faces toward general society and the future.' (Luhmann, 2004, 297).

has no causes or effects. He was simply insistent that one had to identify what constituted legal meaning before one examined its causes and effects. The closure identified by Kelsen is normative, maintaining the fact/norm distinction that runs through so much of his work. But in *General Theory of Norms* we see signs that the closure created by law is not only normative, but also factual. Legal organs establish the conditions for the recognition of a conditional general norm. Law, through its substantive norms establishes what facts are relevant, and through its procedural norms establishes what facts have occurred. This is not an abandonment of the fact-norm distinction, but the beginnings of an acknowledgement that the fact-norm distinction is something established by the legal system by and for itself.

Luhmann takes this further. He insists that the legal system not only generates its own norms, but also its own facts. This is not to deny that there is a reality outside of the legal system, comprising of other systems, general social communication, and the physical universe—but to insist that the openness of law to that environment is mediated through its norms—which leads to the legal system having cognition of the world that is unique to itself. What law will find meaningful, and the meanings that it will generate, are peculiar to law. The nature of this closure can be illustrated by applying this part of Luhmman's theory back against two of the fundamental acts relied on by Kelsen: acts of will, and sanctions. For Kelsen, as described earlier, the world buzzes with acts of will whose objective meaning is established by reference to norms. But the concept of an act of will existing separate from the system of norms that gives it meaning is quite problematic. The identification of an act of will is not a reference to a pattern of activity in a particular part of the brain. It is itself the interpretation of human action. Law's concept of agency, what it means to will, and how will is signified, are all constructed internal to law.[58] Similarly with sanctions. Kelsen takes the application of coercion to be something

---

[58] Using concepts such as intention, purpose, and motive. These concepts, as law's constructions, are then available for philosophical critique.

identifiable without reference to norms, leaving norms with the sole function of authorising what can be identified as coercion, which exists apart from those norms. But coercion is the meaning of acts that can only be established by reference to norms. For example, law not only establishes what constitutes legal sanctions, it also engenders different internal meanings to sanctions. Thus not only can law identify the difference between force applied by a robber and that applied by an arresting police officer, but law will identify both situations as the application of force (one illegal, the other legal). By way of contrast, assisted suicide, although illegal, and perhaps immoral, will not be treated by either system as the application of force. Thus the meaning of force or coercion is grounded by norms. The ability of other systems (religious, moral, or the mafia) or even general social communication contemporaneously to recognise action as sanctions, does not alter the position that each system recognises (and thus creates) facts for and by itself—as becomes particularly apparent when one system is unable to apply the same language to describe an event (in this case sanction) as occurs with another.

Law's closure means that the different meanings attributed to different kinds of law are also internally created. Take one of the best-known criticisms of Kelsen's earlier work, *Pure Theory of Law*, that a positive law theory of sanctions as authorised by law but not by morality would not explain the difference between a sentence of a fine for a crime, and a tax.[59] If we reapply the arguments set out in our earlier discussion of *Riggs v Palmer*, we can begin to understand that law can use communications that have the same linguistic form as occurs within moral systems without duplicating their meaning, or making moral norms into legal ones. Law does indeed have an internally differentiated subsystem called criminal law, in which the application of the code legal/illegal is administered (observed) according to communications couched in terms of good and bad actions, without those legal norms becoming moral ones. Kelsen called these secondary

[59] For a succinct statement of this criticism, see Hart, 1983b, 299–300.

meanings, without investigating, or substantially differentiating, why the secondary meanings of some primary norms is 'don't do X' and the secondary meanings of others is 'you can do X if you pay $£Y$.' Luhmann's theory acknowledges that law can re-use communications outside of itself to explain to itself why and how the code legal/illegal has been applied. Indeed, once it is accepted that the distinction legal/illegal means nothing in itself, observation cannot take place by reference to this distinction, but has to use another distinction. Thus law borrows communications from other systems in order to explain its own previous coding to itself. What within other systems exist as conditioning programmes, leading to an application of a different code, are borrowed by law to explain its own previous coding.

In the case of criminal law, communications with identical linguistic form to those found within moral and religious systems will be re-used within law to stabilise the application of the code legal/illegal. This will result in different conditioning programmes for what is understood within law as criminal law, than exist within tax law. Does the application of morality within criminal law, make criminal law inevitably a branch or application of ethics or religion? The answer is no, for the same reasons that the decision in *Riggs v Palmer* is not the application of moral principles. Law, with its own procedures, its own definitions, re-uses moral communications to explain its own decisions to itself in a manner that severs those communications from the code in which they are used to being applied and the other communications with which they systematically link. To re-use the famous Star Trek quote: 'Its morality Jim, but not as we know it.' Thus, while we see communications that have the identical form to moral communications, these are not moral communications, but remain legal ones (connected to other legal communications systematically, as linking operations, and coding in terms not of good/bad but legal/illegal).

Again, an example may assist. Let us take discretion on sentencing. Judges and magistrates sentence within their tariffs and justify their decisions in terms of public safety, culpability, deterrence, contrition, upbringing and equal opportunity, etc. Is this part of the legal system and, if it is, is it closed? For Kelsen, remember, this moment is the defining moment of the legal system. Choice in the severity of the punishment is not relevant, the punishment, whatever it is, is legal because it is authorised. Again, Luhmann can take us further. Law's closure does not occur just at the parameters of the authority to punish (the tariff). Law can re-use moral communications at this point without those communications having the same meaning that they would have in other systems. The point of application (sentence following conviction) is established by law. Law establishes the crime for which punishment is to be applied. Law establishes the information thought appropriate to put before the judge (formal pleas in mitigation, social inquiry reports, victim statements, etc). The freedom to pick and choose from morality is established by law—incommensurable moral values such as deterrence, retribution, rehabilitation, contrition, plus incommensurable ideas of moral agency versus determinism. Law can plunder all this moral stuff, from decision to decision, in a manner in which it would not operate within the system from which it is taken.[60] Such decisions are not outside the law, but are a microcosm of the use of incommensurable values that occurs throughout the legal system. Closure is maintained not just by formal restrictions on what considerations can be taken into account in sentencing, but also by the application of the code. There is such an important difference between using morality's conditioning programmes to code in terms of good/bad, and borrowing communications about good and bad to code in terms of legal/illegal. Within each system, the coding is the basis for connection with the next communication. Having found a

---

[60] Raz, in drawing out the differences between rules and principles, considers that 'the whole area of sentencing is governed almost exclusively by principles. . . . The law confers certain powers on the agency and directs it to use them to promote certain policy goals in accordance with general principles. The exercise of discretionary powers is typically guided by principles rather than rules.' (Raz, 1972, 841). Thus his 'authority' of law cannot account for law as this very dynamic, and highly individualised set of decisions, namely it cannot account for individualised discretionary sentencing decisions as, in themselves, legal decisions.

person good or bad, in particular respects, some other moral communication can be generated from that starting point. But within the legal system, the starting point for the next legal operation is not the goodness of the defendant, but the legality of their sentence. Through sentence, the fine, imprisonment, etc, is pronounced legal. Law charges on. The legality of the prisoner's continued detention, transfer to prison, application for parole, etc, is established. The 'moral' communications, which have been ripped from the context in which they originate, can be discarded. New decisions on the application of the code (is the prisoner's mail legally intercepted? Is she/he liable to loss of remission for fighting? Etc) can be made by reference to whatever values and communications law selects for use at these new moments within the legal system.

Now we are ready to understand how law creates both itself, and its environment. The norm-fact distinction is something that law establishes for itself, as do other systems. While we presuppose these distinctions at a meta-level, across society and the physical universe, this is not the nature of their existence, as communications, within society. Law in the current—as it is described—postmodern world—exists as communications coding in terms of a distinction: legal/illegal. Validity is the connection between communications that directly or indirectly apply this coding. These communications have the ability to produce internal statements of the differences that these communications make to the social world: law's awareness (observations) of its own applications of its own code can generate its own self-descriptions.[61] But the same operations (applications

[61] The difference between self-observation and self-description is highly significant to Luhmann's theory, and our analysis is dependent on both. 'Self-observation is merely the coordination of individual operations with the structures and operations of the legal system and is thus primarily the implication or explication of the fact that a communication involves legal or illegal communication. However, quite different problems arise if it is a matter of self-description, that is, the presentation of the unity of the system in the system. This is not just the ongoing maintenance of connectivity with the help of selected references but the reflection of the unity of the system in the system, which reflects itself.' (Luhmann, 2004, 424).

of the code) that produce what can be observed by law as itself, also identify what can be observed by law as something other than itself: they are the same moments of application of the code. In this way the world of law, and the world according to (relevant to) law is an outcome of the operations of law, and not something which can be recognised by law outside of its own operations.

Conclusion

In *General Theory of Norms* Kelsen maintained the claim that law was closed, but abandoned the claim that the basis of that closure was logic. Whilst legal operations (the authorisation of sanctions by legal organs) could generate specifically legal knowledge (of the general norms used to authorise sanctions) primacy was given not to this general knowledge, but to individual operations. And, in place of logic, the key relationship linking these operations to general norms is that of recognition. Thus law's closure is not based on what could be authorised with certainty by pre-existing general norms, but by reference to what norms are recognised by legal organs when authorising specific sanctions. Law's separate existence is normative, but the identification of its specific normative content is a mixture of specific kinds of facts (acts of will, the application of coercive force, and the recognition of general norms) and self-reference (these acts have to be undertaken by legal organs). This would seem to produce a position somewhat similar to that attributed to the American Legal Realists,[62] but with the caveat that it is the bodies authorising specific sanctions (which, numerically, will rarely be appellate courts) whose actions constitute the existence of the legal system as a separate normative order.

Whilst this theory accounts for contradiction, gaps, and the general under-determinacy of law, the basis of law's closure and

---

[62] In the famous words of Oliver Wendall Holmes: 'The prophesies of what the courts will do in fact, and nothing more pretentious, are what I mean by the law.' (Holmes, 1896–97, 461).

its openness to the rest of society remain incompletely described. The self-referential nature of the term 'legal organ' supports the claim that what will be recognised by such bodies will have no necessary connection to morals or politics. But this opens the door to theories of soft positivism, which see nothing in the definition of legal organs or the concept of recognition to prevent the norms used to authorise sanctions from being moral or political. Indeed, without further elaboration on the concept of recognition,[63] it is not clear that Kelsen's theory can exclude claims by those, such as Dworkin, who believe that the task of authorising force requires those who undertake this task to utilise moral norms.[64] Kelsen's insistence that the need for recognition prevents moral norms from becoming legal norms remains enigmatic: what kind of closure would be achieved if legal organs routinely and systematically recognised moral or political norms when authorising force?

Luhmann's answer to this question is to go beyond the self-reference of legal organs to the self-production of all of law's elements. Legal organs, using legal procedures, apply legal norms, to legally selected facts, to produce legal remedies, etc.[65] The content of these respective elements is contingent. What is constant is the nature of the communications that generate them, or rather the coding applied by the communications that generate them: legal/illegal. Thus there is nothing inherently 'legal' about any of these elements—norm, remedy, sanction, procedure, etc. A process of coding and observing on that coding establishes all of these. This process establishes a dense and technical basis for the application of future coding: law's conditional programmes. The creation of these programmes out

[63] Such as that undertaken by Raz to distinguish applying norms that had decided matters, and referring to the interests and norms used to produce these decisive norms. It is only the former that can, with adequate clarity, amount to law (see n 45 above).

[64] Or, at least, to provide an adequate conception involving a justification for the application of collective force (see Dworkin, 1986, 93).

[65] In Teubner's terms, we have a hypercycle. See Teubner, 1993a, ch 3 'Law—A Hypercycle?'.

of a common process of coding leads to applications of the code in which the basis of the application is law's observation of itself: legal remedies are applied on the basis of legal norms, in disputes structured through legal procedures, etc.

But if this is the basis of law's closure, what is its openness? Law is potentially open to every other subsystem of communication without becoming part of that system because it continues to code in terms of the distinction legal/illegal. This allows it to remain closed (to retain its separate identity) even in those areas where its operations appear most open to other systems: such as discretionary sentencing. Law's communications connect through its common coding. This allows a complex, technical set of programmes to be developed that, from the perspective of other systems, can be viewed as an irrational collection of incommensurable values. Law can utilise communications from accountancy, morality, economics, politics, general social communication, etc. These communications are changed in the process, by forming links between communications that are coding in terms of what is legal/illegal, rather than in terms of the distinction applied from the system from which they have been taken. Recognising these relationships leads to subjects within law such as the law of housing, banking, accounting, etc. It also generates theoretical endeavours such as political, economic, and moral theories of law. But the connections provided by a common code, and the correspondingly reduced ability of borrowed communications to systematically link together as they would within their own system, maintains law's closure.[66]

To apply these insights from Luhmann back into Kelsen's theory, the process of recognition never amounts to the inclu-

[66] To express this in terms of a pejorative criticism of economic analysis of law: 'If law is economics, it is only A-level economics'. The interpenetration of economics within law is limited by inability of each system of communication to maintain compatible patterns of communication at anything other than a surface level. While law can be described in terms of basic economic theory, the operations (which consist of communications) of the economic system do not maintain a consistent relationship with operations occurring within law. This in turn makes it difficult to apply complex economic theory to legal forms.

sion of moral or political norms within law because recognition is only adopted for the purpose of coding in terms of what is legal and illegal. This is the only meaning of an 'authorised' sanction that law can directly generate. That the communications used to stabilise the application of this coding may (as in discretionary sentencing) have the same linguistic form as moral ones, and form part of conditioning programmes for conclusions on the legality of sentences, will not alter the connection (closure) between legal communications. And it will be the ability to make meaningful communications on what is legal and illegal (law's closure) that will drive law's recognition of communications from morals, science, economics, politics, or any other sub-system of communication.

Postscript on Kelsens' Theory as Self-Description

This chapter has offered an autopoietic critique of Kelsen's theory. What it has not done is demonstrate that Kelsen's theory is autological: that it is a self-description, generated by law's operations, that in turn stabilises those operations. Given Kelsen's generally acknowledged Kantian orientation, this seems quite a major task. A theory of legal science identifying the conditions that enable law to be known, is a commitment to the representation of law within language, with law as an object that can be described separately from its operations.[67] The attributes of self-description, that part of a system are presented as the whole of a system, form commonplace criticisms of Kelsen's theory within jurisprudence. For example, that all of law is presented as if it were an instruction to officials to apply sanctions. Whatever the merits of such criticism, it does not amount to a sociological account of Kelsen's theory, but only a claim that other representations would provide a fuller account of more of the significant features of a legal system.

[67] 'The science of law endeavors to comprehend its object "legally", namely from the viewpoint of the law. To comprehend something legally means to comprehend something as law, that is, as legal norm or as the content of a legal norm—as determined by a legal norm.' (Kelsen, 1967, 70).

To analyse Kelsen's theory as self-description, rather than simply to criticise it from a sociological perspective (for example, by offering our autopoietic critique), one needs to undertake a version of the exercise carried out in chapter 3: to identify the operations of law that produce a theory that in turn orientates legal operations; to show that the theory not only exhibits the characteristics that one might expect from an autological text, but actually is an autological text: a series of communications generated within a system that operate within that system. Such an empirical enquiry will not be undertaken here, though we hope that it will be undertaken, by others if not by ourselves, at a later date. It represents a continuation of the exercise that we self-consciously did not undertake in chapter three, *vis*, an account of the process by which continental legal systems generated operations that altered their self-descriptions from ones that utilised natural law to those that utilised legal positivism. Those undertaking such a sociological study would need to remember Kelsen's status as an international lawyer, and the necessity for self-description to operate at the national as well as the international level. Indeed, the criticism that theorists like Hart neglect international law can be reinterpreted within autopoietic theory to raise a particular puzzle. Whilst the legal system can orientate some of its operations through self-descriptions in terms of national legal systems, how are international law's legal operations carried out (endlessly reproduced) without similarly orientating communications? If legal systems at the national level create themselves and their environment and orientate the process of selection in ways that allow the system to exist with a degree of stability alongside a capacity to evolve, what mechanism other than self-description allows this process to continue at the international level?

6

Law's Politics: Criticising Critical Legal Studies

Critical Legal Studies (CLS) is best described as a movement rather than as a theory. What unite its members are their common commitments, not their adoption of a particular theoretical position.[1] Indeed, one of the attributes of the movement has been the utilisation of an enormous range of theories and methods for the analysis of legal phenomena: Marxism, feminism, critical race theory, deconstruction theory, Foucaultian theory and historiography, etc.[2] An analysis of what autopoietic systems theory could add to the insights provided by all of these theoretical positions would be extremely difficult. Any attempt to reduce all of the positions adopted by members of this movement to a common theoretical core solely for the purposes of carrying out this task would be open to the criticism that the synthesis was both arbitrary and simplistic.[3] Fortunately, neither of these exercises is necessary for our purposes. To analyse what autopoietic systems theory might add to the contributions made by the members of the CLS movement one does not need to identify what unites all of its members—only what might be taken to unite its members by reference to the theory of autopoiesis, and the sociological insights

[1] Collins, 2002, argues that what unites the jurisprudence of the Critical Legal Studies movement is not their theories as such, but their focus on the political quality of law, and a common progressive stance towards the political issues of the day.

[2] See Kennedy and Klare, 1984. Hunt, 1986, 3, fn 7, notes references in CLS literature to Habermas, Sartre, Marcuse, Piaget, Freud, Levi-Strauss, Lukacs, Gramsci, Althusser, Poulantzas, Foucault.

[3] The problems with discussing the movement as a unity are not limited to the diversity of the theoretical approaches adopted by its members, or even their inconsistency. Much of the movement's existence was informal and unrecorded, for example in seminar discussions. See Diamond, 1985, 696.

163

this produces. From this perspective, we offer the following observations, that we shall endeavour to develop in the rest of this chapter. Autopoiesis and members of the CLS movement share a common starting point in their respective acceptance of law's indeterminacy, in the sense that the outcomes of legal decisions are not dictated, but involve choice (they could have been other than what they were).[4] But autopoiesis and CLS adopt a radically different approach to the conclusions to be drawn from this. For CLS law is politics,[5] and attempts to establish any essential differences between the nature of political and legal decisions need to be unmasked and discredited.[6] By contrast, for autopoiesis, law is not politics,[7] just as it is not economics, or media or general social communication; politics are a part of law's environment, which environment it constructs for itself (thus, using the title of this chapter, what law constructs is 'law's politics'). For CLS, the inability of law to predetermine its own content leads to a search for the basis of its determination outside of law.[8] Autopoiesis, with

[4] 'A central assertion of the Critical Legal Studies theorists is that the law—or more specifically, the relationship between authoritative doctrinal materials (like statutes, cases, etc) and the actions of legal decision-makers—is loose or "indeterminate."' (Yablon, 1985, 917).

[5] Hutchinson and Monahan, 1984, 206, call the belief in the political nature of law the 'credo' of CLS: 'Law is simply politics dressed in different garb; it neither operates in a historical vacuum nor does it exist independently of ideological struggles in society.' Kelman, 1987, 2, interprets the CLS critique of law as not politics simpliciter, but of the politics of liberalism: 'The essential picture I propose is that of a movement attempting to identify the crucial structural characteristics of mainstream legal thought as examples of something called "liberalism."'

[6] '. . . a doctrinal practice that puts its hope in the contrast of legal reasoning to ideology, philosophy and political prophecy ends up as a collection of makeshift apologies.' (Unger, 1986, 11).

[7] See, in particular, Luhmann, 2004, ch 9, 'Politics and Law'.

[8] 'The discretionary nature of court decisions, the importance of social and political judgments, and the dominance of the ideology of advanced capitalism characterize our judicial process far better than any notions of justice, objectivity, expertise, or science.' Kairys 'Introduction' in Kairys, 1990, 8. 'Take specific arguments very *seriously* in their own terms; discover they are actually foolish ([tragi]-*comic*); and then look for some (external observer's) *order* (*not* the germ of truth) in the internally contradictory, incoherent chaos we've exposed.' (Kelman, 1984, 293).

its concept of operative closure, insists that law makes its own selections. CLS, having shown that there is no objective basis for the content of legal decisions outside of law ends where it begins, with the essential indeterminacy of law.[9] Legal decisions remain a matter of political choices.[10] For some members of the CLS movement, most notably Roberto Unger, this represents a significant opportunity for those involved in making (or criticising) legal decisions to develop law, and other aspects of society, in consciously chosen progressive and egalitarian directions.[11] For autopoiesis, the indeterminacy of all systems (not just law), and the nature of their respective autonomies[12] (achieved in each

[9] 'The Critics' basic argument—elaborated more fully below—is that by taking the world as we know it as largely determined by impersonal social forces, evolutionary-functionalists obscure the ways in which these seemingly inevitable processes are actually manufactured by people who claim (and believe themselves) to be only passively adapting to such processes. *If there are evolutionary processes in social life, they are processes whose logic is one of multiplicity, not uniformity of forms.*' (Gordon, 1984, 70–71, emphasis added).

[10] 'There was *no such thing* as an objective legal methodology behind which judges could hide in order to evade responsibility for the social consequences of legal decision making. Every decision they made was a moral and political choice.' (Mensch, 1990, 22).

[11] In Unger's writings, constructs of what is regarded as appropriate (what he calls 'formative contexts') not only operate to constitute legal categories, but also are, in turn, constituted by legal categories. (For example, the legal may give a sense of what is possible and appropriate within the political). Such reciprocal relationships offer, to Unger, a possibility for evolutionary change. By choosing to alter the weight given to repressed possibilities within law, participants in the legal system may cause reconfigurations within law that impact, in turn, on social constructs of what is possible and appropriate. Unger calls this praxis 'deviationist doctrine.' (Unger, 1986, ch 5 'Another Politics' especially 109–11).

[12] Hunt, 1986, 28–32, claims that the concept of 'relative autonomy' is implicit within CLS, as the movement attempts to occupy a space between Marxist economic determinism and the autonomy of legal doctrine. But in the case of CLS, this concept remains as a reference to what needs to be described, and not a theoretical account of how law can both remain connected to the rest of society and have autonomy. Luhmann believes that autopoiesis provides this 'account'. In doing so he is critical of the 'useless concept of "relative autonomy". . . . For all these reasons, we prefer a concept of autonomy which is backed by the concept of autopoiesis; that is, one which spells out that autonomy is either given or not and which does not allow for any grey areas. One should

case by their operative closure) leads to a much reduced role for the kind of choices that could be described as a conscious attempt to develop law or other aspects of society in any particular direction.[13]

Common Ground

CLS does not regard all legal decisions as wholly unpredictable. Its proponents accept that law functions routinely in a predictable fashion, so that it is possible for law's participants to offer legal advice, forecast the results of litigation, etc.[14] Thus the claim that law is indeterminate is not a claim that law operates in a wholly random manner. Nor is the claim that law is politics the equivalent of an allegation of the total corruption of the legal system, whereby all decisions are reached in accordance with the particular distribution of political or economic power within the parties. Autopoiesis and CLS both acknow-

---

add preventively that statements such as "more or less" are not excluded by this concept.' (Luhmann, 2004, 96–7).

[13] Contrast Unger's expectations from deviationist doctrine (n 11 above), with Luhmann's description of legal argumentation: 'It appears rather as a massive and concurrent happening in a complex system—without clear lines and with cluster formations around certain texts, but without any hierarchies and without teleology in respect of the system as a whole. Like seeing a rippled sea from an aeroplane window, here a rippled sea of arguments can be seen. The overall meaning cannot be established from the goal of the individual operations or from the aggregate of individual goals, but only as a function of the fact that argumentation takes place.' (Luhmann, 2004, 333).

[14] 'Note that the CLS movement does not deny that judges attempt with some success to justify their interpretations of the law by reference to the coherence of underlying principle or purpose. Nor do they deny that it is possible to predict with considerable accuracy the outcomes of legal disputes. Their argument is rather that the coherence or integrity of the law is always an illusion, because it involves the marginalisation of other principles or policies that do not fit. Furthermore, they also argue that the vision of coherent principles that is typically favoured by judges is one that embodies rather right-wing political precepts.' (Collins, 2002, 288, commenting on the presentation of CLS by Kelman, 1987, 3–4).

ledge that disparities in power affect the abilities of parties to make legal communications (namely, differentiated access to law)[15] but neither simply equates law with power (legal right is not the same thing as wealth, or the ability to coerce physically). And the claim that law, like politics, is composed of decisions that represent choices between competing values does not mean that these choices are equally open to each and every individual. If it did, then one returns to a view of law generated by an unrestricted application of the methodologies (fact and rule scepticism) of the American Realists, whereby the law may be

---

[15] On the CLS side, see the quote by Kairys at n 8 above, but subject to Kelman's discussion (1987, 262) about those who believe that CLS has 'generally rejected crude elite theory instrumentalism—the belief that law-makers are lackeys of the dominant forces, unconstrained by legal traditions or understanding in their steadfast pursuit of their taskmasters' material advantage . . .'. Galanter has written one of the most widely cited articles (listed by Kennedy and Klare in their bibliography, 1984) analysing the reasons why litigation (including doctrinal evolution) might systematically favour elite groups. He noted that regular litigants would have greater interest in pursuing favourable precedents, and greater ability to tell which precedents would affect them financially by altering later transactions (rather than having only symbolic value). Repeat litigants are likely to be better able to restructure their activities to escape the consequences of unfavourable precedents. Lawyers who specialise tend to serve commercial clients and deal in high value low volume work. However, his overall conclusion was that the disadvantages favoured by the 'have nots' in enforcing the law, or procuring legislative changes in their favour, far outweighed their difficulties in securing favourable precedents from litigation. (Galanter, 1974, 95–160). Galanter's analysis is compatible with systems theory in the general sense that one needs to look at the interaction between systems (economic and political, economic and legal, etc) to see how relationships within one induce relationships within another. Tracing these relationships is superior to superficial observation that the 'haves' of society generally dominate: '. . . this is a rather superficial explanation [of evolution] which does not tell us much about the present day. For it goes almost without saying that all forms of communication are tightly linked to the forms of differentiation in their respective societies.' (Luhmann, 2004, 240, discussing the consequences of the evolution of writing). Thinking about the future. Luhmann observes: 'One has a suspicion that the initial problem is that large parts of the population are not included in the communication of functioning systems, or, to put it another way, that there is a stark difference between inclusion and exclusion that, while it is produced by functional differentiation, is incompatible with it and ultimately undermines it.' (Luhmann, 2004, 488).

influenced by what the judge (policeman, citizen, government official, etc) had for breakfast.

The indeterminacy that concerns CLS is the perceived ability of law to be other than it is. This indeterminacy is not the result of the absence of law, but its superabundance.[16] For almost every legal question there are legal arguments pointing towards different decisions.[17] But what, within the legal system, allows those arguments to be given their respective weight? This indeterminacy can be demonstrated through the analysis of doctrine at a particular moment, and is shown even more clearly when doctrine is examined historically.[18] Law changes, and these changes cannot be explained solely by reference to the introduction of new law. Old law (including constitutions) are also re-interpreted. Thus the crucial issue for CLS is not that the content of all law is indeterminate, but whether there is a rationally defensible basis, either within law, or outside of it, that can determine its content. Autopoiesis reaches the same conclusion as CLS: no such basis exists.

When addressing this issue CLS shares with Ronald Dworkin a common disagreement with those legal positivists who rely on sources or a pedigree test of what sources count as legal sources (most notably statute, precedent and constitutions) as the basis of law's predictability.[19] For Dworkin, the weight to be placed

[16] 'The indeterminacy thesis claims that, with respect to every (or nearly every) apparently determinate legal proposition, somewhere in the background rules there is at least one which, if put in play, would provide the basis for a powerful contrary argument of the sort that [supposedly] eliminates determinacy'. (Tushnet, 1998, 229).

[17] In particular, that for each principle of law there is a counter principle: 'the crucial feature of deviationist doctrine is the willingness to recognize and develop the conflicts between principles and counterprinciples that can be found in any body of law.' (Unger, 1986, 17, and the whole of ch 2 'From Critique to Construction').

[18] See Gordon, 1984.

[19] While Dworkin has altered his account of the manner in which law overcomes the indeterminacy that would result from a reliance on sources alone rather than a combination of substantive reasons and institutional sources, his claim that sources alone would be insufficient to produce determinacy in any area of law has been constant, from *Taking Rights Seriously* to *Laws Empire* and beyond.

upon sources is itself a consequence of the reasons that can be given for such reliance.[20] But for CLS, this solution to the problems of the inability of sources to determine the content of law is something to be discredited. Unger sets out this project in terms of the opposition between formalism and objectivism.[21] Formalism—the application of established law to a situation—cannot operate without some judgement that identifies whether the situation is similar or different to that believed to be covered by law created in accordance with a recognised source (such as a precedent). Analogies do not operate in the absence of judgements as to their appropriateness. If these judgements are to be rational, then the interpretation of law requires a hierarchy of reasons. One must have good (moving to better and from there to best) reasons for one's interpretation of the law in a particular situation. But any attempt to establish such a hierarchy of reasons runs the risk of deteriorating into a form of natural law theory. Not only will such an endeavour founder on a lack of consensus on the ethical basis for social life, the complexity of a modern legal system does not allow for consensus on the ethically correct interpretation of legal questions even if there were a consensus on which ethical values to apply. The compromise position, which Unger calls qualified objectivism, is to take existing areas of law and to consider what moral values they may be taken to express.

> Formalism presupposes at least a qualified objectivism. For if the impersonal purposes, policies, and principles on which all but the most mechanical versions of the formalist thesis must rely do not come, as objectivism suggests, from a moral or practical order exhibited, however partially and ambiguously, by the legal materials themselves, where could they come from? They would have to be supplied by some normative theory extrinsic to the law. Even if such a theory could be convincingly established on its own ground, it would be miraculous if its implications coincided with any large portion of the received doctrinal understandings.[22]

[20] See, for example, Dworkin 1986, 108–113.
[21] Unger, 1986, ch 1 'The Criticism of Legal Thought'.
[22] *Ibid*, 2–3.

Having asserted the necessity for qualified objectivism in order to organise the categories of law on a defensively rational basis, CLS proceeds to demonstrate that attempts to present legal decisions as embodiments of, or approximations to, a moral order, are doomed to failure. This enterprise can take many forms. Attempts to present society as a moral order can be shown to be incoherent,[23] leading to, for example, criticism of the organising principles associated with liberal society.[24] In addition, the causal connection between legal categories and any description of society's order can be shown to be no more than a matter of assertion:[25] does the market economy require a doctrine of consideration or not?[26]

If objectivism is not possible, then formalism remains, but in a form that exposes its inherently arbitrary nature. Legal doctrines, the organising categories of legal decisions, are not expressions of or approximations to a moral order within society. Statements of doctrine (the respective weight to be given to different legal arguments on any particular occasion) are a consequence of constructs of what is appropriate that cannot be understood as defensible and rational (coherent). These constructs can include

[23] 'One feature more than any other appears to unite the critical legal theorists. They all engage in critiques of mainstream legal thought directed at demonstrating its incoherence. The general form of critical legal writing is that which asserts the incoherence or contradictions of liberal legalism, of specific areas of doctrine, of specific theorists, judges, or treatise writers.' (Hunt, 1986, 32).

[24] 'The descriptive portrait of mainstream liberal thought that I present is a picture of a system of thought that is simultaneously beset by internal *contradiction* (not by "competing concerns" artfully balanced until a wise equilibrium is reached, but by irreducible, irremediable, irresolvable conflict) and by systematic *repression* of the presence of these contradictions.' (Kelman, 1987, 3). See also Kennedy, 1979.

[25] '. . . the a priori CLS theoretical position [is] that legal practice cannot properly fulfil social needs because liberal discourse in fact sees *conflicting* needs.' (Kelman, 1987, 232).

[26] See Unger, 1986, 6–7. For a more systematic examination of the relationship between legal forms and economic structures, see Kennedy and Michelman, 1980.

matters that are accepted without conscious reflection,[27] and are claimed by CLS to be unprincipled, and even ideological ('making sense out of nonsense').

While autopoiesis can offer a sociological account of the phenomena described by CLS, it would not dispute the correctness of the central conclusions of the CLS project: law lacks a rationally defensible foundation; all of its structures are contingent (have a different form in the past, and will have different forms in the future); there is no determining functional correlation between structures found in the rest of society and those present in the legal system.[28] However, autopoiesis would not accept a claim that the lack of a systematic and coherent basis for legal decisions makes legal decisions indistinguishable from political ones. Nor would it accept that the generation of doctrine is an exercise in ideology whose function is to hide structures that favour dominant interests: white over ethnic minorities, male over female, wealthy over poor, middle and upper classes over working classes, etc. While autopoiesis accepts that the law constitutes and reinforces inequalities of access found in the economic system, political system, media, etc, these inequalities are produced separately within each system. (Thus, if law produces inequalities between individuals that mirror those found in the political system, or even utilises forms of reasoning found in the political system, this still will not make the legal system part of the political system, and vice versa). And the communications, which include jurisprudence, that help to maintain such inequalities are not ideological, if that term is taken to refer to communications that falsely represent the system to itself. For autopoiesis, jurisprudence involves an understanding of how the system presents itself to itself, and how these representations

---

[27] See for example, Kelman's exploration of the unconscious choice of time frames that structure the use of criminal law doctrine, in Kelman, 1981.

[28] There is an ambiguity within CLS literature as to whether the contradictions and incoherence found within liberal legal doctrine and liberal society are actually a feature of all societies. For example, is the contradiction within liberal theory between 'self and other' actually part of the human condition? On this see Hunt, 1986, 22.

assist the system to reproduce itself. The lack of foundation or coherence is not only a problem for law, but for all systems of communication. Jurisprudence, including law's self-observations and the ensuing communication of law's doctrinal categories, includes communications that help the legal system to stabilise itself. While the need to avoid confronting law's lack of coherence or foundation is productive, in that developments that seem likely to expose these absences produce further developments designed to defer that exposure,[29] there is no reason to believe that whole-scale exposure through successful deconstruction will result in the disappearance of jurisprudence, or the radical reconfiguration of doctrinal categories.[30] Legal communications can only continue if the major part of what currently constitutes legal communication remains available for the production of further legal communications. This need to utilise what exists in order to communicate allows the system to overcome through its operations what it lacks in coherence, or foundation (each operation of the system reproduces the system subject to a limited number of variations). While this situation cannot be reduced to the interests of particular actors (all those who seek to make legal communications have to utilise existing legal communications, even when they seek to make novel legal communications), there is some truth in Collins' observation that the CLS enterprise faces considerable resistance from those who wish to continue to make legal communications, including communications about the manner in which law communicates itself to itself:

---

[29] Within CLS writings, such reconfiguration has been linked to a need to restore law's legitimacy. Without reducing legal doctrine to class interests, a 'narrow concept of professional legal consciousness . . . seeks to distinguish itself from orthodox positivist or neo-positivist scholarship by identifying the import and significance of doctrinal development as the production of legal ideology to be understood as mechanism of legitimation or attempts to resolve tensions or contradictions which threaten to disrupt the socio-political assumptions of liberal theory of law as a "system" founded on a normative coherence of its rules.' Hunt, 1986, 14–15; he attributes this view, in particular, to Duncan Kennedy.

[30] A point made by Hunt, 1986, 32–36.

The problem confronting the CLS movement was not just resistance to progressive political positions, but rejection of the analysis of the incoherence of legal doctrine and the (alleged) liberating potential that followed from that insight. Steeped in the doctrinal learning of the common law, few law professors, judges, or lawyers could bring themselves to think that they had always been just 'making sense out of nonsense'.[31]

Systems Theory and the Claim That Law is Politics

What is the nature of the debate between CLS—which seeks to challenge law's presentation of itself as different from politics—and those such as Dworkin and Raz who attempt to show that such a difference does indeed exist?[32] The claim that law is or is not politics does not deny that there is a political system that is not the same as the legal system. Both sides to this debate would have no trouble identifying institutions that belonged to either category. For example, political parties, rallies and interest group lobbying belong to the political system, while courts, adjudication, and litigation belong to the legal system. Of course, political institutions have legal structures, and legal institutions are formed and reformed in response to political choices, so the instinctive allocation of institutions to one or other system may not be as straightforward as it seems. Nevertheless, from a recognition that different institutions and practices can be allocated to each of the two systems the debate within jurisprudence about the similarity

[31] Collins, 2002, 322–23; see also Collins, 1987.

[32] While Dworkin tries to show that all of law (hard and easy cases) is different from politics due to the operation of principles, Raz (following Hart) tries to show that decided law (to the extent and in the manner that law decides matters) is subtly different, despite the 'discretion' available within legal reasoning, from the more open form of discourse associated with politics. In relation to 'directed judicial powers' and the degree of discretion available to the courts, Raz recognises that 'extralegal considerations', including 'social and political considerations', permit the courts 'to develop the law'. 'These are empirical matters which vary between different legal systems. But as it is a necessary fact that courts have law-making powers, it is also a universal fact that in exercising them they base their actions on moral and political tendencies, and that they are *directed by law* to do so.' (Raz, 1994, 253, our emphasis)

and difference of law and politics focuses on moments of apparent cross-over between one system and the other. The creation of a constitution (involving revolutions, assemblies, etc) is an accepted political event, but once created, are the deliberations of courts on the meaning of that constitution in some essential way different from the practices that led to its creation? Similarly with legislation: interest group lobbying, predictions of future electoral success, and ideological conflict are acknowledged influences on the processes that generate statutes, but is the treatment of statutes within the legal system so very different from this?

An autopoietic approach to the relationship between politics and law starts with an appreciation of the implications of operative closure. This seems counter-intuitive, especially at the points of apparent cross-over between the political and legal system. Constitutions and legislation involve communications that apparently co-exist in both political and legal systems. They also appear to represent a move from the political to the legal, with the former providing input to the latter. And as legislation and constitutions both represent attempts to provide stability to the content of political communications, there is surely a sense in which any indeterminacy in the meaning of these forms must constitute a continuation of the processes that the political system hoped to resolve. However, the nature of closure ensures that the manner in which 'politics' operates within the legal system is different from what occurs within the political system.[33] Only the legal system can identify communications as belonging to itself, and likewise only the political system can identify its own communications.[34] As such, the fact that constitutions and statutes are communications in both (that the same text is a communication of, and communicated about, in each system) does not mean that they have the same meaning in each system. The political system can introduce a constitution or statute with

[33] See generally Luhmann, 2004, ch 9 'Politics and Law'.

[34] We refer the reader back to the limited meaning of this statement, as set out in ch 2 of this book, especially in the text following from n 19.

some quite predictable anticipation of how these texts will be treated by the legal system—but it cannot determine that treatment. The meaning of a constitution or statute will be generated within the operations of the legal system—which include all the structures that it has developed for the interpretation of constitutions and statutes.

If we take the example of a statute, and the legislature, the manner in which these two operate as communications within the two systems is not the same. The legal system acknowledges the legislature only as the author of statutes: none, or very little,[35] of its other work registers. Vast amounts of communications (statements from the front benches, prime minister's question time, resignation speeches, lost bills, rejected amendments, etc) are not recognised by the legal system as legal communications. Even such significant aspects of politics as the relationship between the executive and the legislature is either ignored, or examined by reference to authorising statutes, or acknowledged through the doctrine of crown prerogative. Does this mean that the legal system has an impoverished notion of politics? Well yes, seen from the perspective of the political system. But no, once one recognises that the legal system's ability to select from politics what constitutes a communication within its own system allows it to have a fairly stable relationship with the political system. This can be seen to be mutually beneficial to both systems. The fact that the political system can generate texts that are not communicated within the legal system using the same structures as give meaning to those texts within the political system allows the political system to induce something, within the legal system, that it could not create for itself. In the terms of Parsons' systems theory[36] this might be described as an output of the

---

[35] Perhaps '*travaux preparatoire*' can, within some legal systems operate as evidence of what the legislative body intended, but even then, as evidence, it has to be integrated into how evidence is adduced, presented and interpreted, as *legal* evidence.

[36] See Cotterrell's analysis of Parsons, 1992, ch 3 'Law as an Integrative Mechanism', especially 81–91; see also Bredemeier, 1962, and more generally, Parsons 1960 and 1962.

political system (and an input to the legal system). But such descriptions obscure the fact that the ability of the political system to create a reaction within the legal system depends on the basis for the recognition of text and speech established within the legal system. The inducement of predictable reactions within another system does not breach that system's operative closure. Each system remains autonomous in the sense that each system continues to decide for itself what communications are part of itself.

The nature of operative closure may, at this point, seem trite. If the political system learns that certain of its communications will have predictable effects within the legal system, why does it matter if these are described as political inputs to the legal system or not? And if these predictable effects become a regular occurrence, and much of the activity of one system is designed to induce these effects in the other, what benefits arise from insisting that the systems remain closed to each other, that their closure is the basis of their autonomy, and that the relationship between them could be better described as one of structural coupling?[37] The answer to this lies not in the immediate benefits of words chosen to describe such points of close connection between the two systems, but from the fact that a focus on the basis of closure (that only the particular system can identify what constitutes a communication of that system) allows for a much more rigorous analysis of the operations of different systems. Accepting that systems exhibit operative closure (only systems can determine what is a communication within their system) does not involve (as has been consistently stressed throughout this book) a claim that one system has no causal influence on another. So the claim that it is the nature of statutory interpretation that determines what the political system must do in order to create law is not a claim that law is insulated from politics. Rather, by focusing our attention on the communications that law recognises as legal, and the manner in which

[37] For a basic statement on the meaning and importance of the description, 'structural coupling', see Luhmann, 2004, ch 10 'Structural Couplings', section 1. We return to this significant concept in the final chapter of this book.

law insulates itself from all manner of communications that it does not recognise as legal, we are directed towards a far more precise understanding of the manner in which politics influences the creation of law.

The claim that the communications that circulate within the legal system (claims, decisions, precedents, etc) in response to these points of apparent cross-over between the legal and political system continue to be 'political' represents quite a generalised and abstract view of what it means for something to be political. Legal communications are not the same as political ones. This is not because of any ontological difference between the nature of the two systems, but because the two systems have evolved differently. Each has developed its own conditional programmes for applying its own coding. Law has its structures for making legal communications that apply the code legal/illegal: doctrines (including stare decisis), procedures, etc. And politics has its own conditional programmes for applying the code government/opposition: voter registration, parties, conferences, candidate selection, elections, etc. Thus the claim that the law is politics is not an assertion that the communications within the political and legal system are the same, for example, that the interpretation of a statute simply continues the same communications that led to its passage in the legislature (lobbying, calls to have regard to the likelihood of re-election, observations on the record of the opposition parties or promises to pass further legislation in future, etc). Rather, the claim that law is politics is an abstract claim about the nature of both kinds of communications. It refers to politics not as a functioning system, but as a discourse. Politics involves contested ideas as to the meaning of the common good. Politics is not a neutral search for common values but a process that reflects the different abilities of different actors to influence the communications that lead to the establishment of governments and the administration of its programmes. Politics requires choices to be made, which are structured by ideas of what is feasible and acceptable. Such generalised descriptions of what constitutes politics, allows a comparison to be made between politics and certain general features of the legal system. Most notably, whether legal reasoning does or does not share common features with political discourse.[38] There can then be a debate as to whether the deci-

---

[38] For example, in *Taking Rights Seriously*, Dworkin attempts to build a distinction between legal reasoning and politics that relies heavily on the claim that political decisions have to be justified consistently (a theory of political responsibility) and the claim that the degree and type of consistency that can be achieved within the legal system is distinctly different from that available within the political system. Principles, which both reflect and generate political choices, give consistent entitlements to individuals. In Dworkin's opinion, these form a crucial part of judicial reasoning. By contrast, policies, to be defensible, only need to represent a consistent pursuit of some aggregate goal, and are more appropriately left to the legislature and politics. Dworkin asserts that the doctrine of political responsibility is 'relatively weak when policies are in play'. This conclusion follows on from an example of the task facing a Congressman who needs to justify apparent inconsistent voting, the implicit suggestion being that Congressmen could reach inconsistent positions provided that this resulted in a lower aggregate of some undesirable occurrences (in the example, the total number of abortions): 'Suppose a Congressman votes to prohibit abortion, on the ground that human life in any form is sacred, but then votes to permit the parents of babies born deformed to withhold medical treatment that will keep such babies alive. He might say that he feels there is some difference, but the principle of responsibility, strictly applied, will not allow him these two votes unless he can incorporate the difference within some general political theory he sincerely holds.' (Dworkin, 1977, 87). Dworkin's example fails to deal with the fact that principles form part of the communications of politicians throughout the political system. The scope for such communication depends crucially on the point in the political system where such communications occur. And the understanding of the participants that their position is principled cannot be taken out of its institutional context. Thus, for example, senators who feel unable to raise a particular point of principle once a bill has reached a certain stage do not necessarily regard themselves as unprincipled. Nor do they regard themselves as participating in a process that represents a checkerboard, involving no principled basis for consistency in the treatment of individuals. Rather, consistency in the application of legislative procedures (themselves regarded by participants as matters of principle) will structure what arguments of principle can be raised. Of course, exactly the same points can be made about the legal system. The application of substantive principles depends upon institutional context, which includes doctrines of precedent and the hierarchies of courts. This allows positions that seem unprincipled, such as the Supreme Court's consistent upholding of the constitutionality of restrictions placed by States upon access to abortion whilst failing to overturn the Supreme Court decision in *Roe v Wade* 410 US 113 (1973), to be defended by complex arguments that take full account of law's institutions for decision making.

sions made within law, and the manner in which those decisions are structured through discourse, are any more 'neutral' or less 'ideological' than occurs within politics.

As with the study of apparent cross-overs between law and politics, the study of apparent similarities or dissimilarities between the general features of political and legal discourse can benefit from starting with operative closure. If legal communications are the basis for the recognition of a communication as legal, then it is only legal communications that can establish the possibilities of what can be communicated within the legal system at any moment. This does not mean that what can be communicated is always unambiguous. But it does mean that the legal system identifies its own areas of vagueness, for example, its own unresolved issues. And this is actually a two-fold identification. The legal system will identify what constitutes the issue to be decided, and whether that issue is clearly resolved or not. Consider for example, the doctrine of constructive and resulting trusts and its operation in relation to family property. This doctrine deals with the property rights of co-owners when they have not evidenced their co-ownership in formal documentation. While this is not a party-political issue, it is considered to be extremely political in terms of feminist politics. The leading authority, the House of Lords decision in *Lloyds Bank v Rosset*,[39] denies family members a share in property owned by other members of their family unless they can show that they have made a direct financial contribution to the purchase of the property in question, or they can show that the current legal owner has acted towards the claimant in respect of the disputed property in a manner that has caused the claimant to suffer from a detrimental reliance. Whilst the first part of this ruling makes it very difficult for the contributions of women to the welfare of their partners and children to be recognised and rewarded through a share of the partner's property, the second part of the ruling is potentially more liberal. Indeed, if the concept of detrimental reliance is expanded to treat detriment as the usual consequence

[39] [1991] 1 AC 107.

for women that results from their being predominantly the gender which takes responsibility for child-rearing, and silence by their partners as conduct sufficient to justify an expectation of sharing in property, then women in most long-term relationships involving children become co-owners of all their partners assets.[40] A CLS analysis of this question can stress both the indeterminacy within law (the potential of law to be other than what it currently is) and the ideological nature of the choices involved in the current doctrinal position (assumptions about 'normal' relationships between men and women within the 'private' sphere of the family that prevent the courts from assuming that women undertake family responsibilities in the expectation of a property reward).[41] Not only is this issue identified as political via feminist theory rather than legal analysis, but the historical developments that have made this such a burning issue within law cannot be said to be legal ones: the rise of ownership of houses, increases in rates of divorce, the demands for equality for women, etc. In these circumstances, in what sense can the legal system be said to identify its own issues, and establish its own indeterminacy, separately from the political system? Is such a claim no more than the conflation of politics with party-politics and the current system for establishing government?

CLS would accept that the grammar of disputes over family property is peculiar to the legal system,[42] but would regard claims

[40] A similar result occurs if indirect contributions (actions which have value for the other partner) are included in the first part of the ruling.

[41] 'A decision, for instance, to treat the promises of unmarried cohabiters as contractual words rather than as alegal words of commitment puts public force behind what is otherwise legally vacuous. It is hard to see the decision as resting in any significant sense on any particular party's volition, rather than a collective decision about the proper nature of the relationship.' (Kelman, 1987, 105).

[42] Kairys ('Introduction' to Kairys, 1990, 3–4) attacks 'the idealised model [of a] distinctly legal mode of reasoning', while accepting that 'there is a distinctly legal and quite elaborate system of discourse and body of knowledge, replete with its own language and conventions of argumentation, logic, and even manners. . . . But in terms of a method or process for decision making—for determining correct rules, facts, or results—the law provides only a wide and conflicting variety of stylized rationalizations from which courts pick and choose.'

that this grammar prevents such disputes from being different from politics as an example of the ideological nature of legal doctrine. These women's claims have to be equitable not legal, and in terms of constructive and resulting trusts rather than express trusts, because of statutory provisions that prevent changes from occurring in legal titles or beneficial entitlements under express trusts without the requisite documentary formalities.[43] Is this manner of formulating the issue merely a legal grammar for political claims and issues, which leaves courts free to 'pick and choose' from 'a wide variety of stylised rationalizations'?[44]

The first point to make in support of the autopoietic claim that law identifies its own issues is to note that these disputes cannot arise without litigation, which is a legal process. Not every feminist issue can be litigated, only those where establishing the legality of something has worthwhile consequences for the parties involved. The next point to note is the general acceptance that this issue could be decided through Parliament instead of the courts. If a statute introduced a new statutory regime of common ownership of family assets, the basis of these disputes would change. This is not to say that feminist political analysis could not continue to identify feminist issues in, say, the meaning of a statutory definition of 'family property'. But a shift in the legal dispute from the meaning of 'contributions' to property under trust law to the meaning of 'family property' under a statute would not be a shift established through feminist analysis, but would be a result of new communications (a statute) recognised by the legal system.[45] If we accept that the introduction of such

[43] Law of Property Act 1925, s 53.

[44] Kairys, as n 42 above.

[45] Tushnet, 1998, argues that indeterminacy can be produced *whenever* a 'socially significant movement' employs 'well socialised lawyers' (who know what arguments are possible) to conduct litigation. This would seem to discount the ability of the political system to generate communications that alter the possibilities of argument within the legal system. It would also seem to make it pointless for social movements to engage in litigation as a political strategy, since in the face of any socially significant counter-movement, they cannot hope to establish any determinate legal propositions (even within a relatively narrow time-span) or even alter the basis of indeterminacy.

a statute could change the basis of the dispute (that it could determine things currently underdetermined even if it created new indeterminacies) then we also have to accept that it is the absence of such a statute that gives rise to the present indeterminacy. Of course, if we do not believe that a new statute could alter the basis of such disputes, determining issues that are currently underdetermined and raising new issues for determination, then legal categories truly are only an ideological grammar for politics. But this would be a pretty strong claim—that no statute, in whatever terms, could alter the basis upon which the issue of entitlements to property between family members is to be decided. Such a strong view of politics at the level of general political views would not only require us to view the legal system as an exercise in ideology, but much of the political system (all that part orientated around the creation of statutes) as ideological as well.

If the ability of the legal system to identify its own issues by reference to its own categories (statute and common law, particular statutory provision and relevant precedent, etc) is accepted, then what kind of claim is involved in the assertion that law is politics, and that assertions and appearances to the contrary are ideological? This claim can perhaps be understood if we move from what is generally considered law (statutes, common law) to what is generally considered facts, in our example, domestic relations, gender, etc. Law may identify legal issues, and generate rules and principles, but the facts to which those rules and principles are applied (and the subsequent assessment of how those rules and principles should impact on those facts) cannot be generated solely by law, but must include matters that come from outside law, and these will include broad categorisations of activities and roles within society (such as gender roles) that can be described as ideological. Under the second part of the *Rosset* decision, law will select communications about decisions that would not have been made by the claiming party otherwise than in the expectation that they were to share in their partner's property. And these communications will inevitably include descriptions of gender roles generated within general social communication, which exhibit elements of prescription, and a distance from the specificity and diversity of individual experience of gender that warrant the label 'ideology'. What, in the face of this, justifies the claim that law is closed, and that its operations are not, at least in part, ideological?

As with the description of the relationship between politics and law involved in legislation, it is not that autopoiesis does not recognise what is referred to in claims that law involves ideology, but that operative closure gives us a much more rigorous basis to identify the nature of this relationship. The legal system does not create the entire world in which it exists. It does not claim to create the entire physical environment of the world, nor does it claim to create all of the communications in the world. But it does not need to. Just as the legal system can recognise a statute as a legal communication without having to participate in the system that created it (or share all the meanings generated by statutes within that system), so too it can give legal meanings to other communications that it has not created. The treatment of statutes illustrates what closure involves. The legal system does not react to all the communications of other systems, and those to which it does react are not given the same meaning, as they would have in the system that generated them. By the same token, systems do not have to create all of the communications that they utilise. Operative closure involves a system in answering two questions. First, is the communication one that the system recognises? Second, does it recognise the communication as something that is part of itself, or something that is part of its environment? To return to our example of co-ownership within family property, there are many communications about the nature of gender, property and fairness that would not become part of the communications of the legal system. Then, of those that are recognised by the legal system, some would be recognised as part of law itself. These would include the statute that requires claims to co-ownership to be argued about within the law of trusts, and the precedents on the law of trusts that this brings into play. Then there are those communications that law recognises, but regards as not itself (not law). So law, and not the system from which the communications that law is utilising are generated, identifies which communications about disputes are relevant to the issue. That law, rather than social communication, is the selecting system can be seen if one thinks about the problems in generating a feminist theory of law. There are any numbers of points where feminist theory can identify the gender implications of communications utilised within law. And these can include not only the adverse impact of apparently neutral words on each gender, but the manner in which legal description of gender, taken from social communication, in turn reinforces stereo-typical assumptions about the nature of gender roles. But it is extremely difficult to map out a feminist theory of whole areas of legal doctrine (tort, corporate law, trust law, etc) and even more difficult to come up with a theory that accounts for all of the organising categories of law.

This might, in itself, not be sufficient to persuade you that law should be described as being operationally closed to political ideologies. But the case becomes stronger if we can understand *why* it is so difficult to articulate areas of law, or law as a whole, as expressions (having some constant relationship with) political ideologies. This requires us to understand how, in making its selections, law alters the meaning of communications from that arising within the systems that generate them. Here, to think through the nature of the theory's claims, it would assist us to consider an analogy taken from linguistics. Words do not have meanings in themselves, even when they appear to have an immediate referent in the real world (eg tree). Words get their meanings through their differences from (and therefore their relationships to) other words. The ability to make endless distinctions using different words allows us to reach complex and exact meanings. We talk about words from one language 'entering into' another language (eg Norman French entering into Anglo-Saxon English). But in reality, words do not simply enter into other languages, since they cannot duplicate the relationships that they had with all the other words in the language they came from when they are adopted by the language they are perceived to 'enter'. Autopoiesis moves us from the level of language, to that of communications. But it retains the idea that meanings are established not by correspondence with things in the real world, but through relationships between signs. Only, within autopoiesis, one considers the relationships between communications. Communications are generated through the relationships (connections) established between communications. Autopoiesis is based on the recognition that subsystems of social communication can evolve that make connections between communications that would not occur within general social communication. As such, even when the law uses words or phrases taken from general social communication, it does not replicate the meanings of those words as they occur within general social communication. It gives those communications new meanings because it removes those communications from the web of connections (relationships) that gave those words meanings within the system that generated them, and creates relationships between those communications and other communications that are unique to itself. That social communications influence law is not denied, just as communications in the political sphere influence law, most especially when they take the form of statutes. But if those communications are selected by law for its own purposes, and given meanings within law different from those within the communication system that generated them, then law retains its autonomy, and its relationship with the communications it utilises can be studied by reference to how law makes its selections, and how law generates its meanings.[46]

Thus, while the legal system may couple with communications about gender roles at one moment in its operations when deciding about co-ownership, it links such communications to others that do not utilise communications about gender roles.

---

[46] This is also the sense in which autopoiesis claims that systems create both themselves and their environment. By identifying communications that connect to itself (selecting) the law identifies itself (relevant norms such as statutes and precedents) and its environment (communications relevant to those norms such as the history of contributions to, or discussions of ownership of, particular assets).

An assessment of entitlement to co-ownership has implications for the welfare of the parties, and perhaps for women generally, but this is not part of law's continuing communications. Law will move on to communicate about the possibilities of a possession action, bankruptcy, mortgages, fraudulent preferences, gifts, inheritance, and the application of constructive trusts outside of family property disputes. And, if the legal system develops the law on co-ownership (which perhaps diminishes its use of gender stereotypes or its adverse impact on one sex), then unless it can generate adequate distinctions, this may alter all of these linked communications as well. And whilst such changes may be described as a consequence of changes to the law on co-ownership, they will not be an expression of the social communications (political ideology) operating within co-ownership, because these linked communications will not continue to utilise the same ideological aspects of gender descriptions that arise within co-ownership. Thus while it is possible to note the utilisation of 'ideological' communications in an area of law, and to trace the changes that might be required to be made in linked areas of law if the use of these communications altered, it is not possible to give an account of the law (bankruptcy, enforcement, trusts, gifts, inheritance, etc) that demonstrates it to be just an expression of politics (in the form of political ideology), ie that politics is determining the content and form of legal doctrine, without this being both a simplistic and misleading description of what is occurring.

This analysis could be repeated with other attempts to demonstrate that law is an expression of political ideologies (the hegemony of the ruling classes, neo-classical economic arguments, or liberalism). As such, autopoiesis can replicate the conclusions of CLS (that the doctrines of law do not have any coherent relationship to other areas of social life) but provide more by way of positive explanation, both for the lack of coherence, and for the manner in which systems continue to operate without coherent rational relationships either between all of their operations, or between their operations and those of other systems, or those represented within general social communication.

An Autopoietic Explanation of Legal Reasoning

The claim that law has a distinct form of reasoning (as opposed to a different grammar) is regarded by CLS as an ideological claim, through which legal actors mislead themselves and others.[47] While particular examples of legal reasoning might appear to have coherence and rigour, attempts to offer general explanations for substantial areas of the law can be exposed as rationalisations that lack coherence[48] or explanatory power. This is part of the exercise, within CLS, which has been termed 'trashing'.[49] But whereas CLS views such exercises in the rationalisation of legal decisions as an ideological gloss on the operations of law, autopoiesis regards them as also being operations of the legal system. Indeed, as this book is intended to demonstrate, even jurisprudence arguing about the nature of such rationalisations can form part of the legal system.

CLS criticism of legal reasoning stresses the contradiction between oppositions. Kelman's description of this approach is as follows:

> First, the Critics attempted to identify a contradiction in liberal legal thought, a set of paired rhetorical arguments that both resolve cases in opposite, incompatible ways and correspond to distinct visions of human nature and human fulfilment.[50] . . . Second, the Critics tried

[47] In his 'Introduction' to *The Politics of Law* Kairys speaks of a 'judicial schizophrenia that permeates decisions, arguments and banter among lawyers.' (1990, 4).

[48] Both in the sense of having consistent relationships between legal doctrines and interests outside of the law, and in the sense of consistency in the relationships between legal doctrines. For an extensive analysis of these two kinds of consistency, albeit one that argues that together their interrelationship explains both stability and change in common law doctrine, see Eisenberg, 1988.

[49] See Kelman, 1984.

[50] Kelman's three examples are: '(1) the contradiction between a commitment to mechanically applicable rules as the appropriate form for resolving disputes (thought to be associated in complex ways with the political tradition of self-reliance and individualism) and a commitment to situation-sensitive, ad hoc standards (thought to correspond to a commitment to sharing and altruism); (2) the contradiction between a commitment to the traditional liberal notion that

187

to demonstrate that each of the contradictions is utterly pervasive in legal controversy, even in cases where practice is so settled that we nearly invariably forget that the repressed contradictory impulse *could* govern the decision at issue. . . . Third, Critics have attempted to show that mainstream thought invariably treats one term in each set of contradictory impulses as *privileged* in three distinct senses. The privileged term is presumptively entitled as a normative matter to govern disputes; it is simply assumed, as a descriptive matter, to govern the bulk of situations; and most subtly, but perhaps most significantly, departures from the purportedly dominant norm, even if they are obviously frequent, are treated as *exceptional*, in need of special justification, a bit chaotic. . . . Fourth, the Critics note that, closely examined, the 'privileged' impulses describe the program of a remarkably right-wing, quasilibertarian order.[51]

As we shall see, autopoietic theory does not dispute the CLS claim that legal reasoning is incoherent, with relationships between privileged and subordinated communications that cannot be accounted for by reference to a rational moral ordering. However, the distinctions employed by systems theory for the description of legal reasoning do not suggest that this element of arbitrariness can be removed from the legal system, or any other subsystem. Autopoiesis, like CLS, also accepts that any settled legal practice can evolve, and that this may involve the inversion of the hierarchy of what was previously acknowledged and suppressed. However, while CLS critique is itself justified by the assumption that exposing the lack of a rational justification for settled practices will lead to greater support for repressed values

---

values or desires are arbitrary, subjective, individual, and individuating while facts or reason are objective and universal *and* a commitment to the ideal that we can "know" social and ethical truths objectively (through objective knowledge of true human nature) or to the hope that one can transcend the usual distinction between subjective and objective in seeking moral truth; and (3) the contradiction between a commitment to an intentionalistic discourse, in which human action is seen as the product of a self-determining individual will, and determinist discourse, in which the activity of nominal subjects merits neither respect nor condemnation because it is simply deemed the expected outcome of existing structures.' (Kelman, 1987, 3).

[51] *Ibid*, 3–4.

and principles,[52] systems theory analysis does not lead one to expect that radical critique can necessarily destabilise any of the settled practices that are subjected to it.

The starting point for understanding legal reasoning is simply the acceptance that the legal system constantly codes in terms of legal/illegal: thus legal decisions are applications of that code. The paradox implicit within this activity is that the distinction legal/illegal has no intrinsic meaning, it is just a distinction. To repeat the question that brings home the nature of this claim: what would you learn if I told you that an unspecified state of affairs, x, was legal? The only answer that you could give was that x was not illegal. This paradox cannot be either defused or diffused by identifying values that establish, for all purposes and on all occasions, what constitutes the distinction between legal and illegal. For example, legal does not mean 'good' on all the occasions when it is used, nor does illegal always mean 'not good'. If it did, the legal system would not be the one we experience today, but would be some embodiment of natural law theory.[53] Nor is there any other value (or distinction) that can universally stand in for legal/illegal on all the occasions when it is used. But this does not mean that other values are not utilised when the code is applied. Their use arises when the legal system engages in what is called 'secondary observation'. Primary observation is simply the operation of applying the code legal/illegal on a particular occasion. Secondary observation is the process whereby the previous applications of the code are examined in order to identify reasons why that particular application occurred. Secondary observations allow one to consider how the code should be applied in a future case, or cases. They provide a basis for the taking of further legal decisions.

Autopoiesis recognises that secondary observation can be structured through the evolution of norms of competence, whereby the carrying out of secondary observations is allocated

[52] 'These . . . [repressed contradictions] are ready to destabilize settled practice should we ever be forced to articulate or ground that practice.' (*Ibid*, 3–4).

[53] Substantial argument to support this claim has been presented in both ch 2 and 3.

to particular institutions.[54] And in the case of law, these institutions are centrally the courts. With the development of courts, part of the reason for distinguishing particular applications of the code from one another is whether the courts made those applications. With evolution, communications about the basis for the application of the code (secondary observation) that arise from courts form a regular and routine part of what is used (by courts and others involved in secondary observation) to carry out secondary observations.

The development of courts does not remove the original paradox of the code—the lack of any value that can account, on all occasions, for its application. But it does allow for increasing complexity and technicality in the communications that seek to defuse and avoid it. Thus law can develop accounts of its own decisions that present them to itself as applications of doctrine, or responses to interests, or even, within particular localities, as decisions for the achievement of good, or the avoidance of evil. There is no inherent order to this, or hierarchy of reasons. Thus there is much in it that can be described, by CLS, as mere 'rationalisations'. That the courts should be involved in such rationalisations is a result of the need to make distinctions, to account for the application of the code, even when there are no good reasons.[55] And this need arises from the inability of courts to refuse to decide.[56] The Courts cannot limit themselves to decide only

[54] Organisation systems, as Luhmann calls them (2004, 293).

[55] 'Courts have to decide even when they cannot decide, or at least not within reasonable standards of rationality. And if they cannot decide, they must force themselves to be able to decide. If the law cannot be found, it must simply be invented.' (Luhmann, 2004, 289).

[56] This is not to say that courts have no responses to issues that allow them to exercise some control over the issues that come before them. There are time limits, causes of action, staying of actions, or even doctrines (like the doctrine of 'ripeness' which allows the US Supreme Court to refuse to decide an issue that it does not feel ready to decide). But these devices cannot ensure that the courts only decide issues where there are 'good reasons' for deciding an issue one way or another. When matters arise that are not caught by these rather crude filters, then the courts remain caught by their duty to decide (the prohibition against the denial of justice). By contrast, legal practitioners (involved in forward planning) can avoid choosing legal forms that rely on uncertain areas of law.

issues for which there are already good reasons for deciding the matter one way rather than the other. And in making a decision—a new allocation of the code legal/illegal—the courts make a new primary observation that itself may be observed. Such hard cases do not simply fill in gaps in the law. Because they too have to be observed (become the subject of secondary observation) they have the potential to generate shifts in the basis of observation. Thus hard cases (cases for which there is no clear answer based on existing rationalisations of decisions) can later become the easy cases of new doctrines that replace earlier doctrines.

CLS not only acknowledges the presence of hard cases that cannot be answered with any certainty in light of existing legal materials, but at the same time challenges the claim that law, through its own internal resources, can establish easy cases. For CLS, areas of certainty within law are not established through the superiority of reasons, not even within particular localities, but only by a consensus of commitment to the outcomes of so-called easy cases.[57] As such, one needs to investigate the basis of such senses of the appropriate, both conscious and unconscious, and look outside of law for their source. For if there are no inherently 'good' reasons for decisions, how can there be easy cases, except by reference to non-rational factors lying outside of legal reasoning?

To this CLS challenge to legal reasoning, Luhmann offers a distinction that is not itself a legal distinction, and is not part of the self-description of legal systems: redundancy and variety.[58] This is a distinction taken from communications theory, which can be used to understand the distinction between easy cases and hard ones, and between the ability of the legal system both to stay the same (to decide again in the same way as it decided before) and to change (to decide matters differently). Redundancy is that part of a communication which stays the same, whilst variety is that part of a communication which

---

[57] 'Still, the lawyers may know that the judges won't *accept* the arguments. In this sense only, the *outcome* is determinate or predictable.' (Tushnet, 1998, 234—emphasis in original).

[58] See Luhmann, 2004, 316–322.

changes. Redundancy facilitates variety. Only by keeping much of communications the same, can we communicate important differences. For example, only by standardising the reporting of temperatures (using only Celsius or Fahrenheit) can we make the weather forecast easy to communicate. By keeping the format of newspapers unchanged from day to day we facilitate the communication of news (the use of categories like 'politics' and 'business' facilitates the understanding of what is 'new' in politics, etc). By putting bus times into tables we assist our understanding of when the buses will arrive (the headings to each column are addressed identically—redundancy—to each time listed; time itself is reported on a standard basis). Only by communicating in ways that are the same, to an enormous extent, do we make possible the communication of an enormous variety of extremely complicated information.

The aspects of our communications that are redundant can be seen as arbitrary. Nevertheless, the costs of changing them can be quite substantial. For example, changing the basis of our 24 hour calculation of time (decimalising the day for example) would require the re-programming of every computer manufactured up to the date of change, changing the basis of every timetable, mass obsolescence in clocks, major changes to general social communication about experience, etc, etc). And this applies to legal communication too. Secondary observation creates generalisations (doctrine) that constitute redundancy within the system. For example, when something is described as a contract, this can provide a fixed point of reference from which to make arguments about the interpretation of the particular point in dispute. Lawyers are aware that contracts are not capable of being given a direct referent in the real world,[59] and that it is difficult to identify any element of the contract whose presence is essential on all occasions (some contracts exist without consideration, some without agreement, some without privity)[60] so

[59] Hart made the same point about the corporation in 'Definition and Theory in Jurisprudence', 1954; and, see Leff, 1970.

[60] Or to put this another way, since what constitutes consideration is subject to inconsistent interpretation, those who take particular views of what it ought

that disputes over whether something is really a contract can be extremely difficult to resolve on occasion. But it is also problematic to respond to such difficulties by abandoning the concept of a contract, since so much of what is communicated, as law, has already been orientated around the use of that concept. Thus, on the one hand, the law of contract can appear as an exercise in ideology: an incoherent body of rules and principles that cannot be organised into a rational statement of organised principles, and that has no relationship with anything in the physical world or the rest of society that can be expressed with any degree of coherence. On the other hand, maintaining the concept as a self-observation of a particular area of legal activity, and using its sub-categories to organise other legal communications (including the resolution of disputes and the making of legal arguments) continues to facilitate the production of legal communications.[61]

to entail have to concede that the courts have on occasion recognised contracts which lack consideration. Similarly, those who take a strong view of the level of shared intentions necessary to found agreement will have to view contracts recognised with lesser mutuality of intention as contracts lacking agreement, etc (see Dalton, 1985).

[61] This need structures the communications of parties who seek decisions from the courts. To have a legal dispute the parties need to formulate their argument in a manner that is capable of resolution by the court. The plaintiff will present a claim that the facts are A, and that the norms are B, and that this entitles persons in position C (shared by the plaintiff) to an order from the court in the form D. The defendant may simply deny that the facts are A. But if, in addition, she/he wishes to challenge propositions B to D, she/he will have to advance her/his own interpretation of the relevant norms. Whatever the possibilities of further legal arguments within the legal system as a whole, this dispute will normally involve only a choice between, and a ruling upon, the choices offered by these parties. The working principle is one of hypothetical certainty, whereby each party will claim that on the basis of their arguments and evidence, they are entitled to a ruling in their favour. The court will rule 'as if' any person in the winning party's position was entitled to the order sought ie as if the rest of the legal universe had the fixed points adopted by the parties (plus any further fixed points adopted by a judge on the occasions when she/he wishes to consider an argument not offered by the parties), and the ruling established, once and for all, the correct position between them. See MacCormick, 1987.

The legal system, as a complex system, requires large amounts of redundancy in order to communicate variety. And a significant part of this redundancy is the wealth of structures within law that account for past applications of the code legal/illegal. Conceptual categories form a major part of this— common law doctrines, doctrines about statutory interpretation, of precedent, etc. All of the communications that can repeatedly be used to identify something as legal, or to identify what might be novel within a legal communication, can be described as redundancy. Like the example of the use of the 24-hour (60 minutes to an hour, 60 seconds to a minute) system of communicating about time, it is impossible to dispense with all of this redundancy without a substantial cost in terms of the ability of the system to continue reproducing itself. And it is actually impossible to conceive of a legal communication that could require the abandonment of all of this redundancy all at once, since there would be no basis for such a communication to establish itself as a legal communication (nothing that could identify itself as belonging to the legal system).

This distinction between redundancy and variety has implications for the nature of legal arguments. Legal arguments utilise doctrine as fixed points from which to establish reasons. No legal argument can unravel all that has been constructed within the legal system. The precondition of legal communication is that the communication must be recognised as a legal communication, and must link to something also recognised as a legal communication. This precondition is incorporated into legal argument. There must be a selection of something that will not be deconstructed further, but will be reasoned from.[62] And in making selections, one is not involved in what can be understood as a free choice. One can argue for something that has qualities

[62] Such points overcome the fact that only the system can identify a communication as legal, but the system as a totality cannot be connected to, or by, a single communication. The system produces structures that can be used as a local basis for connection. Thus it remains true to say that the system as a whole produces the conditions of connection (since the current state of the system at any moment includes all of its structures) and that connections remain local.

of redundancy (something repeatedly utilised to create varieties of legal meanings) to be itself varied (to lose its status as redundancy). But in so doing, one raises a cost for the system in terms of what can henceforth be communicated within the system.[63]

Consider, for example, the difficulties of the doctrine of statutory construction that requires courts to seek the intention of the legislature. The legislature (as a political system) exhibits nothing that can be adequately described as a unitary intention. And, if the attempts to present the courts as inferior to the legislature can be shown to be based on ideological constructs, can we dispense with them, and begin to make clearer choices about the law that is appropriate to our society? The answer is no, because this doctrine is not simply an ideological construct. It has major effects in terms of organising legal communications, including legal arguments. The doctrine is part of a method for comparing common law doctrines and statutes. Some forms of secondary observation allow for much greater variety of primary observation than would otherwise be possible. So, for example, having applications of the code that do not constitute precedents allows for secondary observations that account for previous decisions without having to find a consistent set of substantive reasons for each decision. The consistent explanation for decisions that have no status as precedents is that their status means that one is not required to give a consistent explanation; and similarly with statutes. Whereas common law reasoning pre-supposes consistent explanations for decisions of a particular kind (based on generalised reasons), statutes allow for new starts, new exceptions. The supremacy of statute over common law allows courts to come to extremely particular decisions that do not create the same need for generalised reasons as would occur within

---

[63] See Luhmann, 2004, 328. Kelman seems to recognise something similar when he says: '. . . internal contradictions . . . do not render daily outcomes wholly unpredictable or random, but simply that commitments to principles that undermine that practice are invariably available. Inertia is powerful; much practice is extremely predictable in the short run because we know that proposed decisions that would greatly change the world will be considered either wrong or too political for lawyers to accomplish.' (1987, 258).

common law decisions.[64] From this perspective the doctrine of legislative intention is simply a communication that describes many other linked communications that in turn facilitate the making of new (variety) legal communications. Given the evolution of our legal system, there is a vast amount of redundancy created by consistent communications about statutes (including consistent self-descriptions of those communications by the legal system to itself as a relationship of legislative hierarchy). Dispensing with statutory supremacy would undo much of this redundancy. As such, one does not have to account for the presence and regular invocation of the doctrine of parliamentary sovereignty in terms of a judicial subservience to the legislature, or an ideological cloak for the supremacy of the judiciary. Nor can the removal of particular doctrines such as this be presented as a matter of choice. Removal of redundancy has a cost in terms of what can henceforth be communicated. At this point in our system, it would be extremely difficult to make sense of our law without assuming that statutes provide new law in this way. For this reason, even the most hardened anti-democratic elitist judge is forced (if she/he wishes to make successful legal communications) to acknowledge the supremacy of parliament (the ability of statutes to make new law even in the face of common law and prior statutes). Interpreting statutes as merely declaratory, or codifications of the existing law (once the normal interpretation of statutes) is no longer considered an appropriate possibility, unless a judge can point to legal communications supporting such an interpretation (Law Commission reports, etc). The earlier interpretation of statutes as declaratory, if applied wholesale, would collapse much of our existing law.[65]

[64] Variety is facilitated by the *ability* to make a new start. The claim is not that decisions on statutes will not follow the pre-existing common law closely (this is one interpretative possibility). Nor are we denying that decisions interpreting statutory provisions build up as a form of common law. But unless the statute is interpreted as a nullity, it is taken to change the common law and earlier statutes in some way, and to be, in itself, a sufficient reason for that change (allowing interpretations of decisions that are not otherwise consistent with earlier decisions).

[65] See our arguments on the relationship between the common law and legislation in ch 3.

This distinction (redundancy/variety) within communication has implications for our understanding of legal reasoning, and the part played within such reasoning by what might, from a CLS perspective, be called ideological self-descriptions. Doctrines arise as secondary observations of past applications of the code. Doctrines may account for large numbers of primary observations. In so doing, they may include not only rules, but also exceptions to rules, and exceptions that grow into sub-rules, with exceptions to them in turn. These doctrines may become extremely technical and complicated, and the twists and turns of their development may represent quite arbitrary choices between values. The need to choose (to make decisions even when there are insufficient reasons for choosing between alternatives) will not produce a doctrinal statement that represents a consistent application of substantive values, or even a consistent application of procedural values (since any attempt to account for a certain coding as procedural, will still generate procedural decisions for which there is no good reason for choosing amongst alternatives). Nevertheless, these twists and turns provide a local basis for making further communications and, in particular, they structure the possibilities of legal argument.[66] If an issue can be decided by making a distinction to establish a sub-rule of a particular area of doctrine, there may be less damage to the redundancy of the system than if one argues for removal of the major rule of which this sub-rule is a part. In turn, if one develops the doctrine through articulating this exception, one may also have added to the

---

[66] Compare this description with Kelman's statement of the CLS position on the nature of rules: 'CLS adherents have modified this [realist] claim [that legal rules were utterly vacuous and question begging] to a significant degree. It *is* possible to establish legal rules, increasingly detailed in covering available cases, that can become mechanically applicable to the vast bulk of actual controversies, but *practice* may well become settled only at the cost of *principled doctrine* becoming chaotic.' (1987, 46).

redundancy that will be lost if the major rule is overruled at a future date.[67]

This account of the legal system points to what is often described as its inherent conservatism: a favouring of the status quo. Those who argue for change within the legal system have to do so by arguments (communications) that are legal. Bald statements that some decision is unfair, or contrary to the interests of the working class, or against the wishes of the prime minister, or contrary to the changing nature of family relationships, will not, unless there is some existing structure that allows such matters to be recognised (such as a statute promoting working class housing, etc) as legal arguments. This need to link arguments to what are already recognisable legal communications serves to prevent many communications (from within both the legal system and its environment) from forming reasons for decisions within the legal system. As rationalisations of earlier decisions, doctrines remove the need to go further back into the history of the legal system. Unless the doctrine relied on as redundancy is challenged in the case in question, the primary observations that are rationalised by the doctrine need not themselves be revisited. In addition, doctrines structure the ability to utilise communications generated outside the legal system from operating as arguments within the legal system. This has already been described in the earlier discussion of the relationship between the political ideology of feminism and legal issues. The selecting mechanism for recognising communications as existing law, or relevant facts, remains the legal system itself, even when the legal system describes that selection to itself as a direct (and subservient) response to matters outside itself (bowing to

---

[67] Considerations of redundancy do not always favour the generation of further exceptions rather than overturning a major rule. The inability to give consistent explanations for exceptions, either in terms of the interests served or relationships between doctrines, may create a situation where overruling provides more reusable redundancy than elaborating further exceptions. On this see Eisenberg, 1988, ch 7 'Overruling and Other Modes of Overturning'.

the will of parliament, responding to developments within society, etc).[68]

The use of doctrines within legal argument should not be understood as reasoning solely by reference to legal concepts. This form of argumentation has its effects, but it would produce a legal system that has lesser capacity to evolve (to introduce variety that produces new redundancy) than operates within existing legal systems. Legal reasoning also involves consideration of consequences, and responses to interests. Concepts are re-examined as reasons (secondary observation) in terms of how they produce consequences, or serve interests. Where considered unsatisfactory, such juxtapositions of concepts, interests and consequences represent reasons for variety that can alter secondary observations of past decisions, and trigger new developments. But does this concession mean that variation and redundancy are simply a response to matters outside the legal system (consequences and interests), and does this undermine the claim of operative closure?[69] It would not be possible for the legal system to respond to *all* of the interests of society, or to take account of all of the consequences arising from its own communications, and make these consequences part of its own deliberations. The impossibility is apparent as soon as one thinks about the totality of interests that exist outside of law, and the infinity of possible consequences that can follow from any given event. The legal system cannot know all the interests that may be affected by any decision. Nor can it take any selection of these interests and apply a calculus that allows it to 'weigh' these

---

[68] Consider, for example, the views of Lawrence Friedman: 'Is law like language? Formal legal thought, in general, assumes that it is. But the example just given—the Russian Revolution—suggests the opposite. Law will be plastic and responsive to social force—most especially when people think so.' (Friedman, 1977, 95).

[69] Supporting views such as: 'The process is one in which the ideas of community and of the social sciences, whether correct or not, as they win acceptance in the community, control legal decisions.' (Levi, 1949, 6). Although Levi also admits that this 'control' is only momentary as, once adopted by the legal system, the ideas begin to mutate through the use of reasoning by analogy (secondary observation). See also Friedman, 1977.

interests against each other. Rather the legal system, in establishing what constitutes a legal issue, also identifies what interests it will recognise as constituting reasons for its decisions. And these interests are themselves not simply given by other systems of communication, but are constructed out of the process of secondary observation: what generalised descriptions can be given of the claims (facts) that law has recognised as open to its consideration in disputes of this kind.[70] In a similar vein, law has no access to the consequences of its decisions in terms of the ramifications of causes and effects within society, many of which will be latent. What the law can know, with considerable certainty, is the likely legal consequences of its decisions: the reconfiguration of doctrine (redundancy) that follows from decisions one way or another.[71]

To re-use an earlier example, if the doctrine of co-ownership is altered to allow cohabitation with children to generate equitable rights against a partner's legal property, then the legal system cannot know the contribution of this to the emancipation of women, or the solvency of companies offering secured credit.

---

[70] At the highest level of generalisation one can attempt to articulate general lists of interests recognised by the legal system as a whole. (See, for example, Pound, 1943.) But describing the legal system as a totality that recognises and weighs social interests in general can only be a communication of self-description. And while such self-descriptions have their effects in terms of facilitating redundancy and variety within the system (and are not adequately described as simply ideologies), they do not actually describe the recognition of interests within law's routine operations, which are always orientated around fixed points (redundancy), which inevitably makes those recognitions local.

[71] See Luhmann, 2004, 334–6. Note that this does not lead to law having a peculiar form of reasoning. What is thought of as legal reasoning is the selection by law of what can be argued: 'First, it is reasoning that is undertaken by those whom the law has given the task of resolving disputes that require legal resolutions: "undertaken according to law, for the law requires courts to reach decisions through such [ordinary evaluative] reasoning." . . . secondly, it is also necessary that those to whom the law has given this task perform this task by employing ordinary evaluative reasoning in a manner that the law permits: "reasoning according to law, reasoning that imports moral and other premises in accordance with the role they have by law, or at any rate consistently with the law."' (Halpin, 2001, 39, quoting Raz, 1998, 5–6).

But it can calculate, to a much higher degree of certainty, the possible knock on effects for the law on property, mortgages, insolvency, gifts and inheritance. In so doing, the legal system can also have regard to the interests that it recognises, one of which is the value represented by secondary observation: the need to treat like case alike. In so doing, the legal system presents itself to itself as an interest. How much uncertainty (loss of redundancy) will be generated by a decision of this kind? How much of the knock on effects can be immediately known, and how much will clearly have to be worked out from further decisions for which there will be no good reasons to decide either way?[72] (Will it apply to all assets or only family homes? Will it apply to all sexual relationships or only heterosexual partnerships? Will the coding of legal communications outside of the courts—mortgages, share-dealings, 'honest' applications for credit, etc—be able to take place despite the variety sought to be introduced? Will the new law on co-ownership affect property acquired before the relationship began, or after the relationship ended? How will actors react to these reconfigurations?). This examination of the 'consequences' for the legal system by reference to the web of connections generated by secondary observation of past and hypothetical future decisions creates an observation of 'consequences' that is unique to the legal system. For example, it will not replicate the cost-benefit analysis that might be associated with a political or economic assessment of the likely consequences of a government decision. And in recognising both interests and consequences in this unique way, one that utilises legal concepts in order to establish

---

[72] It should not be assumed that such hypotheticals always reinforce the status quo. Levi, 1949, 8, describes the process as 'circular'. Decisions will be taken for which there is no good reason, and these can produce situations in which the decisions to be accounted for in secondary observation do not fit easily within the previous doctrinal categories. In such situations, earlier categories cease to contribute redundancy to the system. In these circumstances, making a new start, and allowing a new doctrinal classification to unfold without a clear sense of its legal consequences, may represent little loss of redundancy. See, for example, Levi's description of the evolution of tort law, 8–27.

both the interests to be recognised and the manner in which those interests are likely to be affected, the legal system retains its autonomy. It is not overwhelmed by the totality of communications that could be brought to bear when it needs to deliberate (secondary observation) on the interests that its decisions might affect, and what the effects of its decisions might be. And if one can understand and accept that the basis of selection and weighing of interests remains unique to the legal system—and would not occur in any system except the legal system—one can understand the counter-intuitive claim that expresses the nature of operative closure: law not only selects which communications constitute legal communications, but in so doing, it identifies itself as the legal system, and at the same time identifies (and constructs) its environment. As with the example of the statute, the generation of communications that constitute the environment of law can arise outside of the legal system, but the selection of communications, and the meaning given to those communications by the manner of their selection, remains unique to law. This allows it to react to the rest of society (cognitive openness) without losing the ability to reproduce itself (autonomy), something that it achieves through its secondary observations (which constantly elaborate its normative closure).[73]

Analysis of law's communication by reference to redundancy and variety is not a self-description of the legal system. It is a distinction that operates within all communication, and can be used to analyse all systems of communication. As such it does

---

[73] Luhmann calls this construction of interests and consequences by reference to interlocking legal relationships 'legal imagination'. Unger has famously criticised lawyers for their lack of imagination, in failing to see how legal decisions could be other than they currently are, and has proposed 'legal analysis as institutional imagination'. (Unger 1996, especially 129–182). Systems theory suggests that what Unger criticises is not due to personal cognitive failings, or likely to be changed by personal enlightenment. One has to understand how the legal imagination is constructed through the system, to understand why it has it own particular form. Of course, from the perspective of another observing system, any system's 'imagination' may be described as limited, simply because it fails to see possibilities that the other system would recognise.

not offer an inherently superior description of legal reasoning to that offered by those who seek to synthesise the justifications offered in the courts, whether these be by judges or legal academics. If the point of such descriptions is taken to be the ability to predict when appellate court judges are likely to develop the law, then the need to retain redundancy in order to produce variety tells one little about which appellate court communications, at any point in the legal system, are likely to result in new forms of variety. And from this perspective, many of the contested accounts of this process will have more predictive power than systems theory can hope to offer. However, what systems theory tells one is that these various descriptions of the elements that make up legal reasoning, and the manner in which they combine and lead to evolutions of doctrine, are observations from within the legal system. For example, when Eisenberg, in his 'generative' theory of the common law, accounts for the stability of judicial norms in terms of social congruence between doctrine and social interests on which there is consensus (at least in terms of the communications received by judges), inter-system consistency in the use of legal concepts, and stable doctrine, this is a much richer description than the simple term 'redundancy'. And it may have greater descriptive power than theories such as that of Dworkin,[74] or other rival accounts of the nature of stare decisis.[75] But what systems theory tells us is that all of these theories refer to observations that take place from positions generated within the legal system. So, the 'interests' that have to be congruent, as well as the doctrines that need to be judged as stable, and the inter-systemic relationships that have to be assessed as consistent, are selections of communications made by the legal system itself, and could not be made by any other system. And as such, systems theory by alerting us to what these theories are generalisations of, also alerts us to the

[74] Whether in his earlier writings such as *Taking Rights Seriously* or later writing such as *Laws Empire*.
[75] See generally essays in volumes such as Goldstein, 1987; MacCormick and Summers, 1997.

reasons why such theories have a limited predictive power, and remain matters for endless contestation.

Returning now to the CLS description of legal reasoning, as set out by Kelman, how does the analysis using the distinction redundancy/variety compare? Kelman's fourth point was that principles seen as dominant within the legal system favour groups seen as dominant within the economic, political, media systems, etc. Systems theory recognises that the redundancy found within the legal system is not neutral. There is a social cost (winners and losers) resulting from the establishment and utilisation of redundancy. But systems theory invites one to go beyond the calculation of the social costs of legal forms, to trace the manner in which different systems utilise each other's communications. For example, there are good reasons (found within the economic system) why variety within law may impact less adversely on groups commonly described as dominant. Where the law is unclear, and large sums of money are involved, a considerable part of the expertise of lawyers is employed by business enterprises in procuring legal forms that avoid uncertainty. We can also expect that, where litigation cannot be avoided, those who have access to wealth are more able to repeatedly litigate (or lobby for statutory changes). As a form of sociology, the crude observation that law is not neutral is no substitute for careful tracking through of the processes through which systems induce changes in each other.

Kelman's first and second points are not challenged by systems theory. But his third point deserves development. To repeat it:

> Critics have attempted to show that mainstream thought invariably treats one term in each set of contradictory impulses as *privileged* in three distinct senses. The privileged term is presumptively entitled as a normative matter to govern disputes; it is simply assumed, as a descriptive matter, to govern the bulk of situations; and most subtly, but perhaps most significantly, departures from the purportedly dominant norm, even if they are obviously frequent, are treated as *exceptional*, in need of special justification, a bit chaotic.[76]

[76] Kelman, 1987, as n 51 above.

The claim that doctrines operate through privileging, and that rules operate subject to exceptions that cannot be fully articulated in the form of sub-rules, is not contradicted by systems theory analysis.[77] And Kelman is right to point out that an onus is placed upon communications that urge variety, and seek to displace redundancy. The displacement has to be justified both in terms of demonstrating that it is worth doing, and demonstrating how legal communications can continue to be made (what new redundancies can replace the replaced ones). Indeed, in acknowledging this onus, Kelman is not so very distant from more conventional descriptions of doctrinal development that describe redundancies being displaced when they no longer facilitate the making of legal communications, or inhibit the system's perceived ability to dispose of disputes over interests it has come to recognise.

CLS as Self-Description

The process of generalising from secondary observations produces understandings of relationships between law and society that are unique to law: self-descriptions. Self-descriptions necessarily involve a description of the legal system, and its environment. Law can only describe itself, to itself, through distinctions: distinguishing itself from what it is not.[78] The contingency (lack of sufficient reasons for deciding what must

[77] Exceptionality often offers the 'balance' that 'weighing' principles cannot. The subordinate principle cannot operate in any situation where its generalised application would displace the dominant one. This can generate redundancy—easy cases—where, if the dominant principle were not applied, it would be difficult to understand this part of the system as meaningfully being structured by that dominant principle. An example of the operation of such hierarchies can be found in unfair dismissal. This is not decided on the basis of what is reasonable (which could lead to the tribunal system being overwhelmed) but what dismissals are unreasonable. This standard presumes that dismissal per se is allowed (as does the notion of 'unfair' dismissal) but removes adjudication from a position of endless variety (what is reasonable) to one of considerable redundancy. For a discussion of this move within the law of unfair dismissal, see Collins, 1992.

[78] So, if law is described as a system of social rules, the immediate question is: what distinguishes legal rules from social rules? If law is a kind of reasoning, how is it different from other kinds of reasoning, etc?

be decided) of legal decisions, and the manner in which law selects communications both in order to create its environment and to account for the decisions taken in response to it, generate the legal system's own version of society and law's relationship to the social.[79]

CLS can be seen as an attempt to expose self-description, to reveal that such descriptions do not dictate the results that they purport to justify. But from a systems theory perspective, which starts with the paradox that there is no value that can interpose itself between the distinction legal/illegal to determine its

[79] Which can include a legal version of the moral. Finnis, criticising Unger, acknowledges the lack of determining reasons for legal decisions, yet claims that the process of evolution produced through legal decisions can maintain a coherent relationship to general moral ideas and values: 'Architects, musicians, legislators, and jurists specify and particularize general ideals, commitments and principles, by steps none of which is itself necessary and all of which could reasonably have been in some respect different—so that there is, in these myriads of instances, no uniquely correct solution. Yet all of these steps are reasonable (when things are being done well), and none could without risk of *error* have been taken randomly or without regard to coherence with the larger whole constituted both by the initial general idea or ideas of value, commitment, or principle, and by the steps already taken. It is this requirement of coherence— of the integrity of the system both as a set of rules and principles extending analogously over many different but comparable forms of relationship and transaction, and as a set of interrelated institutions (such as a hierarchy of courts, themselves more or less subject to legislatures)—that distinguishes legal thought from 'open-ended' practical reasoning.' (Finnis, 1987, 160–1). Of course errors will occur, and decisions will be taken that are not reasonable (both of which will still form the basis of later observation). But aside from this, a legal system is not an unfolding of general ideas through steps. Closure occurs when the basis of selection of communications is made by the legal system. Thereafter the possibilities (selection) of moral communications as justifications for decisions are determined by the legal system itself. Intermittent, or even regular selection of moral communications by a system ('interrelated institutions') that is able to subvert and suppress substantive moral reasons when its own redundant communications require it to do so, generates a form of morality that can be understood sociologically with some precision. Describing these operations as an exercise in practical reasoning altered to take account of interrelated institutional arrangements is an alternative description but one that we feel has less explanatory power. For a powerful metaphorical description of this point (God's will subverted by the institutional arrangements God put in place to decide what God wants) see Teubner, 1993b.

application on all occasions, this exposure is no surprise. Indeed, much of the evolution of the legal system is attributed to its attempts to defuse and diffuse this paradox by ever more complicated programmes for the application of the code. Nevertheless, it cannot be denied that CLS takes self-description seriously. Indeed Unger, in his writings, even acknowledges that such self-descriptions are autological. They are part of what they are seeking to describe. As such, if altered, they offer the prospect of changes to the possibility of what will be legal and, with this, changes to law's relationship to the social.[80] However, in its treatment of self-description, much CLS writing is content to assess law in terms of the claims to describe itself, by identifying gaps between those descriptions and the operations they purport to describe.[81] For example, in its potential (if not

[80] With Unger's proposals for deviationist doctrine, we have a programme in which changes to the selection of dominant legal principles are expected to alter the construction of social relations which law helps to constitute, and from which it draws its resources for rationalisations of its own forms.

[81] For an example of CLS analysis that deconstructs self-description, but fails to examine how self-description relates to secondary observations occurring within the system, consider Kelman's discussion of Nozick's defence of the doctrine of duress. Nozick tries to identify duress as threats, and threats as propositions one would rather not hear. Kelman points out (rightly) that this analysis presumes what it aims to demonstrate. If one had no right to shoot people, they would rather not hear the alternative ('hand over your money'). If they have a right to shoot you, you will be very interested in hearing the alternative. This is a criticism of self-description (an attempt to make sense of a legal distinction by reference to standards that are presented as if they existed outside of the legal system, and were in some sense pre-legal). But it ignores the fact that such distinctions are drawn against a vast background of already privileged positions (redundancy) whereby the legal system has established what parties can and cannot do. And in a hard case, these privileged positions are what make sense of the analysis proposed by Nozick: would one welcome a proposition (if the threatened alternative is something the person making the proposition is entitled to do, or is hard to distinguish from things the proposer is entitled to do) or would one rather not hear it (if the threatened alternative is something the proposer is not entitled to do, or hard to distinguish from something the proposer is not entitled to do)? The assessments of what is or is not hard to distinguish may produce arbitrary decisions (for which there is no good reason) but these will still not be the external pre-legal assessments that Nozick's analysis seems to suppose, and Kelman (1987, 23–4) proceeds to deconstruct.

actual) debate with Dworkin[82] over the extent to which law is distinguished from politics, by reference to its mode of legal reasoning, they share a common view of politics. Dworkin's theory of politics is part of law's description of itself. It is a description of how the legal system describes itself as being different from politics: politics is not principles; politics is about choices made in response to vested interests; politics is not objective, etc. This is not a sophisticated model of politics with which to contrast the operations of the legal system. Rather, it represents a focus on one part of the legal system, appellate court decisions, and an attempt to generalise the decision-making processes of the appellate courts to explain law's identity as a totality.[83] The description of politics from which law is distinguished does not focus on any structures within politics that, like the courts, stabilise the identification of what constitutes political communication. Instead, it is a description of law that purports to distinguish law from what it takes to be the nature of communications throughout the political system as a whole. In joining issue with Dworkin, CLS does not move outside this self-description. The CLS reply to Dworkin is not that politics is capable of giving political communications a certainty on occasions which is at least as certain as those of the legal system, or that principles operate within the political system, albeit differently from how they might operate within the legal system. Rather, the challenge from CLS is an attempt to show that this self-description of the legal system does not accurately describe law's operations, because some (or perhaps all) of law's operations share characteristics that law's self-description has attributed to its (political) environment.[84]

---

[82] Unger and Dworkin never debate with each other directly—a point made by Harris, 1989, in which the author attempts to 'bring into sharp focus' their different visions (at 44).

[83] '. . . the legal profession overestimates the importance of interpretation and argumentation precisely because lawyers see the system as belonging to the second-order observation level.' (Luhmann, 2004, 355).

[84] 'Doctrine can exist, according to the formalist view, because of a contrast between the more determinate rationality of legal analysis and the less determinate rationality of ideological contests. This thesis can be restated as the belief that

Autopoiesis, as a sociological theory, not only alerts one to the anti-foundational basis for the legal system, but that this exists within all systems. Each system has to develop its own pro-grammes to overcome the paradox that its own binary code has no meaning except as a distinction, and no way of stabilising the application of that code except by reference to secondary observation on the manner in which it has been applied in the past. Each system develops its own structures for limiting the possibilities of what communications can be made at any point in the system. As such, one needs to be wary of descriptions of communications within any system as 'ideological' rather than real, and even more wary of attempts to present one system as superior to another for being less ideological or objective than that other system.[85]

lawmaking, guided only by the looser and more inconclusive arguments suited to ideological disputes, differs fundamentally from law application. Law-making and law application diverge in both how they work and how their results may properly be justified.' (Unger, 1986, 2). Unger's claim is that no line can be drawn between legal justification and 'open-ended disputes about the basic terms of social life, disputes that people call ideological, philosophical, or vision-ary.' (*Ibid*, 1).

[85] Such superiority (or inferiority) is always communicated from the perspective of the observing system.

7

Law as Sociological Object

Sociological observation on law is not simply critique. Critique is the possibility of observing law using any system of communication that offers insights at variance with the claims that the legal system makes for itself. Critique can show that law is a less satisfactory form of politics than politics, less scientific than science, less artistic than art, less moral than morality, less efficient than economics, etc, etc. Such observation can suggest reforms: more democratic and inclusive legal institutions, greater use of scientific processes within evidence, or economics within judicial training, or ethics within legal education, etc, etc. Observing on law by reference to a system of communication that seeks to show that law is something other than law will give us critique, but what it will not give us is a description that explains how law establishes and maintains itself as an autonomous object, whilst at the same time remaining open to, and part of, the total system of communications that constitutes society. As such, any reforms proposed in connection with such critiques will also fail to have regard to the basis for law's autonomy, with results ranging from 'deafness' (with the legal system failing to make any changes to the criteria it uses for its selection of communications) to distortion or 'misreading', whereby proposals presented in a form that can be selected by law are nevertheless given meanings which vary, often in quite unexpected ways, from the meanings present within the observing system—the background critique—that generated them.

Systems theory observes law as a system that constructs itself, and observes other systems, such as economics, politics, the media and science as systems that similarly construct themselves. Closure is a feature of all systems, as is paradox. Systems develop conditional programmes for the application of their own codes, which programmes never resolve the absence of any value that can account for the application of each system's code on *every* occasion when it is applied. All these programmes do is endlessly apply and account for the application of their integral distinction, and thus constantly 'unfold' their paradox through their own operations. Operations applying a system's codes are open to observation by that system (self-observation), and at a higher or more abstract level of observation such self-observations produce self-descriptions. Self-descriptions are not only constructed by the system, but operate within the system, to stabilise but not determine the operations that produce them.

What this description of systems theory seeks to remind the reader is that systems theory allows self-descriptions (including law's self-description, jurisprudence) to be examined sociologically. One does not only need to ask—as occurs within much debate within jurisprudence as well as debate generated by external critiques—whether a jurisprudential theory is a full or incomplete representation of law's practices. Arguments of this kind about representation give precedence to the perspective of the observer: what does the observer regard as so important that any particular rival description appears incomplete? Such approaches cannot avoid what Dworkin has called the semantic sting.[1] And, in picking whatever is considered to be important within a system, and seeking to present such a feature as a, or the, central feature of that system, there is no boundary with critique. Any jurisprudence that is not felt to exhibit the 'central' characteristic is claimed to be an inadequate or incomplete example of the system. So, for example, we have Hart's presentation of municipal legal systems as 'central cases',[2] and Finnis' presentation of the moral legal system as the 'focal' meaning of law,[3] with the implicit 'critique' that international/bad legal systems are lesser examples of the 'real' thing. More extreme

---

[1] Dworkin, 1986, 45–6, summarising ch 1.

[2] For Hart on international law, see Hart 1961, ch X.

[3] Finnis 1980, 276–81.

critiques, such as the assertion by economic analysis of law that the legal system is 'really' a mechanism for the distribution of resources, lie along the same continuum.[4] Only some sociological theories can move us beyond rhetorical claims about importance and significance. Systems theory takes seriously the legal system's own identification of what is important. This is not simply a matter of accepting what is claimed by the system. The focus is not on rhetoric (semantics) but operations: looking at how the system creates its own identity (its own sense of itself) through its own recurring operations. And looking at how such operations (communications), at the most general level, exist as self-descriptions. 'Importance', when applying such a theory, is not a value judgement, but the conclusion of empirical investigations into concept formation: identifying what communications are generated by what operations. How do they come into being, and what work do they do? This approach to the study of law provides one answer to the puzzle that has occupied those, such as Cotterrell,[5] who have observed the gap between legal theories that seek to organise law's self-understandings, and those sociological and other theories that predominantly fail to take those self-understandings seriously.

We hope that this book has demonstrated the potential of systems theory to offer sociological insights into different jurisprudential theories, and their respective attempts to present particular operations of the legal system as the whole of the legal system. Our most systematic application of systems theory to jurisprudence is chapter three, where we were able to trace the development of law's communications about itself, and suggest what operations within law led to the development of a new self-description, that of legal positivism. Our discussion of the evolution of law's self-description from natural law to legal positivism argued that this change was generated internally: that when the legal system began to experience frequent and particular changes of law it could not organise its own operations in

---

[4] For an introduction, see Nobles, 2002.

[5] Cotterrell, 1998, and further examples from his writings as set out in ch 1.

terms of natural law, but developed self-understandings in terms of authoritative sources. Our discussion of justice and modern natural law in chapter four demonstrated that justice, as an *eigenvalue*, cannot be removed from the legal system, as it is generated by (and in turn stabilises) law's own operations. Neither side in the 'great debate' between natural law and legal positivism can expect a complete victory. Our discussion of Kelsen and closure, engaged with a jurisprudence that treats as central law's description of itself to itself as norms, and its environment as facts. This distinction is essential to law's ability to organise its own operations, but it remains an internal distinction within its own communications. There is no fact/norm distinction outside of law's operations that allows the legal system to exist as only one part of this distinction. This is because facts, as well as norms, are constructed by the legal system through its own communications, while other systems do or do not construct their own fact/norm distinctions within their own operations and coding. And in our chapter on the critical legal studies movement, we presented a challenge to the justifying premise of critical legal theories that law's indeterminacy means that it has no fixed boundary with politics but rather that law *is* politics. As the title of the chapter indicates, we dispute that assertion. Law's politics involves law's construction of politics, which marks a clear boundary between legal communications and those communications generated by the political system.

These insights, through the application of a sociological theory, systems theory, to jurisprudence, go some way to narrowing the gap between legal theory and sociology of law as it has been identified by commentators such as Cotterrell.[6] Systems theory's description of jurisprudence has greater descriptive potential than other sociological accounts of law, because it takes the system it is seeking to describe seriously. It does not simply seek to apply its own organising categories (class, interests, race,

---

[6] Cotterrell, 1998; and see, in particular, Banakar 2000, who proposes a different solution (although not, in our opinion, one likely to be fruitful), based on a different approach to the one we have developed in this book.

sex, etc) and methodologies (most notably statistics)[7] and seek to re-describe law in ways that law does not utilise within its own communications. In this sense systems theory, compared to other sociological theories, provides a fuller sociological description of its object. The gap with jurisprudence is narrowed using systems theory, because traditional sociological approaches have little or nothing to say about jurisprudence, beyond seeing it as an ideological construct which serves to obscure what sociology can reveal (the class, interests, race, sex, etc, basis of law's operations).[8] More sophisticated sociological approaches, like those generated by Weber's hermeneutic methodology (or more recently non or anti-positivistic narrative or rhetorical methodologies),[9] organise themselves around individual actors, and not systems. Again, this approach offers little purchase on theories that purport to present the legal system as a unity. Descriptive sociology along these lines (as opposed to claims to apply it from an Oxford armchair à la Hart)[10] leads to the fragmentation of law into the perspectives of its innumerable actors. From this multiplicity of points of observation, legal theories that attempt to present a single account of the system inevitably appear simplistic representations of reality which, if not ideological, operate only as 'ideal types' available to the sociologist to orientate description of a far more complex reality.[11]

However, in the context of the theory we are using, the concept of a 'gap' has a quite different significance, and the possibility of its being 'narrowed' is quite problematic. A better

---

[7] For example, see Luhmann, 2004, 47.

[8] *Ibid*, 456–7. That said, however, the possibilities of identifying the way in which social stratification could have implications for functioning subsystems, including law, can be considered. Such an exercise would need to utilise the distinction: inclusion/exclusion, and be carefully constructed. Luhmann in the last pages of *Law as a Social System*, 488–90 speculates on how such an analysis could be developed.

[9] See Nelken, 1996.

[10] Lacey, 2004, 229, uses this characterisation of Hart's descriptive sociology, as expressed by critics of *The Concept of Law*.

[11] For a succinct statement of Weber's sociology of law, his social action analysis, hermeneutic approach, ideal types, etc, see Cotterrell, 1992, 148–157.

sociology of law applies a theory that, within a basis of assessment established by sociology, gives a better description of what it observes. And the ability of systems theory to describe law's operations, *including* jurisprudence, therefore offers a superior sociology of law to one that does not. But we have not escaped from the level of critique. Being able to describe and explain legal theories sociologically does not mean that the gap between the two has narrowed in any sense compatible with the application of systems theory. This is not just because systems are closed to each other (so we always end up where we begin); but because the relationship between systems (sociology, as for example sometimes understood, as a branch of science and jurisprudence, as here understood, as part of the legal system) cannot be narrowed or widened by the semantic compatibility of the respective theories. Relationships between systems, like relationships within systems, can only be understood in terms of each system's operations. These are not semantic relationships. In order to talk about narrowing the 'gap' between jurisprudence and sociology or sociological theory, in terms of the relationship between two systems, we have to understand the nature and difficulties of such relationships. Which requires us, at this late stage, to introduce the reader to yet another concept within systems theory: structural coupling.

Structural Coupling

Closure does not allow the relationship between different systems to be one of input and output. Law is not a simple or trivial output of political inputs, just as much as economics is obviously not an output of legal inputs. None of these systems *determines* the other in such a simple way. The communications of one system cannot be simple inputs into another because a communication from one system cannot retain the same meaning when it is selected as a communication within another system. The second system will select a communication for re-use by reference to its own conditional programmes and in order to apply its own code. We might say that the meaning of the

216

communication is changed, by being re-used. Or, to state the process in a more rigorous manner, we should say that the communication only exists as a communication within the second system because the second system has identified it as a communication that connects to itself—that it identifies it as one of its own. However, this process might not prevent us from talking of inputs if every time a communication occurred in one system it was re-selected by another system in a different but nevertheless consistently identical manner—as if communications could exhibit something like a standard deviation within another system every time they were re-used within that other system. But, what we have learned about systems makes this impossible. A communication connects to a system at a particular point in that system, but at the same time, the possibilities of connection are established by the state of the whole of that system at that moment (with systems changing from moment to moment and each system developing at its own rate and along its own trajectories). A communication is selected on the basis of the conditional programmes of that system, and is used in connection with the application of its code. A communication from a different system will have been selected by that system by reference to its own programmes, and used in connection with the application of its own code. Not only will this always result in some change of meaning (sometimes subtle, sometimes gross) but also some communications from one system will not be selected by another system at all. For example, some political communications have no legal significance, and vice versa. (This process was illustrated in chapter two, with our discussion of the use of scientific tests in legal cases, in chapter four, with our discussion of law's re-use of moral communications, and again in chapter six, when we discussed how the legal system selected some political communications for re-use as legal communications). The fact that systems are closed to each other in this way does not mean that they cannot have effects upon each other. In particular, it does not prevent communications from one system from inducing communications within another. On the contrary, closure is what makes it possible for systems to influence (be open to) each other, without losing their autonomy ie their ability to process billions of communications, which they identify as belonging to themselves, in a single moment.

Structural coupling refers to the relationships that come about between closed systems whereby each develops expectations as to the communications that will occur in the other at the same moment. To quote Luhmann: '[C]oupling mechanisms are called structural couplings if a system presupposes certain features of its environment on an ongoing basis . . .'.[12] We have already provided one example of structural coupling in our discussion of statutes in chapter six. The political system expects the legal system to generate certain interpretative techniques in response to the texts that it generates through the passage of parliamentary bills. The nature of this relationship can be understood if one imagines, for example, an encounter between two tribes who do not speak each other's language. Assume that one tribe found that every time a metal cross was left at a particular spot, it was replaced within one week by a quantity of gold. This recurring event might, within one tribe, be experienced as trading, and within the other, as a religious rite. Over time one tribe might build a temple orientated around the religious 'miracle' of deposited crosses, whilst the other build a vast iron works for the production of metal crosses. As neither tribe (or ourselves given the poverty of this hypothetical) knows what processes result in the replacement of their offering by its substitute, we cannot claim that the relationship of substitution is mechanical. Nor can we assert that the deposit of crosses determines the deposit of gold, or vice versa. But if, for whatever reason, the actions of one tribe generate a predictable response within the other, then there is potential within each tribe to invest more in relationships that are facilitated by the substituted materials: temples within one tribe, manufacturing processes within the other.

What this short story is meant to draw out is that neither shared communication, nor causality, is a prerequisite to stable and productive relationships between separate systems. The

[12] Luhmann, 2004, 382.

term used within systems theory to describe the process whereby closed systems induce reactions in each other without the necessity for shared meanings, or relationships determined by causality, is 'irritation'. Irritation is any operation (communication) induced in one system by events that are attributed to its environment: the physical world, other subsystems, or general social communication. For systems to irritate each other, an operation of one must be treated as an event by the other, and vice versa. Where irritations become regular and predictable, such that operations within one system are expected to trigger responses in another (and vice versa) one can talk of structural coupling. The term is apt, as what occurs is indeed a coupling of structures. Structures (such things as rules or norms within the legal system, and prices within the economic system) are a precondition for each system to have expectations of the other. Without such structures, there could be no communications generated within each of these systems, because there would be nothing that would enable each system to recognise what occurs within the other as a significant event. (The religious communications of one tribe allows it to respond to crosses, and the economic communications of the other leads it to understand itself as undertaking trades). Moments of mutual irritation represent opportunities for each system to develop further structures that increase the mutual triggering of operations. It is these *ongoing* mutual couplings that constitute relationships of structural coupling. There is always an ambiguity of identity involved in coupling between systems, whether this occurs on an occasional or ongoing basis. This is because the event is selected (identified) only through the separate recursive operations of each system. Thus even where the same language is involved, this will not mean the same thing in each system. For example, contract in the economic system is a transaction involving exchange which alters the possibilities for payments to be made, while in the legal system it is a (re)configuration of legal relationships. The contract as an event takes place at the same time in both systems. The contract represents a configuration of costs and benefits within the economic system (can a party afford to breach the contract?) whilst it represents an array of duties and powers within the legal system (is a party under a duty to comply with the contract, or to pay damages if the contract is breached?). The separate meanings can never be reduced to each other (the cost and benefits of the contract within the economic system are affected by legal duties but cannot be reduced to them, or vice versa). Despite all these differences of meaning, a contract still gives a stability to the economic system: it allows the economic system to communicate about the costs and benefits of something that it identifies as relevant to, but different from, itself.

Systems theory, with its concept of structural coupling, offers a different answer from other sociological theories to the question of relationships between law and the rest of society. It is not an arid answer, whatever the challenge represented by the terminology employed. Nor is it a reductive answer, in the sense that these relationships are reducible to general meta-variables such as class, interest, race or sex. It is, in fact, both a complex and empirical answer. One has to examine the self-referential generation of meanings within separate systems in order to study their relationships. One needs to find out what was communicated as meaningful within the political system, and what in turn (if anything) was communicated as meaningful within the legal system, to find out how these systems have influenced each other. Similar investigations can be undertaken with reference to law and the economic system, the media, science, etc. One commences such empirical investigations with an understanding that even when common language and terms are utilised in both they are not sharing a common meaning (though one can speak of productive or creative misreading by each system of the other). In our own work, we have considered the different meanings circulating around criminal justice generated within law and the media, with a particular focus on the different meanings given to convictions and appeals within the two systems, as well as law's construction of rights and truth.[13] Others have looked at the 'same but different' communications generated within law,

[13] Nobles and Schiff, 2000, ch 4, 2004b, 2001 and 2006.

child welfare and children's rights,[14] industrial relations,[15] contracts,[16] mental health practice,[17] etc.[18]

If this book were intended to be a contribution to the relative advantages of systems theory as a sociology of law, then we would need to expand considerably this discussion of structural coupling, and compare its utility with concepts more traditional to socio-legal studies, such as relative autonomy. We hope that this book has alerted the reader to the productive possibilities of such analysis. However, as this book is intended to make a contribution to the relationship between sociology and jurisprudence, we are content to refer the reader who wishes to learn more about this theory, and its productive potential to illuminate socio-legal studies, as a starting point, to some of the works listed in footnotes to this chapter. Our focus on jurisprudence leads us, rather, to consider the narrower question of what—if any—structural coupling is possible between sociology of law—informed by systems theory—and jurisprudence.

Jurisprudence and Sociology: The Possibilities for Structural Coupling?

Our consideration of more traditional jurisprudence leads us to be aware of the difficulty of claiming that changes in the sociology of law will invariably lead to changes in law's self-description. Could autopoietic insights on the nature of systems be expected to increase the ability of actors to make communications that are likely to irritate other systems in more predictable patterns? In many ways the theory simply increases awareness of operations that already occur: politicians and lawyers make communications about law in forms that are likely to be selected by the media as

[14] King, 1991 (and for a critical comment, James, 1992); see also King and Piper, 1995; King 2000.

[15] Rogowski, 2001.

[16] Teubner, 2000.

[17] Peay 2005, 52–56.

[18] See Paterson and Teubner, 1998, and other essays in Priban and Nelken, 2001.

part of their conditional programmes to code news/not news;[19] lawyers take social communications about family and responsibilities and produce communications that the legal system recognises as wills and trusts. What the theory adds is a greater awareness[20] of the nature of the operations that lead to such activities, their difficulties and their limitations. The enormous number of communications that occur within systems, and the lower (but still enormous) number of structural couplings that occur between systems, offer only limited possibilities for the self-conscious guidance of communications within (let alone between) different systems. As we tried to show in our discussion of legal reasoning in chapter six, systems develop when they select novel communications. Only with hindsight can we refer to successfully selected novel communications that have established new structures and talk about a system being 'guided' by what was offered. However, assuming that an autopoietic self-consciousness of the nature of communications would alter some of the communications available to the legal and other systems, and the resultant selections made, is there any reason to believe that the legal system could exhibit greater structural coupling with other systems at any of its levels, including that of self-description—jurisprudence?

Our discussion of jurisprudential theories indicates the difficulties involved in such an enterprise. Our discussion of the evolution of law's self-description from natural law to legal positivism argued that this change was generated internally: that when the legal system began to experience frequent and particular changes of law it could not organise its own operations in terms of natural law, but developed a self-understanding in terms of authoritative sources. Our analysis questioned any explanation of this change in terms of the legal system learning, or 'taking on board' a superior account of its operations from an outside source. Thus, whatever the quality of Hobbes' deconstruction of the jurisprudence of the common law, the legal

---

[19] Or, to be more precise, for Luhmann, information/non-information (Luhmann, 2000, 17).

[20] That is, of the ability within the observing system, to observe.

system continued to generate this jurisprudence until such time as it was no longer generated in that form—when it no longer served to stabilise law's own internal operations. This example serves as a warning against claims that the legal system will 'learn' from external critique. There is no inherent reason to believe that sociological theory will prove superior to political theory in teaching the legal system what its jurisprudence ought to be. Indeed, systems theory, taken seriously, indicates exactly why neither should expect to succeed.

Our description of the legal system 're-using' communications from other systems points to one part of the possibilities for relationships between systems, and what is traditionally described as learning. The wealth of communications developed within society's different functioning systems not only increases the complexities of these systems, but also offers increased resources to each other, by increasing the ability of other systems to select (re-use) communications that they have not generated themselves. But the need for the system in question to make the selection for re-use to occur (and the presence of the opposite alternative—not to select—'deafness'), inevitably means that opportunities are necessary but not sufficient conditions for selection. With respect to the issue we are addressing in this chapter, the possibilities of inter-system relationships between sociology and law, sociology's generation of systems theory offers a possibility for communications to be selected by law as part of its operations that was not present before. But the question still remains, what evidence is there that law would be likely to select such communications for re-use within its operations? And, even if it did, why would the episodic use of such communications build into a new self-description? Systems theory provides explanations as to why positivist jurisprudence arose. And the concept of justice as an *eigenvalue* indicates why modern natural law continues to offer an alternative self-description, which operates autologically to stabilise many of law's operations. But the wealth of other kinds of communication utilised by the legal system drawn from many of society's subsystems, economic, political, religious, accounting, ethical, scientific, etc, whilst they may assist to stabilise communications within particular localities, face enormous, if not insuperable, difficulties in colonising all of law, or organising sufficient operations to generate a jurisprudence that presents the unity of the legal system to itself.

A further caveat is necessary at this point. The re-use of communications is not exactly the same thing as structural coupling. Coupling involves re-used communications, but at a quite minimal level. Take again the example of contract. Given that a common language is being used by different systems, where there is a specific contract, the word 'contract' will occur in the economic and legal systems at the same moment (at least some of the time). The use of the same word in two different systems, and its re-use at the same time in the different systems, facilitates the mutual recognition of events by each system. But this does not mean that each system needs to incorporate much of the different conditioning programmes that surround the use of the word 'contract' within the two systems. Structural coupling involves only the mutual expectations of events generated by another system. It operates like our story of the tribes. The same 'something' has to be selected by each system at the same time, but it does not have to have the same meaning, and the amount of syntax that each system may need to re-use in order to explain the meaning of the event to itself can be large, minimal, or in our example, zero.

Systems Theory as Jurisprudence

If one looks at systems theory as a complex body of concepts, there is little reason to believe that it is capable of engaging in structural coupling with law. Luhmann himself conceded that it was a complex theory that was unlikely to be readily selected by the legal system in order to undertake self-observation, let alone self-description. For example, what legal concept is going to be explained within the legal system (ie in a manner that is capable of generating further observation which guides future decisions) in terms of irritation, redundancy, coupling, code, conditional programme, paradox, tautology, *eigenvalue*, etc. (However, one notices a similar lack of legal decisions explained by the legal system to itself in terms of 'relative autonomy' and 'class interests'.) And, to move from re-used communications to structural coupling, what is the chance of the legal system developing a legal concept that allows for a shared use of such words? Nevertheless, one needs to remember that Luhmann also pointed out that natural law operated as the self-description of the legal system without the necessity for magistrates to thumb 'through the *Summa Theologiae* after a hard day at the sessions'.[21] What he was alluding to, which we tried to develop in chapter three, was that the operations of law generate self-descriptions, not that every operation in law is experienced in terms of that self-description. Following this, the question would be what, within law's operations, is capable of generating a self-description compatible with systems theory? This does not require the adoption of systems theory terms. Rather, it requires us to consider whether the legal system is ever likely to generate a self-description that replicates the insights of systems theory. This, yet again, is quite problematic. The evolution of the legal system, and other systems, is based on operations of self-observation that implicitly deny the paradox that their code offers a meaningless distinction. The paradox that codes are simply distinctions without foundations, and totally contingent in their application in the long term, is constantly 'unfolded' by the evolution of increasingly complex conditional programmes to account for the code's application. Luhmann describes this denial or unfolding of paradox through operations as productive.[22] In everyday terms, when a communication that explains the application of a system's code creates major problems the system is likely to develop a new one—one that better facilitates

---

[21] Luhmann, 2004, 425.

[22] Luhmann, 1988b. And, see Teubner, 2005, for his recent exploration of how this might be so: 'The interplay of paradoxification-re-paradoxification is anything but a cumulative sequence of negations, a "transcending" of contradiction, a progress of the spirit. It is more a case of the return of the same, a continual oscillation between paradox and structure, a dialectic without synthesis.'

the system's operations. Self-descriptions that seek to account for the unity of a system fuel this process. They represent an assertion that the application of the system's code is not arbitrary, because there are features within the system that are essential, and always present. What is the potential, by contrast, for a self-description that recognised that the law is a closed system that constructed itself and its environment, and that the basis of its construction is the endless application of a code, which has no inherent meaning?

Both natural law and legal positivism have been, and remain, the dominant self-descriptions of law despite unceasing critique that by now should have succeeded in their dislocation. That this has not occurred can be explained by understanding the autological role of each of these self-descriptions. On the one hand one finds the *eigenvalue* of justice as the treating of like cases alike (as a precondition for any attempt at self or secondary observation)—and on the other, the utilisation of authoritative sources as a self-description of operations that apply the symbol of validity (which is no more than the connection between each and every communication whose meaning is the application of the code legal/illegal).[23] Given the present state of legal operations, a dislocation of these two self-descriptions seems unlikely. Jurisprudence reads or misreads external critique, but no matter how powerful that critique might be, jurisprudence *cannot* learn, as its conditions (at least those of natural law and legal positivist theories) are grounded in their autological operations.

The only qualitative observation that systems theory offers on the nature of the general processes represented by the evolution that occurs within all systems as a result of their operations is that 'complexity' increases.[24] Such a conclusion with its comparative resonance to Darwin's evolutionary theory, from

[23] On the intrinsic role of the symbol of validity, see Luhmann, 2004, ch 2/*VIII*.

[24] Luhmann, 2004, 231.

difference to adaptation,[25] is mirrored at the level of self-description. Both natural law and positivist legal theories have become ever more complex appendages (with further differentiation and adaptation) to the enormous numbers of legal operations and their communication that they attempt to capture within their self-thematisations.

Whilst this analysis makes one pessimistic as to the possibilities of a systems theory version of 'closing the gap' between sociology or sociological theory and jurisprudence, one needs to recognise the potential for systems to develop, and the operations within the legal system that are likely to displace existing self-descriptions. The positivist self-description—law as authoritative sources—may continue to facilitate legal communication at the level of nation state legal systems, but it does not offer similar possibilities when looking at international legal operations.[26] At the level of public international law, the difficulties of generalising self-observations of the application of the code into positivist self-descriptions (reliant on sources, or a test for sources) may be compensated for by the constant utilisation of natural law (especially, in the modern era, in the form of human rights[27] as representing a discourse of continuity from natural rights). But within private international law, one finds legal operations that the system cannot explain to itself as either the application of authoritative sources, or the unfolding of a moral order.[28] Under these conditions the possibilities for a jurisprudence of legal pluralism is no longer exceptional. Self-observation and self-description of the operations of the various agencies that make such private international legal decisions, or at least that adopt the distinctive code legal/illegal for this purpose, is expressed through conditional programmes that seem to

[25] This has been elaborated further in ch 6 through the dynamic analysis of legal reasoning in which law's evolution is reflected in the possibility of variation, selection and stabilisation.

[26] See Hart, 1961, ch X.

[27] See Verschraegen, 2002; van Hoecke, 2002, 167–70.

[28] See Fischer-Lescano and Teubner, 2004; Teubner, 1997a; Teubner, 1997b.

reflect differentiated internal unifying themes. Fischer-Lescano and Teubner have described these themes not as policies, in the sense that these would be generated within political systems, but as 'contradictions between colliding sectors' offering 'fragmentation' as a characteristic of global law.[29] Such agencies understand themselves as providing legal form to particular social interests (world health, world economic order, etc), and experience pluralism through their acknowledgement that decisions have to take account of an environment that includes more interests than the particular one to which they provide legal form. The various international legal forums that undertake these operations have the potential to develop a self-description in terms of relationships between the legal system and other functioning systems and the rest of society, which might replace the existing dominant self-description of legal positivism. The latter, with its orientation around authoritative sources, is the legal system's internal reconstruction of one particular system in its environment: the political system. At the international level, the developments identified by Teubner and others[30] point to the possibility of structural coupling with other systems in a form that would generate new self-descriptions in terms of the legal system responding 'directly' to more aspects of their environment. This might in turn (and this can only be a speculation) provide some purchase to self-descriptions that contain some of the insights (if not the terminology) of systems theory.

Jurisprudence and Autopoiesis—Nascent Possibilities for Further Analysis

We hope that this book will succeed in introducing readers with a knowledge of jurisprudence to the nature of systems theory and its potential to illuminate many of the issues central to this subject. In seeking to make the theory accessible to those unfamiliar with Luhmann's writings we have inevitably opened

---

[29] Fischer-Lescano and Teubner, 2004, 1004.
[30] See n 28 above.

ourselves up to criticism from experts on his work on the grounds that we may have been superficial, or misrepresented his position. If readers who have been introduced to Luhmann's works through this book are stimulated to read further into systems theory, and re-examine our observations on jurisprudence using a more rigorous and informed understanding of Luhmann's works than we have been able to show here, then we would be delighted. Our aim has been to introduce the theory, and show its potential to inform jurisprudential debate, not to provide the definitive work on the theory. Nor would we claim that our understanding and application of the theory in this book, even if correct, exhausts all of its power to observe jurisprudence. We are firmly convinced that other theories and issues than those which have been discussed in this book are ripe for reconsideration using the insights that result from the application of the concepts of systems theory. The potential for such further work lies firstly in the fact that Luhmann himself tackled far more issues than we have been able to address here, such as the nature of freedom, procedural justice, social exclusion from law and other systems, the role of norms in constructing time, the role played by sanctions, the position of the courts within the legal system, the limitations of economic analysis of law, etc. And secondly, those stimulated to read more of his writings, and reach an understanding of his theory that allows them to address matters not directly discussed by Luhmann himself, will, we believe, be able to continue the sort of analysis undertaken in this book, and achieve insights that, even if glimpsed without the aid of this theory, could not be so clearly perceived and analysed without its assistance.

What we seek from our readers is an engagement with the theory, as it has been presented in this book. And we do stress that it is an engagement with the theory that we seek, and not a reaction to the ideas suggested by one or two of its terms.[31] Engaging with systems theory to the extent that one can generate insights and criticisms of existing jurisprudence results, at the very least, in existing theories having to respond and

---

[31] See the text above in the paragraph containing n 21.

develop. In this way autopoiesis can enrich our understanding of existing jurisprudence, even if it is eventually rejected by those who have accepted its challenge.

Systems theory is fairly described as a post-modern theory, in the sense that it is anti-foundational. Systems apply distinctions that have no inherent meaning, and the contingent meanings that are developed by systems' operations are always open to change. Whatever the role played by any structures at a particular time, over time, nothing can be said to be essential. In denying essentialism, systems theory shares ground with theories that engage in deconstruction and, in so doing, it may seem to invite rejection from those who see deconstruction as a negative exercise. This reaction is misplaced, for it misses the extremely positive aspects of the theory. Deconstruction tends to engage with claims as to the foundation of matters such as knowledge and, by demonstrating their absence, leaves us without a basis for understanding what has been deconstructed (except perhaps in terms of its arbitrariness). But systems theory engages with the absence of foundations, and seeks to account for the manner in which modern society functions in their absence. What can be shown to be arbitrary through the use of rational deconstruction, is not arbitrary when understood in terms of complex and constraining systems of communication.

Lastly, systems theory offers a sophisticated form of realism. Naïve forms of realism seek to find the reality that underlies communications, and tend to treat certain kinds of communications as ideological, in the sense that they distort or disguise some underlying reality. This theory treats communications, and different subsystems of communication, as a totality, as society. They are its existence, and its reality. As such there is no reason to treat some communications as less 'real' than others. The task, instead, is to examine what operations are performed by different kinds of communications, both within, and between, different systems of communication. The potential for insights through this form of analysis, with its possibilities, to inform and structure both jurisprudence, and interdisciplinary approaches to the study of law is, we believe, enormous and, as yet, largely untapped.

230

Bibliography

Aquinas (1959) *Aquinas Selected Political Writings* (Oxford, Basil Blackwell, trans JG Dawson, ed AP D'Entreves)

Alexy, R (2002) *The Argument from Injustice: A Reply to Legal Positivism* (Oxford, Clarendon Press, trans BL and SL Paulson)

Andreski, SL (1981) 'Understanding, Action and Law in Max Weber' in A Podgorecki and CJ Whelan (eds) *Sociological Approaches to Law* (London, Croom Helm) ch 3

Aubert, V (ed) (1969) *Sociology of Law* (Harmondsworth, Penguin)

Austin, J (1955) *The Province of Jurisprudence Determined* (London, Weidenfeld and Nicolson, first published 1832)

Banakar, R (2000) 'Reflections on the Methodological Issues of the Sociology of Law' 27 *Journal of Law and Society* 273–295

Banakar, R and Travers, M (eds) (2002) *An Introduction to Law and Social Theory* (Oxford, Hart Publishing)

Bankowski, Z (1996) 'How Does It Feel To Be On Your Own? The Person in the Sight of Autopoiesis' in D Nelken (ed) *Law as Communication* (Aldershot, Dartmouth) 63–80

Bentham, J (1977) *A Comment on the Commentaries and A Fragment on Government* (London, Athlone Press, ed JH Burns and HLA Hart)

Berger, PL and Luckmann, T (1967) *The Social Construction of Reality: A Treatise in the Sociology of Knowledge* (Harmondsworth, Penguin)

Blackstone, W (1765–69) *Commentaries on the Law of England*, 4 vols (Oxford, Clarendon Press), full text at: <http://www.lonang.com/exlibris/blackstone>.

Bredemeier, HC (1962) 'Law as an Integrative Mechanism' in WM Evan (ed) *Law and Sociology: Exploratory Essays* (Glencoe, Illinois: Free Press) 73–90

Brown, GS (1969) *Laws of Form* (London, Allen and Unwin)

Bulygin, E (1998) 'An Antimony in Kelsen's Pure Theory of Law' in SL Paulson and BL Paulson (eds), *Normativity and Norms: Critical Perspectives on Kelsenian Themes* (Oxford, Oxford University Press) 297–315

van Caenegem, RC (1973) *The Birth of the English Common Law* (Cambridge, Cambridge University Press)

Bibliography

van Caenegem, RC (1995) *An Historical Introduction to Western Constitutional Law* (Cambridge, Cambridge University Press)

van Caenegem, RC (2002) *European Law in the Past and the Future: Unity and diversity over Two Millenia* (Cambridge, Cambridge University Press)

Celano, B (1998) 'Norm Conflicts: Kelsen's View in the Late Period and a Rejoinder' in SL Paulson and BL Paulson (eds) *Normativity and Norms: Critical Perspectives on Kelsenian Themes* (Oxford, Oxford University Press) 343–361

Clark, M (2002) *Paradoxes from A to Z* (London, Routledge)

Coleman, JL (2001a) *The Practice of Principle: In Defence of a Pragmatist Approach to Legal Theory* (Oxford, Oxford University Press)

Coleman, JL (ed) (2001b) *Hart's Postscript: Essays on the Postscript to the Concept of Law* (Oxford, Oxford University Press)

Collins, H (1987) 'Roberto Unger and the Critical Legal Studies Movement' 14 *Journal of Law and Society* 387–410

Collins, H (1992) *Justice in Dismissal: The Law of Termination of Employment* (Oxford, Clarendon Press)

Collins, H (2002) 'Law as Politics: Progressive American Perspectives' in JE Penner, D Schiff and R Nobles (eds) *Jurisprudence and Legal Theory: Commentary and Materials* (London, Butterworths) ch 7

Cotterrell, R (1984) *The Sociology of Law: An Introduction* (London, Butterworths)

Cotterrell, R (1992) *The Sociology of Law: An Introduction* (London, Butterworths, 2nd edn)

Cotterrell, R (1995) *Law's Community* (Oxford, Clarendon Press)

Cotterrell, R (1998) 'Why Must Legal Ideas Be Interpreted Sociologically?' 25 *Journal of Law and Society* 171–192

Cotterrell, R (1999) *Emile Durkheim: Law in the Public Domain* (Edinburgh, Edinburgh University Press)

Cotterrell, R (2001) 'The Representation of Law's Autonomy in Autopoiesis Theory' in J Priban and D Nelken, 2001 80–103

Cotterrell, R (2003) *The Politics of Jurisprudence: A Critical Introduction to Legal Philosophy* (London, Lexis Nexis, 2nd edn)

Cotterrell, R (2006) 'From "Living Law" to the "Death of the Social": Sociology in Legal Theory' in M Freeman (ed) *Law and Sociology* (Oxford, Oxford University Press)

Dalton, C (1985) 'An Essay in the Deconstruction of Contract Law' 94 *Yale Law Journal* 997–1114

Diamond, S (1985) 'Not-So-Critical Legal Studies' 6 *Cardoza Law Review* 693–711

Dias, RWM and Hughes, GBJ (1957) *Jurisprudence* (London, Butterworths)

Dickson, J (2001) *Evaluation and Legal Theory* (Oxford, Hart Publishing)

Durkheim, E (1960) *The Division of Labor in Society* (Gelncoe, Ill, Free Press, trans G Simpson, 2nd edn)

Duxbury, N (2001) *Jurists and Judges: An Essay on Influence* (Oxford, Hart Publishing)

Dworkin, R (1977) *Taking Rights Seriously* (London, Duckworth)

Dworkin, R (1985) *A Matter of Principle* (Cambridge, Mass, Harvard University Press)

Dworkin, R (1986) *Laws Empire* (London, Fontana)

Eisenberg, MA (1988) *The Nature of the Common Law* (Cambridge, Mass, Harvard University Press)

Ewald, F (1988) 'The Law of Law' in G Teubner (ed) *Autopoietic Law: A New Approach to Law and Society* (Berlin, Walter de Gruyter) 36–50

Finnis, J (1980) *Natural Law and Natural Rights* (Oxford, Clarendon Press)

Finnis, J (1987) 'On "The Critical Legal Studies Movement" ' in J Eekelaar and J Bell (eds) *Oxford Essays in Jurisprudence* (Oxford, Clarendon Press, 3rd Series) ch 7

Fischer-Lescano, A and Teubner, G (2004) 'Regime-Collisions: The Vain Search for Legal Unity in the Fragmentation of Global Law' 25 *Michigan Journal of International Law* 999–1046

Fish, S (1982) 'Working on the Chain Gang: Interpretation in Law and Literature' 60 *Texas Law Review* 551–567

Fitzpatrick, P (1992) *The Mythology of Modern Law* (London, Routledge)

Friedman, L (1977) *Law and Society: An Introduction* (Englewood Cliffs, NJ, Prentice-Hall)

Galanter, M (1974) 'Why the "Haves" Come Out Ahead: Speculations on the Limits of Legal Change' 9 *Law and Society Review* 95–160

George, R (ed) (1996) *The Autonomy of Law: Essays on Legal Positivism* (Oxford, Clarendon Press)

Goldstein, L (ed) (1987) *Precedent in Law* (Oxford, Oxford University Press)

Gordon, RW (1984) 'Critical Legal Histories' 36 *Stanford Law Review* 57–125

Bibliography

Guest, AG (ed) (1961) *Oxford Essays in Jurisprudence: A Collaborative Work* (Oxford, Oxford University Press)

Hale, Sir Matthew (1971) *A History of the Common Law of England* (Chicago, University of Chicago Press, ed CM Gray)

Halpin, A (2001) *Reasoning with Law* (Oxford, Hart Publishing)

Harris, JW (1989) 'Unger's Critique of Formalism in Legal Reasoning: Hero, Hercules, and Humdrum' 52 *The Modern Law Review* 42–63

Hart, HLA (1954) 'Definition and Theory in Jurisprudence', 70 *Law Quarterly Review* 37–60

Hart, HLA (1958) 'Positivism and the Separation of Law and Morals' 71 *Harvard Law Review* 593–629

Hart, HLA (1961) *The Concept of Law* (Oxford, Clarendon Press, 2nd edn 1994)

Hart, HLA (1983a) 'Kelsen's Doctrine of the Unity of Law' in Hart, HLA, *Essays in Jurisprudence and Philosophy* (Oxford, Oxford University Press) 309–342

Hart, HLA (1983b) 'Kelsen Visited' in Hart, HLA, *Essays in Jurisprudence and Philosophy* (Oxford, Oxford University Press) 286–308

Hart, HLA (1994) *The Concept of Law* (Oxford, Clarendon Press, 2nd edn)

Hobbes, T (1960) *Leviathan: or the Matter, Forme and Power of a Commonwealth, Ecclesiastical and Civil* (Oxford, Basil Blackwell, ed M Oakshott, originally published 1651)

Hobbes, T (1971) *A Dialogue between a Philosopher and a Student of the Common Laws of England* (Chicago, Chicago University Press, ed J Cropsey, originally published 1681)

van Hoecke, M (2002) *Law as Communication* (Oxford, Hart Publishing)

Holmes, OW (1896–97) 'The Path of Law' 10 *Harvard Law Review* 457–478

Hunt, A (1986) 'The Theory of Critical Legal Studies' 6 *Oxford Journal of Legal Studies* 1–45

Hutchinson, AC and Monahan, PJ (1984) 'Law, Politics, and the Critical Legal Scholars: The Unfolding Drama of American Legal Thought' 36 *Stanford Law Review* 199–245

Ibbetson, DJ (2001) *Common Law and Ius Commune* (London, Seldon Society)

James, A (1992) 'An Open or Shut Case? Law as an Autopoietic System' 19 *Journal of Law and Society* 271–83

Kairys, D (ed) (1990) *The Politics of Law: A Progressive Critique* (New York, Pantheon Books, revised edn)

Kelman, M (1981) 'Interpretive Construction in the Substantive Criminal Law' 33 *Standford Law Review* 591–673

Kelman, M (1984) 'Trashing' 36 *Stanford Law Review* 293–348

Kelman, M (1987) *A Guide to Critical Legal Studies* (Cambridge, Mass, Harvard University Press)

Kelsen, H (1945) *General Theory of Law and State* (Cambridge, Mass, Harvard University Press, trans A Wedberg)

Kelsen, H (1967) *Pure Theory of Law* (Berkley, University of California Press, trans M Knight)

Kelsen, H (1973) 'Law and Logic', in H Kelsen, *Essays in Legal and Moral Philosophy* (Dordrecht, Kluwer, ed O Weinberger, trans P Heath) 228–53

Kelsen, H (1991) *General Theory of Norms* (Oxford, Oxford University Press, trans M Hartney)

Kennedy, D (1979) 'The Structure of Blackstones Commentaries' 28 *Buffalo Law Review* 205–382

Kennedy, D and Michelman, F (1980) 'Are Property and Contract Efficient?' (1980) 8 *Hofstra Law Review* 711–770

Kennedy, D and Klare, KE (1984) 'A Bibliography of Critical Legal Studies' (1984) 94 *Yale Law Journal* 461–490

Kerruish, V (1991) *Jurisprudence as Ideology* (London, Routledge)

King, M (1991) 'Child Welfare Within Law: The Emergence of a Hybrid Discourse' 18 *Journal of Law and Society* 303–22

King, M (2000) 'Future Uncertainty as a Challenge to Law's Programmes: the Dilemma of Parental Disputes' 63 *The Modern Law Review* 523–43

King, M and Piper, C (1995) *How the Law Thinks About Children* (Aldershot, Arena, 2nd edn)

King, M and Thornhill, C (2003) *Niklas Luhmann's Theory of Politics and Law* (Basingstoke, Palgrave MacMillan)

Kronman, AT (1983) *Max Weber* (London, Edward Arnold)

Lacey, N (2004) *A Life of HLA Hart: The Nightmare and the Noble Dream* (Oxford, Oxford University Press)

Laski, H (1967) *A Grammar of Politics* (London, Allen and Unwin, 5th edn)

Lawson, FH (1955) *A Common Lawyer Looks at the Civil Law* (Ann Arbor, University of Michigan, The Thomas M Cooley Lectures, 5th series)

Bibliography

Leff, AA (1970) 'Contract as Thing' 19 *American University Law Review* 131–157

Levi, EH (1949) *An Introduction to Legal Reasoning* (Chicago, University of Chicago Press)

Lieberman, D (1989) *The Province of Legislation Determined: Legal Theory in Eighteenth-Century Britain* (Cambridge, Cambridge University Press)

Lobban, M (1991) *The Common Law and English Jurisprudence 1760–1850* (Oxford, Clarendon Press)

Luckmann, T (2005) 'On the Communicative Construction of Reality' Lecture at LSE, February 2005 (<http://is.lse.ac.uk/Events/LuckmannLecture.pdf>)

Luhmann, N (1982) *The Differentiation of Society* (New York, Columbia University Press, trans S Holmes and C Larmore)

Luhmann, N (1986a) *Love as passion: The Codification of Intimacy* (Cambridge, Mass, Harvard University Press, trans J Gaines and DL Jones)

Luhmann, N (1986b) 'Closure and Openness: On Reality in the World of Law' (San Domenico (FI), Badia Fiesolana, EUI Working Paper No 86/234)

Luhmann, N (1988a) *Die Wirtschaft der Gesellschaft* (Frankfurt am Main, Suhrkamp)

Luhmann, N (1988b) 'The Third Question: The Creative Use of Paradoxes in Law and Legal History' 15 *Journal of Law and Society* 153–165

Luhmann, N (1988c) 'The Unity of the Legal System' in G Teubner (ed) *Autopoietic Law: A New Approach to Law and Society* (Berlin, Walter de Gruyter) 12–35

Luhmann, N (1989) *Ecological Communication* (Chicago, University of Chicago Press, trans J Bednarz)

Luhmann, N (1990a) 'The Cognitive Program of Constructivism and a Reality that Remains Unknown' in W Krohn, G Kuppers and H Nowotny (eds) *Self-Organization: Portrait of a Scientific Revolution* (Dordrecht, Kluwer), 64–85

Luhmann, N (1990b) *Essays on Self-Reference* (New York, Columbia University Press)

Luhmann, N (1990c) *Die Wissenschaft der Gesellschaft* (Frankfurt am Main, Suhrkamp)

Luhmann, N (1992–93) 'The Code of the Moral' 14 *Cardozo Law Review* 995–1009

Luhmann, N (1993) *Das Recht der Gesellschaft* (Frankfurt am Main, Suhrkamp Verlag)

Luhmann, N (1995) *Social Systems* (Stanford, California, Stanford University Press, trans J Bednarz and D Baecker)

Luhmann, N (2000a) *Art as a Social System* (Stanford, California, Stanford University Press, trans EM Knodt)

Luhmann, N (2000b) *Die Politik der Gesellschaft* (Frankfurt am Main, Suhrkamp)

Luhmann, N (2000c) *The Reality of the Mass Media* (Cambridge, Polity Press, trans K Cross)

Luhmann, N (2002a) 'What is Communication?' in N Luhmann, *Theories of Distinction: Redescribing the Descriptions of Modernity* (Stanford, California, Stanford University Press, trans J O'Neil and E Schreiber) ch 7

Luhmann, N (2002b) 'How Can the Mind Participate in Communication?' in N Luhmann, *Theories of Distinction: Redescribing the Descriptions of Modernity* (Stanford, California, Stanford University Press, trans J O'Neil and E Schreiber) ch 8

Luhmann, N (2004) *Law as a Social System* (Oxford, Oxford University Press, trans KA Ziegert, eds F Kastner, R Nobles, D Schiff, R Ziegert)

MacCormick, N (1981) *HLA Hart* (London, Edward Arnold)

MacCormick, N (1986) 'Law as Institutional Fact' in N MacCormick and O Weinberger, *An Institutional Theory of Law* (Dordrecht, D Reidel) ch II

MacCormick, N (1987) 'Why Cases have *Rationes* and What These Are' in L Goldstein (ed) *Precedent in Law* (Oxford, Clarendon Press) ch 6

MacCormick, N and Summers, RS (eds) (1997) *Interpreting Precedents: A Comparative Study* (Dartmouth, Ashgate)

McIlwain, CH (1910) *The High Court of Parliament and its Supremacy: An Historical Essay on the Boundaries between Legislation and Adjudication in England* (New Haven, Yale University Press)

Maine, Sir Henry (1875) *Lectures on the Early History of Institutions* (London, John Murray)

Maitland, FW (1926) *The Constitutional History of England* (Cambridge, Cambridge University Press)

Maturana, HR and Varela, FJ (1980) *Autopoiesis and Cognition: The Realization of the Living* (Dordrecht, Reidel)

Maturana, HR and Varela, FJ (1988) *Tree of Knowledge: Biological Roots of Human Understanding* (Boston, Shambhala, trans R Paolucci)

Bibliography

Mensch, E (1990) 'The History of Mainstream Legal Thought' in D Kairys (ed), *The Politics of Law: A Progressive Critique* (New York, Pantheon Books, revised edn) ch 1

Milsom, SFC (1985) *Studies in the History of the Common Law* (London, Hambledon Press)

Moreso, JJ and Navarro, PE 'The Reception of Norms, and Open Legal Systems' in SL Paulson and BL Paulson (eds) *Normativity and Norms: Critical Perspectives on Kelsenian Themes* (Oxford, Oxford University Press) 273–291

Nelken, D (1996) 'Can there be a Sociology of Legal Meaning?' in D Nelken (ed) *Law as Communication* (Aldershot, Dartmouth) 107–128

Nelken, D (1998) 'Blinding Insights? The Limits of a Reflexive Sociology of Law' 25 *Journal of Law and Society* 407–426

Nobles, R (2002) 'Economic Analysis of Law' in J Penner, D Schiff and R Nobles (eds), *Jurisprudence and Legal Theory: Commentary and Materials* (London, Butterworths) ch 17

Nobles, R and Schiff, D (2000) *Understanding Miscarriages of Justice: Law, the Media, and the Inevitability of Crisis* (Oxford, Oxford University Press)

Nobles, R and Schiff, D (2001) 'Criminal Justice: Autopoietic Insights' in J Priban and D Nelken, 2001 197–217

Nobles, R and Schiff, D (2004a) 'Introduction' to N Luhmann, *Law as a Social System* (Oxford, Oxford University Press, trans KA Ziegert, eds F Kastner, R Nobles, D Schiff, R Ziegert)

Nobles, R and Schiff, D (2004b) 'A Story of Miscarriage: Law in the Media' 31 *Journal of Law and Society* 221–44

Nobles, R and Schiff, D (2006) 'A Sociology of Jurisprudence' in MDA Freeman (ed) *Law and Sociology* (Oxford, Oxford University Press)

Nobles, R and Schiff, D (2006) 'Theorising the Criminal Trial and Criminal Appeal: Finality, Truth and Rights' in A Duff et al (eds) *The Trial on Trial II* (Oxford, Hart Publishing)

O'Sullivan, R (1965) 'Natural Law and Common Law' (Transactions of the Grotius Society 1946) in R O'Sullivan, *The Spirit of the Common Law* (Tenbury Wells, Fowler Wright) 117–138

Parsons, T (1960) *Structure and Processes in Modern Societies* (Glencoe, Illinois, Free Press)

Parsons, T (1962) 'The Law and Social Control' in WM Evan (ed) *Law and Sociology: Exploratory Essays* (Glencoe, Illinois, Free Press) 56–72

Paterson, J (1996) 'Who is Zenon Bankowski talking to? The Person in the Sight of Autopoiesis' in D Nelken (ed) *Law as Communication* (Aldershot, Dartmouth) 81–104

Paterson, J and Teubner, G (1998) 'Changing Maps: Empirical Legal Autopoiesis' 7 *Social and Legal Studies* 451–86

Paulson, SL (1986) 'On the Status of the *Lex Posterior* Derogating Rule' in R Tur and W Twining (eds) *Essays on Kelsen* (Oxford, Oxford University Press) 229–247

Paulson, SL and Paulson, BL (eds) (1998) *Normativity and Norms: Critical Perspectives on Kelsenian Themes* (Oxford, Oxford University Press)

Peay, J (2005) 'Decision-Making in Mental Health Law: Can Past Experience Predict Future Practice?' 6 *Journal of Mental Health Law* 41–56

Penner, J, Schiff, D and Nobles, R (eds) (2002) *Jurisprudence and Legal Theory: Commentary and Materials* (London, Butterworths)

Pickthorn, KWM (1934) *Early Tudor Government* (Cambridge, Cambridge University Press, 1934)

Postema, GJ (1986) *Bentham and the Common Law Tradition* (Oxford, Clarendon Press)

Postema, GJ (1987) 'Some Roots of our Notion of Precedent' in L Goldstein (ed) *Precedent in Law* (Oxford, Clarendon Press) ch 1

Postema, GJ (1996) 'Law's Autonomy and Public Practical Reason' in R George (ed) *The Autonomy of Law: Essays on Legal Positivism* (Oxford, Clarendon Press) ch 4

Pound, R (1943) 'A Survey of Social Interests' 57 *Harvard Law Review* 1–39

Pound, R (1959) *Jurisprudence*, vol 1 (St Paul, Minn, West Publishing)

Priban, J, and Nelken, D (eds) (2001) Law's New Boundaries: the conequences of legal autopoiesis (Aldershot, Dartmouth)

Rasch, W (2000) *Niklas Luhmann's Modernity: The Paradoxes of Differentiation* (Stanford, Stanford University Press)

Rawls, J (1973) *A Theory of Justice* (Oxford, Oxford University Press)

Raz, J (1970) *the Concept of a Legal System: An Introduction to the Theory of Legal Science* (Oxford, Clarendon Press)

Raz, J (1972) 'Legal Principles and the Limits of Law' 81 *Yale Law Journal* 823–854

Raz, J (1986) 'Dworkin: A New Link in the Chain' 74 *California Law Review* 1103–1119

Raz, J (1994) *Ethics in the Public Domain* (Oxford, Clarendon Press)

Bibliography

Raz, J (1998) 'Postema on Law's Autonomy and Public Practical Reasons: A Critical Comment' 4 *Legal Theory* 1–20

Reiner, R (2002) 'Justice' in J Penner, D Schiff and R Nobles (eds), *Jurisprudence and Legal Theory: Commentary and Materials* (London, Butterworths) ch 15

Rogowski, R (2001) 'The Concept of Reflexive Labour Law: Its Theoretical Background and Possible Applications' in J Priban and D Nelken, 2001 179–196

Ross, A (1958) *On Law and Justice* (London, Stevens)

Rottleuthner, H (1989a) 'A Purified Theory of Law: Niklas Luhmann on the Autonomy of the Legal System' 23 *Law and Society Review* 779–797

Rottleuthner, H (1989b) 'The Limits of Law—The Myth of a Regulatory Crisis' 17 *International Journal of the Sociology of Law* 273–285

Royal Statistical Society (2005) 'Statistics and the Law' vol 2(1) *Significance* (Oxford, Blackwell)

Schiff, D (2002) 'Modern Positivism: Kelsen's Pure Theory of Law' in J Penner, D Schiff and R Nobles (eds), *Jurisprudence and Legal Theory: Commentary and Materials* (London, Butterworths) ch 5

Simmonds, N (1990) 'Why Conventionalism does not Collapse into Pragmatism' 49 *Cambridge Law Journal* 63–79

Simpson, Brian (1986) 'The Common Law and Legal Theory' in W Twining (ed) *Legal Theory and Common Law* (Oxford, Basil Blackwell) ch 2, 8–25

Stoner, JR (1992) *Common Law and Liberal Theory: Coke, Hobbes, and the Origins of American Constitutionalism* (Lawrence, Kan, University of Kansas Press)

Sunstein, CR (1996) *Legal Reasoning and Political Conflict* (New York, Oxford University Press)

Tamanaha, BZ (2000) 'A Non-Essentialist Version of Legal Pluralism' 27 *Journal of Law and Society* 296–321

Tamanaha, BZ (2001) *A General Jurisprudence of Law and Society* (Oxford, Oxford University Press)

Teubner, G (ed) (1988) *Autopoietic Law: A New Approach to Law and Society* (Berlin, Walter de Gruyter)

Teubner, G (1989) 'How the Law Thinks: Toward a Constructivist Epistemology of Law' 23 *Law and Society Review* 727–757

Teubner, G (1993a) *Law as an Autopoietic System* (Oxford, Blackwell)

Teubner, G (1993b) 'And God Laughed . . .' in G Teubner, *Law as an Autopoietic System* (Oxford, Blackwell) ch 1

Teubner, G (1997a) 'Global Bukowina: Legal Pluralism in the World Society' in G Teubner (ed) *Global Law Without A State* (Aldershot, Dartmouth) 3–28

Teubner, G (1997b) 'Breaking Frames: The Global Interplay of Legal and Social Systems' 45 *The American Journal of Comparative Law* 149–169

Teubner, G (2000) Contracting Worlds: The Many Autonomies of Private Law' 9 *Social and Legal Studies* 399–417

Teubner, G (2005) 'Dealing with Paradoxes of Law: Derrida, Luhmann, Wietholter' in O Perez and G Teubner (eds) *Paradoxes and Inconsistencies in the Law* (Oxford, Hart Publishing) 41–64

Teubner, G, Nobles, R and Schiff, D (2002) 'The Autonomy of Law: An Introduction to Legal Autopoiesis' in J Penner, D Schiff and R Nobles (eds) *Jurisprudence and Legal Theory: Commentary and Materials* (London, Butterworths) ch 18

Thomas, P (1971) *The House of Commons in the Eighteenth Century* (Oxford, Clarendon Press)

Tur, R and Twining, W (eds) (1986) *Essays on Kelsen* (Oxford, Oxford University Press)

Tushnet, MV (1998) 'Defending the Indeterminacy Thesis' in B Bix (ed) *Analysing Law: New Essays in Legal Theory* (Oxford, Clarendon Press) ch 11

Unger, R (1986) *The Critical Legal Studies Movement* (Cambridge, Mass, Harvard University Press; first published in 1983, 96 *Harvard Law Review* 561–675)

Unger, R (1996) *What Should Legal Analysis Become?* (London, Verso)

Verschraegen, G (2002) 'Human Rights and Modern Society: A Sociological Analysis from the Perspective of Systems Theory' 29 *Journal of Law and Society* 258–81

Watkin, TG (1999) *An Historical Introduction to Modern Civil Law* (Dartmouth, Ashgate)

Watson, A (1981) *The Making of the Civil Law* (Cambridge, Mass, Harvard University Press)

Weber, M (1954) *On Law in Economy and Society* (Cambridge, Mass, Harvard University Press, trans E Shils and M Rheinstein)

Weinberger, O (1986) 'Logic and the Pure Theory of Law' in R Tur and W Twining (eds) *Essays on Kelsen* (Oxford, Oxford University Press) 189–190

Yablon, CM (1985) 'The Indeterminacy of the Law: Critical Legal Studies and the Problem of Legal Explanation' 6 *Cardozo Law Review* 917–945

Index

Index

Index

Index